POPPY DREAM - THE STORY OF AN ENGLISH ADDICT.

Joe South

authorHOUSE®

AuthorHouse™ UK Ltd.
500 Avebury Boulevard
Central Milton Keynes, MK9 2BE
www.authorhouse.co.uk
Phone: 08001974150

In order to protect people, places and institutions I have changed names where it is appropriate. The famous, however, remain famous.

First published by AuthorHouse 8/13/2008

ISBN: 978-1-4389-0128-2 (sc)

Printed in the United States of America
Bloomington, Indiana

This book is printed on acid-free paper.

To Fred and Annie

"I Can Resist Everything Except Temptation."

Oscar Wilde.

"Being Born With A Penis Is Like Being Handcuffed To A Maniac For Life."

Kingsley Amis.

1

CHILDHOOD IN HENRY STREET

Late summer 1953

We watched the flames take hold of the meadow and send thick, grey smoke up into the clear, blue, summer sky. Patrick, Sidney and I gazed transfixed by the crackling, whooshing, angry blaze.

We were hiding behind some trees on the outskirts of the woods that bordered the pasture next to our school. "Bugger me, we'll be flayed alive for this," I whispered. Fear tingled between my legs and in my backside; the damp smell of moss mixed with tree resin filled my nostrils as I hugged the old elm close to my face and body. The grass was very dry and now the fire was spreading rapidly up towards the three of us in the woods. I heard Sidney crying softly at the next tree. "I've had it now, I really have. They'll send me away for certain this time," he whispered.

"The fire brigade are here. Look, there at the gate," said Patrick. Sure enough three fire engines had drawn up on the Marston Road and firemen were pouring into the hay field carrying their hoses and beaters.

Early that morning Patrick, Sidney and I had rounded up a few of the Henry Street lads for a game of Crazy Horse and General Custer. Cowboys and Indians in the field behind our street. It was the school holidays and it was hot. We were all happy, free and looking forward to re-enacting the Battle of Little Big Horn. The Dalton lads were there, and Brian, Tim and young Kevin were charging around through the long grass on their pretend gee-gees. "How do you make a galloping noise and a gunshot at the same time," asked Kevin to nobody in particular.

"Take this white man, bollock brain," yelled Sidney, jumping on to Kevin's back and wrestling him to the ground. "Stop messing about fellas, let's get organized," I yell at the two boys scrapping furiously in the long grass. "OK I'm Crazy Horse and Patrick you can be Custer," I commanded. "Pick your men. I'll have Sid."

"That's not at all fair," whines a resentful Patrick, "that just leaves the nippers."

"Listen Goldilocks, Custer Sir, they are Henry Street nippers after all - do be quiet," says I. A sulky Patrick began to choose his cavalry and soon we were divided and ready for the game.

We decided to pretend that the concrete air raid shelter behind the school was a cliff top on the side of a narrow canyon and that Custer and his horsemen would ride through it straight into an Indian ambush. Us Sioux braves lay down on the warm concrete roof and waited for the arrival of the US Cavalry. At last, from behind a vast blackberry bush below us, five small boys clip-clopped, in single file, behind General Custer and into the canyon below. I watched them squinty eyed, injun fashion and then when the soldiers were directly below us I gave my warriors the signal to attack and charge. "Aiieee! Death to the palefaces!" I yelled. With that we all jumped off the shelter roof and engaged the enemy. Guns, tomahawks, bows and arrows and finally knives were used in the close quarters fighting. As usual, most of us died at least twice and were wounded several times during the fierce confrontation, but finally, the Sioux nation won and the cavalry were subdued.

Puffing hard and running with sweat I ordered that Custer be staked out, spread-eagle fashion, whilst we thought of a suitable death for him. We bunched the long grass at his wrists and ankles and tied him to these green anchors with baler twine. "OK you paleface lot, you are now Indians by order!" I dictated. "Let's all do a victory dance around the helpless cur, Custer." As the lads whooped, hollered and danced around the prostrate Patrick I took out my matches from my khaki shorts and began to set light to the dry grass surrounding his body. The braves, delighted by the exciting development, stopped their prancing to watch the delicious flames gather in strength. "Frying tonight! General Custer frying tonight! Frying tonight!" sang a young, happy Brian. Suddenly both Sid and I realised that Patrick was in danger and that he was powerless to escape the fire creeping towards him. We both jumped through the knee high flames to cut him free with our sheath knives. Patrick was on his feet quickly and we all charged through the encircling flames. Once outside we saw that the little 'uns had vanished; probably terrified of the consequences of being found anywhere near our crime, they had run to their homes to become innocent school children once more. For a while the three of us tried to beat out the flames using our grey, school shirts but it was no use and the fire grew and spread out, fanned by the gentle summer breeze. "It's no good, it's hopeless," I shouted through the bitter sweet smoke. "Make for the woods. Run."

Reaching the shelter of the trees we dropped down to the ground where we watched from a crouching position.

It was 1953 and I was 9 years old. Of course, I didn't know it then but throughout the rest of my life I was going to watch scenes like this play out in front of my eyes. Sometimes I'd watch with horror at the unfolding disaster or, sometimes, I'd marvel and look with pleasure at the beautiful creation in front of me. This fire had been a picture in my head early that morning and now I had released the creature from my brain and it had taken on a malevolent life-force of its own. The fantasy was living outside of me and worse, it was out of my control. The young ringmaster was now the victim.

A song thrush sang in the branches above Sid's head. A clear, pure sound; a counterpoint to the drama that I was watching in the field below. I didn't know it then but it marked the beginning of my journey through decadence, jails, madhouses, addiction, love affairs and miracles.

We watched the firemen fight the blaze for an hour or more until all that was left of our meadow was black, scorched earth and drifting smoke. The tired firemen moved through the fire ground beating out hotspots and dousing the small flames that sprang up here and there. "I'm dying for a fag, let's go to the den," said Patrick. We needed to get our alibi straight. We needed to talk before we went home.

We reached the camp in the woods. Weeks before, we had built it out of straight branches, stolen planks and corrugated iron sheets. It was situated on the other side of Half Acre Orchard and it was our HQ where we would shelter from the rain: smoke, chat, plan devilment and occasionally cook on the campfire outside. We ducked down and entered the cosy, dark den. Sid reached the Woodies out from our safe, a rusty old biscuit tin, and the three of us lit up gratefully. "That's better," sighed Sid as he exhaled the blue smoke. I noticed that his tears had washed clean tracks down both of his soot covered cheeks. He was scared and so was I. We sat there for a while, sucking on our fags and looking at the earth floor. "Right," announces Patrick. "We deny everything, say nothing. Agreed?"

"Agreed," Sid and I mumble.

"OK, where have we been this morning?" he asked warming to his self allotted task of 'Liar-in-Chief to parents, police and other nosy sods asking awkward questions.'

"Let's say that we went to The Pitt Rivers Museum to look at shrunken heads," I suggested.

"That's the one," agreed a nodding Patrick. "We know that place inside out and back to front. That's really easy to fib about." We stubbed out our cigarettes and felt pleased with our plan. "Sid you'd better wash your face in the stream before you go home. You look like a shrunken head yourself," I laughed. We walked back to our street through the woods.

Henry Street was a cul-de-sac off the Marston Road in New Marston, Oxford. There were allotments on one side, a meadow on the other and woods at the end of the street. It was built on a small hill which stretched from Marston to Headington, just a short mile to the beautiful city I came to love so much. There were about 80 houses, all in varying styles and built at different times starting in the mid 1800s. Mostly they were two up and two down with long gardens and outside lavatories. They were bitterly cold during the winter and I would often wake to find thick ice coating the inside of my bedroom window.

My parents Frank and Kate had come down from the 'hungry North' some years before to seek work in the more prosperous South. My dad was a butcher and a talented artist. He also made model steam trains, by hand, that he sold now and then to make extra cash. He was a quiet, subservient man who constantly caved in to my mother's more dominant and critical manner. They were both bright and liked poetry, literature, music and art. My mother loved to argue and battled with most of her acquaintances at one time or another. She looked black eyed and furious when she scrapped with our neighbours, usually about some aspect of my more unacceptable behaviour. I remember when she stood toe to toe with Mrs Mayhew as she defended my good name and honour against her neighbour's wicked accusations. "He bit my front gate; I was watching him from my front window. It's been freshly painted and now it's covered in your son's teeth marks," she screamed. Of course if my mother had chosen to go and inspect the Mayhew front gate she would have seen the evidence but she chose not to, she preferred to fight.

The night before the fire, on my way up the stairs to bed, I lay face down on the stairs and peeped through the tiny spy hole which I'd gouged weeks before with my sheath knife through the panelled wall on the staircase. It gave me a limited view of our sitting room but, better still, I could hear everything said in the room below if I put my ear to the hole. Frank was talking in a tired, droning, exasperated monotone. "They've painted bloody swastikas on our front gate again. Five this time – big un's." My mother sighed and I heard her knitting needles click together as she dropped them into her lap. They were facing one another in front of the empty fireplace. It was warm and it was summer. "The war has been over for eight years and the Adlers left us four years ago. What are they thinking of? They are just plain ignorant and that's a fact," exploded my mother quietly. "We'll never be accepted here tha' knows. They hated us before we took the Adlers in, long before. At least we've got something about us and that is what they don't like. Intelligence and character for instance. Ignorant Oxford folk - peasants, that's my opinion."

Just before the war started, before I was born, there came a knock at our front door. My mother opened the door to a couple and a young girl, all warmly clad in thick woollen overcoats. The man was carrying a small brown, leather suitcase. The woman spoke in heavily accented and faltering English, "We are Jews and we are seeking shelter." Nothing more was said for several seconds. My mother looked at them and at the little girl and said, "Come in, come in. Let's see what we can do."

In the house they sat down, drank tea, gulped down hot pea soup and then began to tell my mother their story.

Frantz Adler, the husband and father of little Amabel spoke, "We are from Austria and we had to flee when we heard that our parents had been captured by the Nazis and sent to Bergen-Belsen. We came to Oxford because we believed that we had a distant relative here, who would take care of us for a while, but alas, we cannot find him. We have knocked on many doors in the city and you are the first to let us in to your home." In the weeks and months that followed my mother and father learned that the Adler's parents were later transferred to the death camp at Auschwitz. Naturally they feared the worst. Frantz told my mother that the Jews were starving in the ghettos and gradually all being moved to the concentration camps.

My mother listened to their story and loved this little fugitive family on sight; she wanted to help them. Without consulting my Pa she told them that they could stay, "You are welcome to stay with us for as long as you like," she offered with a sad smile. Both Frantz and Hilde smiled through their tears and hugged my mother jabbering thanks and endearments in German to her. Amabel started to sob, big heaving wails. "Thank God she's crying at last," breathed Hilde. "It's the first time since we escaped the ghetto, thank God." She hugged the little girl tight and rocked her back and forth.

My mother was like that. Brave, intelligent, tough and she knew what was right and what was wrong. I don't believe that my father, Frank, or my mother, Kate, considered the consequences of their kindness to the Adlers should the Germans have successfully invaded England. No, you simply did the right thing and trusted in the Almighty. They were both heroes in their own ways but it was only much later that I could see it clearly.

Although my mother insisted all her life that she was working class, she was not and neither was my father. Both their families had some money and respected positions in their communities. My mother was born to a Preston farmer and milkman, who owned his own house and business, and her mother was a matron in a local mental hospital. My grandfather was an alcoholic and often behaved violently towards my grandmother. When my granddad failed to return home after a day delivering milk it was my mother's job to go and find him.

She toured the Preston streets and when she spotted a pub with the horse and float tethered outside she knew she would find my grandfather inside and probably dead drunk. Often, after assessing the state of her dad, by peeping through the pub door, she would decide to leave him there and drive the cart back home alone through the dark, cobbled streets. The booze finally claimed him and he died of cirrhosis at 48. My mother, the eldest child in a family of six, took care of all her sisters, her brother and probably her father too, when he was too drunk to function.

My father Frank was born, in India, to a Captain in the Ghurkha Rifles and a rather mysterious lady who nobody remembered much about. The family legend ran that she was fatally wounded by a gunshot, but no one ever told me more than this. When young Frank returned to England after her death he was cared for by an aunt who loved him to the exclusion of everything else in her life. My dad taught me how to fish and how to draw; he was patient and he had a quiet manner. He was born with one leg shorter than the other and consequently had failed his army medical. He was handsome and in spite of walking with a pronounced limp he sported a muscular body. Obviously though, my mother did not love him and all through my childhood I sat through her daily verbal attacks upon my dad. After work he would sit in the corner of the sitting room quietly reading his newspaper as my mother taunted him, "Just look at him, the useless article. What have I done to deserve this?" I suspect that they did not make love after I was born. On the top of my father's wardrobe sat a single condom. The same French letter sat there for years, gathering dust and probably crying out for a good home. I was interested you see – I checked these things. Certainly in the years that I was growing up and the subject was brought up, no matter how tentatively, my mother would splutter her standard response, "Sex – yuck!" Much later, and too late, I believe that she began to understand that perhaps she had missed something precious. She would watch me with various girl friends, especially Hilary, and I think I saw regret and sadness in her eyes.

My sister Angela was about five years older than me and for some reason I cannot remember much about her. We only drew closer much later in life, after the terrible troubles. Of course, we had different sets of pals because of the age gap, but I have no warm affectionate memories of her as a child. It was probably my fault that we had no relationship - too sensitive, I often reacted to her facial expressions. I saw a superior sneer and it made me angry and withdrawn. I have no evidence, either then or now, to prove that she was judging me with contempt but I suffered under my subjective impression of her. Besides, my hero was Billy the Kid and Angela's were Mario Lanza and Albert Schweitzer.

On the day of the meadow fire nothing was said until late evening and I became complacent in the silence following the incident. Patrick, Sidney and I had spent the afternoon watching Jed Higgins from a patch of nettles and long grass in the vacant lot next to his small crumbly house where he lived with his spinster sister. Julie Smith had insisted that we go with her to watch Jed and his antics. Jed Higgins was the one man in Henry Street who could make us children run for cover when we saw him approaching on his sit-up-and-beg bicycle. He was very tall and very thin with a grey, gaunt face. He wore a long, belted, Harris Tweed overcoat and a dark blue flat cap. If you were caught in his mad, grey eyed stare Jed had the power to freeze you rigid. Once you had eye contact with this child cannibal, you simply could not move because he was so terrifying to look at. Often he would chase us if we could not drop our gaze quickly enough but he never caught us, thank God.

That hot, summer afternoon the four of us watched in the grass as he stood, stark naked at his upstairs bedroom window. It was the only time that I saw him smile as he beckoned to us through the dusty glass and jerked his erect penis. We watched him with complete fascination for a long time until dusk began to set in and the street gas lamps started to light up. We wandered back into the street and began to play rounders outside Patrick's house. After twenty minutes, more children and some parents began to join in the game. We had no television then and street games were one way of amusing ourselves. Nick Knock Nanny, British Bulldog, Truth, Dare or Promise, Rounders, Hopscotch were just some of the games we played regularly.

We were all getting tired and just about ready to pack it in when my mother arrived, out of the gloom, and stood under the flickering yellow gas lamp. "Where were you this morning?" she asked with her hands on her hips. Hands on hips generally meant that my immediate future was going to be uncomfortable, or worse, painful. "In The Pitt Rivers looking at shrunken heads," answered a petrified Sid. I swear that I could see his skinny knees knocking together below his grimy, khaki shorts.

"I wasn't asking you Sidney," said my mother in a quiet, menacing tone.

"In The Pitt Rivers looking at shrunken heads," I said. I felt pale in the darkness.

"And now Patrick, let me guess that you also were in The Pitt Rivers looking at shrunken heads," queried my doubtful mother.

"Yes that's right," answered Pat, clearing his throat nervously.

"Why?" said Sidney's mum holding the street rounders bat and looking worried. Wrong thing to ask I thought, you really should not ask questions like that. "Someone has set light to the meadow next to the school and done serious, serious damage," replied my mother.

"Oh dear!" said Sidney,

Sidney never, ever said 'Oh dear!' Things were not looking good in this particular interrogation. My mum was already streets ahead and poised for the kill. "Do you know who did it?" I ventured.

"We've all got a pretty good idea who it was, but when I find out for certain they are going to catch it," declared my mother pointing at me, "Bed you, it's time for bed, come on."

I could not sleep that night for fear of what was likely to happen. This was the first of many guilt, soaked nights in my life when I went without sleep. If guilt and shame, tears and sleeplessness were the currency of my misdeeds, then I've paid my fines to the heavenly court, with interest, throughout the years.

2

LOVE AND SEX AT TWELVE YEARS OLD

Mid summer 1957

I remember the smell of creosote as I peeped through the vacant knot hole in the old wooden fence. The game that we were playing was called Spot the Biggest Knob and it was a regular pastime for Patrick, Sidney and me as we waited for Bert to open up Dame's Delight for the day.

The year was 1957, I was 12 and it was summer. A hot, still day in August; a perfect day to swim and lounge around. Parson's Pleasure, a nude male swimming enclosure was situated across the punt rollers from its sister bathing place, Dame's Delight, a clothed, mixed sex swimming hole. Local legend had it that Dame's Delight had also been a nudist colony, strictly for women, but before our time. Both pools were on Mesopotamia in the University Parks where the River Cherwell divides into two.

We had placed our cozzies, wrapped Swiss roll fashion, along with our day's supply of sandwiches, on the brown, dead leaves which carpeted the ground near to the wooden fence. Hardly anyone in today, too early, about a dozen I reckoned. Dons, professors and churchmen from the University and the City. All queer of course, we knew that for sure. One fat, white one attracted my attention. He was sitting with his seal back against a tree reading the Times and enjoying a chunky cigar. I watched as he lowered his paper and glanced from left to right. Standing up, purple and proud against his plump belly was the most enormous, erect penis I had ever seen. "Fuck me, Patrick, Sidney look to your left under that tree. He's smoking a cigar, look for the smoke," I shouted in a whisper.

"Fuck," says Pat, "I see it, that's a whopper."

"Where, where?" howls Sidney. Just too late to see this wonder as the newspaper is lowered back into its original position, covering the large, red column. We watched for a while longer and giggled as an aged, skinny gentleman skipped and tripped across the grass to execute a near perfect belly flop into the grey, green water.

We picked up our cozzies and ambled over the rollers to Dame's Delight. The rollers were a dozen or more metal cylinders, mounted on a concrete path, and connecting the high part of the Cherwell to the lower bit. It saved you trying to navigate your boat up a weir! It was prohibited for women to enter Parson's Pleasure, so ladies were supposed to disembark the punts and boats at the rollers and walk around the outside of the bathing spot to meet their transport and their men, at a landing stage on the other side. We always cheered when an intrepid female student hid herself under coats and towels in order to make the voyage through the pool.

"It was fucking plum coloured, it was enormous, it reached right up to his chest," explained an impressed

Patrick to Sid. He stroked his thick black locks and lovingly patted his 'duck's arse' hairstyle into place.

"Wish I'd seen it," whispered Sidney.

"You'll be glad tomorrow when we both have horrible nightmares tonight," I said.

"No, I'd like to have seen it. It's interesting, things like that."

"How do you get something that size up an undergraduate's bum?" pondered Pat.

"They use butter to grease it," says I knowledgeably.

"We can try it later and see if it works. In the girl's cubicles before they come," suggests Sid.

"No butter," I say miserably.

"We've got sandwiches," said Sid, "we can scrape the butter off the bread."

"Good idea Watson," I reply.

We crossed the metal rollers and opened the gate to Dame's Delight. Bert was inside on the boardwalk hauling up a kettle of river water, on a life-ring rope, for his morning tea. He was dressed, as usual, in a white shirt, grey braces and smart grey trousers with razor sharp creases. He was around 50 I suppose, Brylcreamed silver hair and a military moustache. He never smiled, leastways, never at us very much.

"Morning Bert," I said. We were first in.

"Morning Bert, lovely day," says Patrick.

"Morning Bert," says Sidney in a cheery friendly tone.

"Hmmph," replies Bert as he carried his kettle to his tiny wooden ticket office at the entrance. We handed him our tanners and he tore off our white tickets in return. **Dame's Delight. Oxford University Parks Dept.**

Admit One Child. 6d. The swimming hole was ours for the day." Thanks Bert, you're an officer and a gentleman," I smiled.

"No diving on young girls or pushing 'em in today. I've 'ad complaints," mumbled Bert.

"Right lads, in future, we'll push 'em out not in," I respond.

"Just fuck off smart arse," muttered an already irritated Bert.

We fucked off slowly to the changing hut, a corrugated iron fence enclosure which smelt of Jeyes Fluid and stale urine. It comforted me, that smell. I relaxed in the luxury of the security that the strong odour offered me. Even at 12 I was alert and fearful most of the time, always watchful and noticing many things. It was good to find something, a smell say, which rescued me temporarily from this sensitive and painful state.

When we had changed into our woollen bathers we walked across the lawn to the empty girls cubicles. "Bring the sandwiches Sid," I ordered. "You keep a look out for Bert and we'll try the experiment." The green wooden cubicles stood in a long line and were built on stilts about 15 inches high and there was just enough room inside for Patrick and me. "OK, bend over then and pull down your trunks," I commanded. He did as I asked and rested his hands on the low wooden plank that served as a seat. He thrust his white bottom towards me and giggled. I rubbed my erect penis between his buttocks slowly. "That's lovely," I murmured.

"Delightful my dear," joked Patrick.

"Is it all clear Sid? Where's Bert?" I queried through the almost closed cubicle door.

"It's OK, he's reading his newspaper," replied Sidney. I was getting more excited and started to push the head of my dick into Richards' back passage when something shocking occurred to me. "Um, there's nothing up there is there?" I asked gently.

"What do you mean, mice, rats?"

"No, no, you went to the lavatory this morning didn't you? No turds or anything up there?"

"Nothing. Clean as a whistle. Launch the torpedo Captain," says Pat.

He wriggled impatiently despite the fact that he was sporting a hard on. It curved up and to the left like a bouncy banana. "Sid, hand me the sandwiches, I need the butter," I whispered through the slightly open door. The sandwich was handed to me and I scraped off a fair amount of the yellow grease with my thumbnail. I massaged it well into my member and then tried to force the tip into Pats anus. "Christ it hurts," he complained.

"Your arse is too small, it won't go in, it's impossible," I reported.

"It feels like it's in to me. It hurts like hell - burning like."

"I swear I'm only just pushing at the gate and I haven't gained admittance yet," I muttered. I grunted and pushed again but it was no use and my cock was starting to act disappointed and began to bend against his bum. "It's no use, its not working. Perhaps homosexuals tell lies." I said resentfully.

"Sid's got a thinner knob let him try," suggested Pat. I pulled up my trunks and jumped down out of the cubicle. "You try it, take another sandwich, you'll need it for Mr Tight Arse in there," I said to Sid. He hopped up and closed the door. I sat outside and gazed out over the big lawn to the river.

Weeping Willows were hanging over the green fencing that surrounded the pool. The sky was bright blue and nothing was moving except for the tiny flies and midges flitting over the still Cherwell. Apart from the grunting behind me in the cubicle there wasn't another sound. Bert was in his office and all was well on this sunny summer morning. I could smell the green grass, the muddy, fishy water and the butter. It was quiet.

I hoped that Charlotte would come today. This posh girl usually came at the weekends with her best friend Bunny. They walked from high on Banbury Road in North Oxford. Charlotte spoke like the Queen. My feelings of fascination for her were not related at all to the feelings which I had when I gazed at the penises through the fence across the water. Quiet, powerful speechless awe was what I experienced in the presence of this blonde haired, blue eyed girl. A chivalrous knight was required here, certainly not a hard dick. Lust was not in my body or in my mind when I dreamt of Charlotte. When she was around I hardly ever spoke. I was struck dumb by her closeness and by her smell. Ahh!...her smell. I think it was the mixture of Wright's Coal Tar Soap and her girlish sweat. What ever it was her scent was sublime to me. I really hoped that she'd come today.

"Fuck it, it's no good, it won't go in," explodes a frustrated Sid from inside the changing hut. "Right we'll have a wank instead," he suggested to Pat. Two minutes later after a few loud sighs and appreciative "fucks" they both emerged from the cubicle and jumped down on to the grass. Bert looked up as we charged hollering and screaming across the grass towards the water. When I eventually surfaced I was looking directly at Bert who was now out of his office and leaning against the wooden railing near to the shallow part of the pool. His day had just begun and he looked sad standing there in the sunlight. "Would you like a fag Bert, we've got some Woodbines with us," I offered, trying to cheer him up.

"Bugger off you cheeky sod, you're too young to smoke," but he half smiled as he walked back to his small wooden hut. We swam and horsed around for half an hour and then collapsed exhausted on to the grass, hands trailing in the luke warm water. I smelled the damp earth and remembered things, day dreamed and pondered.

Sex was proving to be a painful thing to experience. A couple of months before, when I was taking my weekly bath, I had masturbated in the bath tub using carbolic soap as a lubricant. Immediately after I had come I experienced the, now familiar, guilt and shame which appeared like magic after my desire had subsided. I prayed earnestly to God, "Please show me a sign, even a little one will do, to tell me if wanking is right or wrong. Thank you Lord. Amen." The next day my penis was as sore as sore could be. I'd rubbed it raw with my frantic lustful jerkings. I decided that this was the sign I was looking for, clearly The Lord God Almighty was telling me that masturbation was a sin. I must stop all sexual activity until I was married.

A few days later I was walking along Harberton Mead, a private road running through an estate of lovely old houses, with my mother and Lulu, my pet spaniel. We were kicking the autumn leaves and teasing Lulu. Suddenly I spied something glossy and colourful lying under a pile of leaves at the roads edge. I instinctively knew that it was a 'nudey' magazine. I'd seen them in a newsagent in St Clements. They looked enticing in the shop and I always hovered nearby trying to see more than just the cover. I would return to pick it up that evening without my mother and Lulu in tow. Later, at dusk, I arrived at the spot on my bicycle to collect my find.

That evening, alone in my bedroom, I carefully inspected the magazine. The book was called 'QT' and it was full of ladies showing off their very large breasts. My heart was thumping as I turned the pages. Sometimes I stopped breathing as I looked at these black and white posing images. Pouting lips, bee hive hairstyles, surly looks and carefully, carelessly arranged bits of clothing. What was it that made this marvellous bursting pressure in my shorts? The deep, dark cleavages, the full roundness of the breasts or was it the look of insolence in their eyes? The magic effect on my body was instant and overwhelming and it signalled the end of my wanking ban. I'd just have to live with the guilt and lump it.

The pages smelled damp from the leaves and today, 50 years on, the smell of wet, glossy paper has the power to turn me on.......click .....I'm horny. A girl called Pearl particularly excited me. There were 4 or 5 photos of her in 'QT' pushing her large bosom through a fishing net which was hanging, usefully, from a hook on the studio wall. In each photo pose she was looking straight at the camera, unsmiling, almost sneering at the lens. Pearl brought me to sticky orgasm many times and I never, ever, shared her with Sid or Pat. 'QT' lived under my bed along with a semen stiff handkerchief until I left home a few years later.

The day was getting hotter and Dame's Delight was filling up with swimmers but still there was no sign of Charlotte. I felt gloomy as I sucked on my butterless sandwich. Perhaps we should go to Cheney Woods tonight. A girl called Liz walked her black Labrador in Cheney Lane during the long summer evenings and she always accepted our invitations to join us near the bamboo in the middle of the woods. Liz occupied the 'sex' section of my brain and not the 'love' section.

Blonde, pink faced Liz had breasts and she allowed us to extract them from her school blouse and caress them. She stood obediently as we exposed her small tits to the night air. Sometimes there were 5 or 6 of us lads and she liked us all to take a turn stroking her body. The black Labrador lay at her feet, tired and panting, occasionally looking up at the action. I used to imagine that the dog knew more than he was letting on and when he looked up at me like that I felt guilty. Liz came to Cheney most evenings that summer.

Janice Oldman and Julie Smith were two other girls who both allowed us to 'capture' them and undress them in the long grass of Half Acre Meadow or against the crumbling brick wall behind Morgan's Garage. Janice would see us walking towards her down River Road and with a girly, 'Ooooh', skip off down the road to hide behind the garage. We always found her in the same place. Back against the dusty wall hissing at us, "No, no, keep away, please don't." Dark eyes, black almost, in the half light of dusk she stroked her hair with podgy fingers loaded with cheap plastic rings. Janice was always wet and ready to admit my finger, breasts smelling of her bitter sweat. She panted and so did I, but I never got my dick touched once. She had a shiny, yellow blouse and a big, thin nose. I loved to look at her nose. Dare I tell the others that I loved her broken nose? I wanted to tell Janice but I never did. Later, the tired gang would all return to our street, up River Road smelling each others fingers and making appreciative noises.

Several months previously the boys and I were taking advantage of the absence of Harry Timpson's mum and dad and we were all lounging in the attic bedroom of their Henry Street house. It was a large three storey yellow brick house that stood at the end of our cul-de-sac and overlooked Half Acre Meadow and Orchard. The four of us, Pat, Sid and me along with Harry were lying on the huge feather bed, knobs out, masturbating ourselves and each other. Despite Harry's slight build he sported a colossal penis, thick and long. I was mesmerized by this monster and liked to touch it and rub him. It had a long foreskin which gave off a faint odour of mild cheddar when I pulled it back. I had been circumcised when I was a baby but I didn't really understand why.

Hearing rustling and giggling outside the bedroom door we all hurriedly covered up and tucked in. Julie Smith hurtled through the door, pushed from behind by Harry's sister Mary. Julie was a couple of years older than us, plain, close-together, mocking, green eyes, a lisp and enormous breasts. I liked her a lot. "Go on then, show them. You said you would," jeered Mary at Julie.

"Shut up you," giggled Julie. "I never did."

"You told me downstairs that you wanted the boys to feel you up," protested Mary.

"Never, you liar," blushed Julie. Collectively stunned by the implied offer we were all speechless until an enterprising Harry asked Julie to join us on the bed and to calm down.

Gradually during the course of the next hour Julie's blouse was opened and her bra lifted above her abundant breasts. They were red, shiny and full. She lay on the bed or sat against the battered, varnished headboard as four boys, with erect penises sticking out of their trousers, stroked, kissed and sucked her tits. Mary, who unfortunately had no breasts yet, had left the bedroom to make toast in the kitchen downstairs.

All of us were hot, panting and bursting but not quite sure where to go from here. Then Julie raised herself from the crumpled sheet and announced, "OK I'll let one of you do it to me."

"Who?" we chorused. None of us, I'm certain, knowing what we would do if we were chosen. I was scared, so it was a relief when a cunning Julie declared her candidate to become her lover. "Sidney, you can do it to me." A look of horror spread over Sid's timid face as he fumbled with his buttons, trying to do them up in a hurry. He said something as he left the bedroom, stumbling over Harry's shoes. I think he said, "I've got to go home now," but I wasn't sure. Julie, red breasts hanging, lounged against the headboard and smirked triumphantly.

The lapping water and the children shouting gradually brought me out of my reverie. Dame's Delight was filling up. We swam some more and studied the newcomers. Some swimmers we already knew, they were regulars like us, and some were strangers. These particularly, we stared at. It was interesting to see a family of African Natives spreading their colourful rugs on the grass, giggling and berating their children at the same time. We'd seen black families like this in The National Geographic Magazine except that they were not wearing very many clothes. Black people were not exactly a rarity in Oxford during the fifties but they were still unusual and good to stare at. They didn't seem to have cozzies like us. At least the women didn't, just colourful sheets wrapped around them.

A strong blast of Wright's Coal Tar soap told me that Charlotte had arrived at last. She was already sitting beside me, her long legs dangling in the water. She had entered the pool completely unnoticed by anyone. She said a cheery hello to us but I could only manage an incoherent "'lo" in reply. I was inflicted, yet again, with 'love dumbness' and all I could do was occasionally glance at her out of the corner of my eye and do little smiley grunts in her direction. She took my breath away, she was my Princess and I was going to save her one day.

Suddenly Charlotte was up on her feet and she began to back away from the river bank. Then, she barrelled towards the water and launched herself into the beginnings of a perfect racing dive, but something happened to her just as she was about to enter the river. She crumpled and folded like a broken, balsa wood, toy airplane caught up in a strong gust of wind. She dropped into the water in an untidy knot of arms, legs and torso. Seconds later she surfaced, water streaming from her wet hair, and grinned a proud smile at her audience on the grass. I thought, with some embarrassment, that she was completely unaware of how her dive had turned into such a disaster in the last moments. Her failure to make the perfect dive gave me confidence somehow. I felt better.

She swam amongst the other noisy swimmers sporting their coloured rubber swimming caps and then she floated on her back for a while. I loved her slim, brown legs and her long fingers. Turning to us she hollered across the surface of the water in her best Queen voice, "My father says I mustn't mix with oiks." She grinned and then giggled in a cruel way, showing her white teeth. I hadn't a clue what an oik was but it sounded like it might describe me and that it wasn't very nice. "What the hell is an oik?" whispered Sid.

"I don't know," I said quietly. I gazed at her floating on her back and I was saddened. 'I'm an oik and she doesn't like me,' I thought. The pain of rejection was too great to bear and I retreated to the changing room to find the Woodies. I needed a smoke.

Later that night in bed I cried silently into my quilted eiderdown. Before I fell asleep I remembered, with a deal of hope, that Sue Dobson and Elizabeth Page and Susan Moore all had the capacity to make me 'love dumb' and that they hadn't yet rejected me or called me an oik.

3

SONIA THE SCHOOL GODDESS

Mid winter 1959

Wearing our green blazers we stood in a line as Colin Palmer moved quietly and swiftly up and down our row dealing the playing cards. We were the boys of Form 5a, Cheney School, Oxford and we were enjoying a game of pontoon during school assembly. Palmer was so small, for his 15 years that he could not be seen by the singing teachers on the stage, far away at the front of the hall.

The school of technology, art and commerce was opened in 1954 and its two storey, bleak, 'modern' appearance was in some way redeemed because it lay in such a beautiful place. Surrounded by mature trees it was situated at the top of Headington Hill and Morrell Avenue and was close to Cheney Woods and South Parks. The pupils of Cheney thought of themselves as fairly privileged simply because they were allowed to specialise in their particular fields of interest and consequently the place exuded a friendly atmosphere.

The headmaster, 'Wammer' Wainwright, had already led the school in The Lord's Prayer and now we were all singing Onward Christian Soldiers. There were several hundred of us gathered in the school hall arranged in alternate lines, according to the sex of the pupil. Boys, girls, boys, girls; from the first-years at the front, to the upper sixth at the back. We usually stood behind the girls from our form during morning assembly and, beside cards, another pleasant pastime was trying to lift, without being detected, Margaret Farrell's grey, pleated skirt so high we could see her knickers. I remember that she had rather a plump bottom and I felt moved by the sight of it, albeit clad in large white drawers. To my fellow pupils it was a thing to deride – 'Coo! what a fat arse!' kind of thing, but I secretly admired and lusted after Margaret Farrell's delectable rump. One of my many fantasies, at that time, involved me gallantly losing a wrestling match to Margaret and being subdued by her sitting on my head as I lay on the ground. For some reason the day dream only happened beneath a spreading cedar tree. Like John Betjemen I rather enjoyed the idea of arriving in the next life as a saddle on a girl's bicycle.

The banker, Palmer, served the cards to the whispered orders of, 'twist, stick, twist, stick, stick, twist,' up the line of lads. It was the last hand because the hymn was drawing to a close and it was difficult to play during the day's reading and announcements. There were only fifteen pupils in 5a. Nine boys and six girls but we liked to think that we had two claims to fame. We were known as the school outlaws and we also had in our midst the most beautiful girl in the school – Sonia Brookes.

I first laid eyes on Sonia at the beginning of the third year intake. We were amongst several pupils who had come to Cheney after successfully passing the 13+ examination.

We were both artistic in temperament and aptitude so we were allowed to specialise in the arts, hence 3a - or 3 art. I was standing with a bunch of new boys in a corner of the vast playground, on that first September morning at Cheney, when I overheard Harris say to Palmer, "Strewth, look at her. Magnificent, I hope she's in our form." I looked in the direction of his gaze and located the target of his keen appreciation.

She was walking towards a bunch of girls and dressed in her brand new Cheney uniform: green blazer, white shirt, black and green striped tie and a grey skirt. She was smiling as she walked towards the gaggle of new girls huddled in a corner of the playground and she looked radiant in the weak, morning sunlight. Goodenough, Kilpatrick and Lacey joined Palmer, Harris and me as we stared at this remarkable creature. Without doubt she was the most beautiful girl I had ever seen. She had long, wavy, black hair, grey/green eyes and she wore an expression of otherworldly serenity: soft, gentle, inviting and female. I was dumbstruck and she frightened me to death.

For the following year and a half I barely spoke a sentence to Sonia Brookes. I was tongue tied, my hands shook and I blushed uncontrollably when I was in her presence. Within half a term, after arriving at the school for the first time, she had elevated her status even higher by starting to go out with a boy who looked exactly like Elvis Presley and he was in the year above us. Most of the boys in the school adored her and after a while this mass worship really began to get on my nerves. I had to develop a tactic to deal with my paralysing feelings around Sonia, so for eighteen months I told my pals that she did absolutely nothing for me at all. "No I don't fancy Sonia, not my type at all I'm afraid," I repeated endlessly. Then, in an art class, at the end of the fourth year, whilst I was painting a vast mural on the wall she told me that she liked me. I finally looked into her marvellous eyes and wearing my blushes with bravery, I fell in love.

After the card game in assembly we made our way down the corridors to 5a boy's geometry lesson. I walked behind Harris who was humming Buddy Holly's latest, 'It Doesn't Matter Any More.' The title just about summed up our collective mood before we entered any class with the dreaded Percy Flagstaff. You simply had to keep your head down and stare at your work for an hour and a half in order to survive Percy unscathed.

The nine of us sat down at our drawing boards and waited patiently and quietly for the arrival of the 'Horror from Headington.' A full five minutes had elapsed when David Prowse got up from his desk and walked to the front of the class where he picked up some chalk and a long wooden pointer. The tall, thin Prowse faced us and in a faultless imitation of Percy's voice and mannerisms began to address us. Poor Mr Flagstaff had a cleft palate and his voice came down his long, beaked nose in a loud, whining buzz. Sometimes his words all blended together much like the nasal hum of a model aircraft engine. We watched Prowse as he began to draw a parabolic shape on the blackboard next to the classroom door, the whole time explaining the diagram in an Oscar winning 'Percy' voice.

Once we got over our shock at the audacity of the stunt we began to laugh at his antics until we reached a near hysteria of mirth. We were all gagging for breath when, very suddenly, Percy appeared in the open doorway of the form room. We stopped laughing immediately and gawped, horrified at our strict master. We froze as he stared in at us from slightly outside the doorway. Prowse, unable to see him, continued his portrait of the deranged geometry teacher not five feet away from the spectral Percy Flagstaff. Narrow shouldered, bald Percy watched us through his thick, pebble lensed glasses. They made his blue eyes look enormous in his small, pointy chinned face. He had a rather disconcerting tic which twitch-flashed across his left cheek every few minutes. He reminded me of someone I'd seen before somewhere, as he stood there scrutinising his 5a 'victims,' but in my fear I couldn't recall who it was. Unfortunately, there was only one word to describe Percy and that word was 'sinister.'

Waving his long arms about and slapping the board with his stick Prowse 'power whined' into a finale with, "If the angle of the bi-section is less than 45 degrees then, for God's sake, give it to the bloody cat." He gave us the most enormous grin and bowed low, confident of his superbly funny performance. He was totally unaware of our sudden lapse into silence, but then with a panic stricken look of terror it dawned on him that we were not clapping or laughing but all gaping at the open doorway beside him. Like a long, thin spider in a green jacket he tip-toed back to his drawing board and very quietly sat down. It was some seconds before he dared look up and peep at the open doorway. Percy stood there, still and silent, watching us. During one of my quick glances up it came to me that he reminded me of Heinrich Himmler, Adolf Hitler's Reich Leader of the SS and German Police. I looked down and with a chill began to calculate the quality and severity of our punishment for the insulting crime that we had just committed.

We sat there for several minutes staring at our desk tops and the next time I looked up there was no Percy – he had vanished. Slowly 5a's heads came up and the whispering began. "He's gone, oh God, where's he gone?" said Harris. Prowse, deathly white and trembling, announced quietly and with some certainty, "He's gone to fetch the cane."

"Wrong. He's gone to get five canes, big 'uns with 'severe' written on the handles," I said. The muffled giggles started but died down as we realised our awful predicament. "Nice knowing you Prowse," whispered Palmer.

We sat there silently for a full fifteen minutes, trying to understand our situation. After what seemed like an age Percy arrived in the doorway. He quietly closed the door and headed for his desk at the front of the class. "I apologise for being late 5a. Something came up. Very pleasant to walk into such a quiet, well behaved class though," he buzzed and meowed. After the class there followed an urgent and immediate discussion between us in the corridor. "That's what you call applied psychology," offered Kilpatrick. "He's going to leave us in limbo, suffering like, until the end of term. I'm scared shitless and so are you lot. He's clever. Very, very clever because there's nothing worse than having something unresolved." Kilpatrick was dead right of course. We never did find out why Percy behaved like that but now we were even more terrified of him than ever.

There was a 5a party that night at Annie Barbour's house. I think that we were quite unusual as a class because we held drinky get-togethers in each other's houses about once a month. Obviously because we were fond of one another and we felt close. We clubbed together for the drink and Goodenough brought the latest LPs for us to listen and dance to: the Everly Brothers, Elvis Presley, Eddie Cochrane and Buddy Holly were special favourites at our parties.

To cope with being alone with Sonia I learned fast that I could pacify my trembling hands and cure my speechlessness by guzzling a cider as soon as I arrived for the festivities. After just one drink I felt confident and normal. I sat with Sonia on the Barbour's front room sofa, under a standard lamp as The Shadows twanged away in the background.

My girl friend was wearing a soft pink cashmere twin set, a knee length tartan skirt and shiny pink lipstick. Pink lipstick! She looked exactly like a young sophisticated, beautiful woman and she scared me, but the booze helped. I loved the way that Sonia kissed me, her soft, full lips promised me everything. The powerful romantic feelings I experienced with her somehow subjugated the 'beastly, beastly' desires that surfaced within me around my neighbourhood girlfriends. I saw her as a gentle saint, and breast and fanny fondling were not in my thoughts at all. Cuddled in her arms the smell of her Johnson's Baby Powder began to create its own receptor site in the sensual part of my young, developing brain. Her powder had the power to send me to another unknown and wonderful place.

When I was with Sonia I sometimes wondered why she had chosen me from all the fellows that she could have had. I took my life in my hands one night and asked her directly, "Why do you like me?"

"I love your body and you make me laugh a lot," she whispered. Looking away from me she added, "and I love your nose too." I could not believe what I was hearing but it felt marvellous. No one had ever said such things to me before and I felt confident and manly.

Needless to say the feeling and the mood had disappeared by the next morning as I donned my worthless worm garb yet again. But at least I was beginning to gain knowledge which would help me through life. For example, with just one drink, I could change from a dithering Stan Laurel into a cool sophisticated Marlon Brando and handle just about any situation that fate decided to chuck at me.

4

THE RANDOLPH STAR BAR

Mid winter 1961

"Of course they shot the bastard down, he was spying on their country," Ginny the Witch declared angrily. She was referring to the American U2 spy plane incident earlier in the year, when the Russians had shot down the US plane with Capt. Gary Powers on board.

"I can't believe this. You're a pacifist, a liberal, a member of CND and you're defending an act of aggression by the Russians," countered Irish Playwright, pulling his ancient donkey jacket around him as if he was cold, although the plush bar was pleasantly warm.

"Well, you are right of course but sometimes there is no other choice," said Ginny. "I'd always rather talk than fight."

"I smell liberal double standards here," muttered Irish.

"It's common knowledge that anyone from the left always takes the cowardly line of least resistance," exclaimed Cosmo.

"Yeah that's right, if you are ever in a tight corner don't count on a liberal to dig you out," sneered Pete the Sheep.

"War is wrong, wrong, wrong plain wrong," screeched Gin the Witch.

"Oh do listen to naïve Nellie sounding off. You can't negotiate with autocratic regimes you know," said Irish leaning back and picking up his pint. "No one in their right mind wants war but sometimes there is no other option but to fight and defeat the rapers, pillagers and bad fuckers when they threaten us. Fuck CND I say."

We were all in The Star Bar of The Randolph Hotel in Oxford's city centre. Steve O'Donovan, Nigel, Bob Painter, Linda, Jenny, Mick Mulligan, Pete the Sheep, Hank Lamar, Denis Cornell, Cosmo, Pluto, Skolimoski, Irish Playwright, Dick, Max, Felix, Sonia and me. I could never quite work out why we chose to drink in this very classy 5 star hotel. Was it a conscious, considered statement I wondered? Every last one of us was dressed in a super-distressed manner and our clothes were none too clean either. Plus, I could never figure out why The Randolph management let us, the 'filthy beatniks,' into their prestigious establishment. It was all very mysterious.

That November evening I was dressed in a dirty and ripped combat jacket, a long-sleeved French matelot T-shirt, tight Varlsen jeans and worn-out baseball boots with flapping soles. We sat in the corner, at a large, polished table, our feet sinking into the deep pile of the luxurious carpet, drinking and talking, as the rich and powerful aristocrats and academics of England milled around in the bar pointedly ignoring the noisy rabble at the far end of the room.

Soon after leaving school I had met Gin the Witch at a popular jazz club near Carfax. I had watched her singing, on stage, for an hour or more and after her performance I approached her and we started to talk. Gin was my introduction to the Oxford 'beat' scene where I began to meet others who shared my attitudes and doubts about the bourgeois English life. We talked endlessly about art, politics, revolution, poetry and films. Our heroes were Cocteau, Genet, Ginsburg, Bergman, Bunuel, Fellini and we were all fairly convinced that our opinions were the 'right' ones and it was time for the older straights to move over. We were 'anti' just about everything belonging to the establishment and we knew that the establishment owned most things: but not us.

All we needed was the extra seasoning of marijuana and other drugs to complete our scene, but in those early days I never saw much evidence of dope. I'd often bump into Pete the Sheep or Cosmo somewhere in the city centre and they'd enthuse about the weed that they had just smoked. "No, sorry, none left. Bit of a Mary-Jane famine at the moment I'm afraid," they'd reply to my requests. I came to believe that that the smoking of the reefer was just a myth and a fantasy for some of our more boastful Oxford characters.

I'd spent that afternoon in Walton Street with Hank Lamar. He'd picked me up in The Crown Inn at lunchtime and pleaded with me to go back to his room in Jericho. I first saw Hank in the Star Bar about a month after I had started my first job. I had also left home and got my own room, in St. Clements, pretty much as soon as I left Cheney School. My parents had had enough of my drunken, late night arrivals at Henry Street. It was too much for my mother to bear, probably recalling the painful memories of her father's dreadful drinking.

Hank had sidled up to me in The Crown bar and introduced himself afresh although I already knew him by sight from The Randolph. "You must know me Joe. Hank Lamar – Pennsylvania Steel – well, I'm it." I stared at the small, plump American and wondered why he bothered with the self-aggrandizement. When you looked like Hank it was better to keep quiet I would have thought. Overweight, sweaty, pink, short with bulging, bloodshot eyes. He was a great friend of Denis Cornell, a lawyer, and another old queen, who regularly gave advice to the young city boys who got into trouble. I grew to like both Americans a lot over time. "Come back with me this afternoon and I'll give you £20," he urged. Twenty pounds was a month's wages for me. "What's involved," I asked nervously. He leaned into me and whispered, "I just want to look at your naked body that's all."

"Just posing yeh?" I said, seeking reassurance.

"Well......," he trailed off, knocking back his gin and tonic.

I had been doing daily exercises since I was 13 years old when I had met a real muscle man in Dame's Delight and he had given me sets of Charles Atlas 'Dynamic Tension' body building exercises. I remember that he had spent a couple of hours, on the grass near the water that summer, lovingly writing out the exercises for me complete with little matchstick men demonstrating the exercise moves. I had so admired his big, toned, muscular body that it was a pleasure to go through the pain twice a day doing the exercises because of the promise of a marvellous body just like his. Now, at 16, I was muscled and fit looking.

Hank unlocked the door of his room and invited me into his untidy, book littered domain. The place smelled of paper, ancient semen and alcohol. "I'll just get us a drink and then we can get on with it," he suggested, breathing hard from the effort of climbing up the stairs to his room. "I'm a Harvard man you know. I'm doing a PhD here," he said handing me a gin and then sinking, with a sigh, into his battered sofa, clutching his drink in his podgy fingers. "What's your subject?" I asked. "Nude boys and homosexuality in an English city?"

"Very funny. Why don't you just take your clothes off so that I can see you?"

"Give me the 20 quid first and then I can relax," I said.

I spent that grey afternoon, naked, in a grimy room, drinking gin and following instructions from a pink and sweaty Hank. "Stand over by the window and pretend to look out. That's right, hold the curtain back slightly. Yes, wonderful, hold that," or "Bend over the back of that armchair," or "Lie on the sofa and put your hands behind your head." I posed for Hank for the best part of two hours and I felt scared and excited by the weird session, but I felt important, needed, worth something.

As dusk arrived he produced a dozen or more black and white photographs from between some books on his packed bookcase. "Do you like these?" he asked, handing me the pictures as I sat naked in front of his two bar electric fire. Most of the photos looked like they were of couples, semi-clothed, smiling at the camera and participating in obscene activities and lewd poses. However, two of the prints showed a naked adolescent boy, bending over a leather armchair and being penetrated from behind by an elderly gentleman with a long beard. He was fully dressed in what looked like Victorian fashion complete with a top hat and a frock coat. The thin, white skinned boy was smiling at the camera as he was being buggered by the old man. I was entranced by these forbidden images and studied them for some minutes. When I looked up I saw that Hank had been watching me closely and was madly, yanking at his small, erect penis. His eyeballs drifted upwards as he came to a sticky finale over his brown corduroy trousers.

I sank back into the sofa, the room made warm from the buzzing electric fire. I understood that I was beginning to live two lives. One, as a kind of bohemian, a life I shared with Sonia, and another altogether secret life: an addictive, shameful, pleasurable, sinful life. I slumped into the soft couch and felt as if there was a thick sheet of plate glass between me and Hank. I'd experienced this 'plate glass' phenomenon before. I wanted to knock on the glass and shatter it so that I could move closer to the person on the other side, but the thick, clear barrier prevented the kind of intimacy that I craved. I was an intruder, an interloper in this life and when they found me out I'd be in deep trouble. I'd started to wake each morning with a pounding heart and full of fear. It felt as if something dreadful was about to happen, but then the feeling would leave after half an hour. Also, sometimes, when I was alone, I burst into tears – great gulping sobs which lasted for several minutes. No reason......it just happened. Much later I was to learn that this kind of chemical fear is common with people who are predisposed to addictions. I felt every feeling in an exaggerated way but fear was the worst.

I watched Hank frantically rubbing his trousers with his handkerchief and I knew that we were separate; that we were all living our own lives and that we were all alone.

Since leaving home and moving into my St Clements' room I had worked for a stationary company in the city, selling paper, typewriters and pens to the good citizens of Oxford. After work and at weekends I became a creature of the night and I was infatuated with the concept of undermining the establishment by using crime and theft.

One night, after taking Sonia home to Granpont, I stumbled, half drunk, down an alley in the town centre to take a piss. After I had relieved myself in the darkness I noticed that there was a small window further down the passage and something urged me to go and have a look. The room that I looked into was lit by the moon shining through a roof light above and I could see dozens of cardboard boxes stacked in neat rows. Obviously the place was a storage shed for a tobacconist on the High. I could see exotic brands like Camel, Citanes, Gauloise Disc Blue, Marlboro, Passing Cloud, Sobranie Black Russian etc. I knew that there was a ready market for these items and I hatched a plan.

The following evening, after seeing Sonia home safely, I borrowed an old van that was always parked at night in the Cowley Road. The van door was not locked and I reached under the dashboard to rip off the ignition wires and twist them together. The old machine coughed into life with a bit of a splutter but gradually warmed up. I had stolen cars before but I was not an experienced driver at all......but, if I kept stealing cars, I would eventually learn. It was around 11.30pm when I pulled up outside the alley in High Street. I stepped out on to the quiet pavement and put on my brown storeman's coat that I'd brought from work. Hopefully, I'd judged the time just right. Not too late for loading the next day's deliveries and I would not attract the attention of passers by and the lone policeman at Carfax. I was simply a delivery man getting ready for the morning.

It was easy to break the window and gain entry to the stock room and I discovered, to my great delight, that the old wooden door pushed open easily. I spent half an hour carting box after box up the alley to my trusty van. Several late night strollers walked by but continued with their chatter and barely gave me a second glance. As I loaded the last box of Gauloise a policeman on the other side of the road wished me a cheery goodnight and I replied in what I hoped he would recognise as an Irish accent.

The burglary was complete and I drove off to my stash. During my childhood rambles and adventures I had discovered a set of outhouses and sheds that belonged to an empty, derelict house in Old Headington. I decided to park my cigarettes there because I could access the sheds through a large hole in a hedge on a secluded lane that ran behind the large house. The entrance I chose was hidden from view and was away from the busy London Road and main driveway to the house. I'd toyed with the idea of buying a new lock for the shed but quickly abandoned the idea when I realised that it would attract attention to the decrepit outhouses. I had to trust to luck on this one. During the next few months I became a supplier of quality fags to the intellectuals and ne'er-dowells of my beloved city. I told no one about the theft and consequently lessened the chance of being captured in the future.

"Why don't you put your clothes on, you must be cold," suggested Hank as he raised himself out of his armchair facing me. It was dark outside now and I guess we must have fallen asleep for a little while. I was chilly in spite of the heater close by. "Are you still a virgin Joe?" asked Hank lighting up one of my Disc Bleus.

"No," I replied and hoped that he wouldn't pursue the matter. I wanted to present as a sexually experienced guy in this sophisticated, cool, company. "When did you first make love then," he pressed me. "Was it with a girl called Ruth, a friend of Seymour's?" I was so surprised that he already knew that it was impossible for me to lie as the truth was written clearly across my face. "Yes two months ago with Ruth, course I've been with loads of women in my time," I boasted, "but this was the first time I went all the way. How did you know anyway?"

"Pandora Seymour told me a few weeks ago. She said that she had watched you from her bed whilst you screwed Ruth on the floor. She said that she asked to join you both on the floor but Ruth told her to fuck off," reported Hank with a knowing half-smile. "It's true," I laughed, remembering that first night in St Aldates, in a room above Alice's Sweet Shop. "They say that Pandora is a nymphomaniac," said Hank, idly fiddling with his tie, "she'll screw anything, anytime."

"Yup, I suppose that's right, although I feel that I'm a bit like that myself. Lady Lust takes me over and I'm her slave," I said.

Fully dressed again I relaxed back into the sofa and picked up a freshly poured Guinness. "Are you queer like me?" asked Hank.

"No, not at all."

"They all say that. You're only hiding your true sexual inclination because you are ashamed," he countered.

"Look, I don't even think of myself as bi-sexual........I just feel.......sexual. I think I could have sexual relations with anything."

"Not anything," he screeched.

"Men, women, animals, trees, statues, anything," I tried to explain with a concentrating frown.

"Oooh, you are so wicked. I just don't believe you at all. You're a queer-in-waiting, a faggot in the closet," Hank howled, pointing an accusing finger at me as he rocked back in his chair, giggling madly.

"Let me ask you a question to try and explain," I suggested. "Do you feel attracted to women, to their faces, breasts, arses, legs etc?"

"How could you ask me such a repulsive question? Of course not."

"Well, I am attracted to women's bodies and, also, a little bit to men's, but my sexual desire doesn't seem to be dictated by either sex. I just feel sensual and sexual about everything," I said.

"Young man you are a strange, utterly weird, perverted individual and I'm very proud to call you my friend. Cheers!" laughed the American, lifting the remains of his Guinness in a toast to, "Decadence!"

"Does Sonia know these things about you," he probed.

"I'm sorry to say that I tell her very little. I don't trust her for some reason. I want to be free you see," I replied.

"Come on. Time to go to The Randolph," announced Hank. "Lovely afternoon, let's do it again soon."

We were an hour off closing time in the Star Bar and we were all fairly drunk. Bob Painter was discussing his forthcoming trip to India. He intended to make the whole journey alone, by train, and his ambition was to stay stoned for the duration of the trip – about a year he reckoned. "The problem is that once I start smoking that quality Charas in Pakistan I'll never want to come back," he declared earnestly.

"Send some back for Christ's sake. There's nothing in this God forsaken city," said Steve.

"As soon as I hit Paris I'll start mailing stuff back. I'll send it through Mick here. You will all have to buy from him," said Bob.

"It'll never get through you know. Customs always gets it, is my experience," put in Pete the Sheep.

"Well, I can only try can't I?" answered a belligerent Bob.

"Are you getting your hair cut before you go?" asked Skolimoski. He, Bob and Mick all had shoulder length hair and it was still rare to see it worn this length by young men.

"Yes, you must," pressed Ginny. "I've heard that some countries will arrest you on sight with hair that length."

Close to our corner of the bar a rather elegant woman in an evening dress was watching us all and she suddenly declared loudly to the man that she was with, her husband I presumed, "It really is too bad Arnold. Why does the manager let those 'beatniks' come into the hotel? One can't get a seat for love nor money and they do smell. Goodness, they smell, such creatures! God help England that's all I can say." We all listened to her judgement in a delighted and stunned silence and some time after she had finished we all burst into loud, delighted laughter and cheers.

During that final hour before closing time, I sat seriously calculating the evidence of need for marijuana and uppers and realised that if I could supply it I could make a lot of bread. There were very few illegal drugs available at that time in Great Britain. A bit of weed here and there and a small registered heroin addict population, but nothing spectacular, and clearly the newly emerging 'beat' scene was hungry for chemical highs to fuel the coming revolution. I made up my mind to supply the new freedom fighters with dope.

5

A BUSY, BUSY, NIGHT IN SOHO

Autumn 1962

"Fucking hell, we're airborne Joe," screeched a delighted Georgie. He was absolutely right – the Mini that we had stolen an hour ago in Oxford was flying quietly through the foggy air, high above the ground. Suddenly, with a back snapping crash we hit the tarmac on the far side of the roundabout. The little car continued to move forward for a few yards but we could hear big important parts falling ominously from her body. The front bumper and number plate went first and then we heard the exhaust pipe and silencer drop off with a loud metallic clatter. The Mini engine started to steam and then stopped altogether. Georgie and I stared at each other and after a few eye-popping and amazed seconds we collapsed into helpless, hysterical giggles. The steaming battered Mini rocked from side to side in the fog with the force of our convulsing, laughing bodies.

Georgie had asked me earlier that same evening, in La Fantasia, if he could come with me to London. I had three thousand Drinamyl, 'Purple Hearts,' which I needed to sell in Soho, and I made regular trips, in stolen Minis, to supply my customers in the West End. Drinamyl was sold over the counter up until 1958 but was made a 'prescription only' medication after that date because cases of amphetamine psychoses and addiction were being reported, mainly amongst dieting women using the drug as an appetite suppressant. Later it became popular in the Blue Beat clubs of London and with the young, mod hipsters of English cities.

Early in 1962, just turned 17, I recognised that there was a big market for 'hearts' and that the supply was small and infrequent. I knew that I had to make a relationship with a drug company warehouseman, in Oxford, in order that I could start supplying customers. Drinking in the Crown at lunchtime I'd noticed, over time, that several guys in brown storemen's coats met most days for a pie and a pint. I knew that they were employed by a large chemist chain that had an outlet in the city centre. One of the fellows looked like a very suitable candidate as my future supplier and I got excited checking him out over a week or two. He was small, middle-aged and, on his left hand, on the webbed flesh at the base of his thumb and forefinger, he had a crude prison tattoo depicting a hangman's noose. No doubt, he was a villain, but he looked steady and cautious. He always smiled at me and nodded a pleasant hello when he saw me in the Crown. I felt that we were made for each other.

Finally the day came when I decided to make my move. I waited until he was at the bar, ordering a fresh round, and away from his mates. "How're you doing? I need to speak to you about a matter of mutual interest which could benefit us both," I spoke low and close to his ear.

"Where and when?" he asked, without dropping a stitch.

"The Scala Cinema, middle back row, on the left hand aisle. Saturday at 3 pm."

"I won't speak to you again in here OK?"

"OK, see you"

The following Saturday I entered the darkened flea pit to find that 'brown coat' was already there, munching popcorn, and admiring some perky, Scandinavian breasts on the big screen. The cinema was only about a third full and we were able to talk without inhibition. "OK, what's your proposition," he opened.

"Do you work near the prescribed medications?" I asked.

"Yeh! All day, every day, tons of drugs.

"I need a regular supply of Drinamyl. I'll pay £10 for every 1000 and take any amount that you can give me," I said, encouraged by the forward movement of our discussion.

"Cash up front," he demanded, not taking his eyes of the black and white moving images. The cinema was thick with blue cigarette smoke and there was a loud ticking noise from the projection room above our heads.

"As soon as you give me the Purple Hearts I'll pay you on the spot. Guaranteed," I reassured him. "We don't need to know each others moves. We just need a mutually agreed signal to buy and a meeting place to do the transaction."

"I'd prefer to steal to order, on a weekly basis. They come in tins of a 1000, about 9" high and 3" in diameter you know. I can get up to 8 tins a week, no worries," he said earnestly.

"OK. I'll see you in the Crown every Wednesday at 12.30pm and give you the order for the coming Friday. There's no need for us to talk or acknowledge each other. I'll wear paper clips on the pocket of this combat jacket. One for each thousand."

"Make sure they're big shiny paper clips, I'm getting older and my eye sight isn't what it was," he chuckled.

"You don't seem to have sight problems at the moment," I said as we watched a young, blonde nymphet plunge naked into a fjord somewhere in Norway.

"The Friday handover can be in the public bogs at Elliston and Cavell at 1pm. Go into the end cubicle and have the dubes in a carrier bag. You can pass them under the partition and I'll pass you the cash the same way."

"Course I've got to make sure that you are in the bog first," he sniggered, pleased with his fantasy of giving the drugs to an unsuspecting old geezer taking an innocent crap after his cup of tea and iced bun in the department store's café.

"Yeah, good point. I'll put a copy of the Beano slightly under the partition so that you know it's......"

"Dennis the Menace," he laughed. "Sounds good. No need to talk or meet up again in public. Sweet." Thus began a long and profitable partnership with my warehouseman. After a few weeks and several successful hand-overs we began to trust each other and my business supplying amphetamines gradually took off.

Back on the Western Avenue, in the fog, when Georgie and I finally ceased our merriment we began to realise that in order to reach the West End we'd need to steal another motor. It was around midnight and the dual carriageway was deserted thanks to the thick, January, pea soup fog. "Come on man, let's split. Time for another jam jar. Wipe everything you've touched for God's sake," I gently instructed him. Georgie Wilberforce was a little bit older than me and spoke in a BBC 'received pronunciation' voice. He had wild, curly brown hair and a permanently red face. The son of an important civil servant, he was nevertheless, rebellious and likeable.

He owned an old, bright green Austin Seven which was his absolute pride and joy. One evening, in the Star Bar, a few weeks previously, Sonia had brought in a copy of the Oxford Mail and pointed out a news item about Georgie. The paper reported that he had been arrested and charged with speeding at 75 mph on the Oxford By-Pass. After the fuzz had presented their evidence to the court the magistrate asked if Georgie had anything to say. He replied, "Sir. I drive and maintain a 1937 Austin Seven motor car. My car will not normally exceed 30 mph, therefore I can only assume that on the day in question there was a strong following wind." That evening, in the Randolph, Georgie became a new Oxford star within our hedonistic mob. He'd recently turned on to hearts for the first time and he had liked the experience so much that he began to buy a 100 every week from me. I liked Georgie a lot and worried about his instant and insatiable appetite for the amphets, but I continued to supply him.

We left the steaming vehicle on the side of the road and walked towards White City. I was clutching a carrier bag containing 3000 Purple Hearts, packed in blue Basildon Bond envelopes in 25, 50, and 100 tablet deals. After a couple of hundred yards we spotted the neon and dim, night lights of a parade of shops on the left hand side of the road. It was deathly quiet as we crossed the duel carriageway and walked along the row of shops. Almost at the end of the parade we spotted a narrow service road that curved behind the shops. "Up here," I whispered. "There's bound to be a motor." Sure enough there was a car, just one, a Mini. We couldn't believe our luck and smiled at each other in the dark. I leaned on the door handle until I heard the soft, distinctive snap as the Mini door lock broke and allowed me to climb into the small car.

In the newly stolen Mini we reached the Bayswater Road in no time and we would be in Soho in less than 20 minutes. We were both high and smoking Capstan Full Strength cigarettes one after another. Thick fog outside our vehicle – thick smoke inside, but we were happy. "I even enjoy the come downs," ventured Georgie. "I just lie back and close my eyes and watch my own pornographic films. I call them mind movies. Do you have them?"

"Yes, every time, complete with a thumping hard-on, it's nice," I replied. My fantasies often revolved around some women that I was seeing at that time for paid sexual services. By definition, they were wild and desperate simply because they were willing to pay me. Nevertheless, I did have big affectionate feelings for most of them, especially a young Jewish undergraduate that I was seeing once or twice a week.

We spent long and pleasant afternoons together in her rooms in North Oxford. Her name was Anna and she stared at me with big, sad, brown eyes. She seemed to be pleading with me for something but I could never work out what it was and, for some reason, I felt scared to ask.

I got the strong impression that she would take her own life one day, such was the depth of her sadness, but she was loving and passionate with me. When I arrived she would beam a huge smile and chatter excitedly. She smelt of musk and spices and I loved to smell her hot skin between her large, drooping breasts. Anna demanded anal sex and seemed to receive more satisfaction from this method of loving. I think I was a little bit in love with Anna and I thought about her a lot, even when I was with Sonia.

"Last weekend, during a comedown, I had an amazing fantasy about a couple of academic sisters in their thirties," I related to Georgie. In fact the women were not part of a 'mind movie' at all but real people who had been paying me for sex since I was 16. I guess that I wanted to talk about it to Georgie without revealing my customers identities. Game playing really. I first met the sisters at a party in the Woodstock Road. We sat in a corner, chatting and drinking, until very late and the party had died a death. The older one invited me back to their house in Rawlinson Road and once we were there in that vast, empty roomed house they delivered their proposition.

They would pay me £5 and drinks if I agreed to visit them once a week after 11pm. "We want to undress you and tie you up," explained the younger, plumper sister. She looked enthusiastic about the prospect and her blue eyes were shining and flashing. "Uhh….and then what?" I asked apprehensively. "Oh God Joe, don't worry, it's only a nice, little game that we like. It's quite harmless and we'll untie you after," said the older woman persuasively.

"Uhh…..after what?" I persevered.

"Don't be a silly boy now. Come on, we'll show you," giggled the younger sister. "Come on. Beddy-byes and we will undress you in the big bedroom." She took me by the hand and clutching our drinks we stumbled through various rooms and up two flights of stairs to a large bedroom, panelled in dark oak. I lay on the bed naked and helpless with my wrists and ankles tied to the large, lumpy bed. The two women, half clothed, rubbed themselves against my captured body. And so began my weekly erotic adventures with the two sisters.

During the two weeks that followed I began to look forward to the late evening appointments in Rawlinson Road. These sessions contained an essential ingredient in the making of an addiction. Highly seductive, sensual and pleasurable they always promised more than they delivered. Always, just falling short of ecstasy but leaving me with the firm belief that the next time I'd go to Pleasure Heaven. In fact I was only to visit that sublime place once in my life and that was still a few years off yet. For me, lust, greed, intoxication and power were all tricks; cruel deceptions, but again, I never found that out until decades later and after the deaths of many of my friends.

"You know Georgie, for hours I just lay there, spread-eagled, until finally they took it in turns to climb on top of me and satisfy themselves," I recounted to my friend who was now smoking, chewing gum and doing peculiar, forward motions with his jaw.

"Please do stop it, you are making me randy. I could fuck a camel you know," he fizzed.

"You couldn't," I said.

"Why not?"

"They are too tall and they've always got the hump," I smirked. The fog had lifted as we drove up Wardour Street into Soho.

We parked a couple of blocks away from the Limbo and eased ourselves out of the car. "Can you remember where we're parked Georgie? I've totally forgotten on my last three trips," I asked.

"I've got a memory like an elephant mate. The exact location is safely stored in my large brain," he replied. It was early and the Limbo was fairly quiet when we entered but there were already a few couples dancing to Prince Buster on the juke box. The large basement was, as always, in semi-darkness lit only by a couple of small red lights and the fluorescent light behind the bar. There were a lot of girls sitting around and some were dancing with slim spades in Blue Beat, pork pie hats. I loved Blue Beat and Ska and the jerking music lifted me up even higher.

As we walked across the dance floor to the soft drinks counter I remarked to Georgie, "You know, it always pisses me off that there are rarely any black chicks around. I dream about marrying a beautiful West Indian girl one day but I don't think that they are allowed out at all."

"You've already got a beautiful chick – the most beautiful – you've got Sonia," said a bewildered Georgie.

"Yeh," I muttered, spotting one of my customers in the far corner by himself. "Get some orange juice or something. I've got to see the guy over there."

"Hi Zim, how's it going?" I greeted my man.

"I'll take a 1000 now and 2000 this time next week," said the small, wiry East Londoner. "It's safe enough to hand over in the bog. Come on I've got valued customers waiting." The dimly lit lavatory stank of stale piss, Jeyes fluid and vomit but it was OK to use as an office for a couple of minutes. I handed Zim ten envelopes containing a hundred tablets each and he handed me £25. "Nice.

See you next week, same time and same place," he said opening the flimsy door to leave.

"Take care man," I said.

Back in the club I found Georgie sitting next to a young girl wearing bright red lipstick and a scarlet coloured blouse. She was watching me as I crossed the floor towards them. I accepted the orange juice from Georgie and scanned the club for my other dealer. I couldn't see him amongst the jerking dancers but didn't doubt that he would turn up eventually. I noticed that the red chick had a Midland's accent when she spoke quietly to me, "Got any PH?"

"What's PH?" I replied coolly. She dug me playfully in the ribs with her elbow and giggled. "Amphets, you know. I've seen you in here before, well at it you were."

"Do you mean these?" I asked showing her a glass jar with 500 tablets inside.

"Christ! You idiot! Put them away before we get busted," she whispered. I felt stupid and embarrassed to have made such a foolish error. It was a purely impulsive desire to impress her and I'd put us both in danger. "Let me have 50 can you?" she smiled. I was about to reach into my pocket for an envelope when Georgie nudged me and nodded towards the drinks counter. I replaced the envelope in my pocket and looked over at the dark suited guy talking to Harry, the Limbo boss. It was Ronnie Kray and the place had gone awful quiet. The music played on but most of the dancing couples had deserted the floor so that they could sit and stare at the notorious gangster. His broad shoulders stretched the material of his Italian suit jacket as he leaned into Harry across the bar. They were in quiet, earnest conversation and Ronnie was staring at the Limbo boss with the manner of a man who was used to being obeyed. He emanated badness did Ron.

I knew that the Krays owned a warehouse in the East-End which housed, amongst other things, Drinamyl for sale in Soho. I was in his territory now and I knew it. If he knew what I was doing here I was yesterday's news. Ronnie continued to stand at the counter, talking quietly to Harry Bidney. He had his back to the dance floor and the seating around it. He appeared to be alone. As Kray continued his chat with Harry my contact entered the club and came down the stairs. He spotted me immediately and grinned a big beaming hello. As he sat down next to me I told him, "We've got company, let's wait a bit." The North Londoner followed my gaze and I watched the blood drain from his face. "Fuck, we're dead men," he muttered.

"Stay cool," I whispered. "He's looking for young rent boys. He's not interested in us. That's why he's talking to Harry." It was an educated guess but it could have been an accurate supposition because less than 5 minutes later Ronnie turned and walked towards the staircase and exit.

Instantly the Limbo sprang to life again and people started to dance and chat. The four of us were a bit slower to recover though. I was desperately trying to work out why Mr Kray was here. One of my regular customers, back in Oxford, in the Swan and Castle, was an East-End villain who worked alongside Jack 'The Hat' McVitie whom I knew was currently in a power struggle with Ronnie and Reggie. I assumed that this hood was buying for Jack and it had always puzzled me why McVitie should buy from me when he could have scored direct from his overlords. Jack had an amphetamine problem himself so maybe there was some pride and paranoia motivating him to score from me. The more I thought about it, wired as I was, the more appealing the monastic life appeared. The problem was I had no way of knowing what was happening, so I had little or no control over events. I was scared.

"Come on you lot. We can hand over in the Take Five doorway, it's usually empty," I suggested to the girl and my dealer. "How many do you want Fred?"

"Let me have 1,500."

"OK get the cash ready," I instructed. The four of us climbed the stairs and picked up our pass-out tickets at the Limbo exit. We did the deed in the drain smelly entrance to Take Five and the dealer and the chick left us and walked out into the streets of Soho. "Where to?" asked a red faced Charlie. "I need to drop some more hearts."

"OK just let's get out of here and think later. I've still got around 400 left to get rid of but I think I'll phone in sick. I feel that I have a nervous condition coming on," I declared, feeling miserable and ratty. As we made our way out to the main street a big guy in a dark suit appeared out of the Limbo and walked towards us. He was indicating with his hand that we should move to the side of the alley. "One of Ronnie's," hissed Georgie and I felt for the steel button on my flick knife which lived in my right hand jacket pocket. In one glorious and spontaneous moment I dropped the chiv as a bad idea and both Georgie and I hit the hood simultaneously: a left from him and a right from me. He fell back against a group of metal dustbins and then lay still, groaning a little bit. As we hared off down

Old Compton Street we could not believe our luck. Pure chance - a divine, enchanted escape from the clutches of evil.

When we were certain that we were not being followed I asked Georgie, "Where did we park the car, where did we leave the fucking thing?"

"Now there is an excellent question," he pondered. We'd lost another car. I could not believe it. After a few seconds, both turning round in bemused circles, we collapsed on to the pavement in hysterical laughter. "The life and times of a young master criminal," I spluttered, taking in deep breaths and holding my stomach.

"Those punches were pure luck you know," giggled Georgie. "A fluke - a million to one chance that we both caught him at exactly the same time."

"Let's go home, I've had enough," I croaked, my laughter gradually winding down.

"No car," screamed Georgie slapping me on the back and we were off again, helpless with mirth on a pavement somewhere in Soho. After we had recovered sufficiently we easily located another Mini in Dean Street and drove back to Oxford. High on the 'hurry up' tablets, we yakked and chattered non-stop all the way back to our city of dreaming spires.

It was around 7am when we arrived in the city. The fog had lifted and we abandoned the Soho Mini in St Clements. We walked to Mick's Café on the Cowley Road. Mick's was a workmen's and yobboe's joint: it was always open early and it was sufficiently seedy to relax and talk business in. This dodgy establishment was near The Plain and Magdalen Bridge, the very beautiful entrance to the City of Oxford. The contrast between the Cowley

Road and The High was dramatic to say the least. Michael Dibden once wrote, in one of his fine novels, that there should be a passport control on the Plain roundabout to clearly separate the two districts. Mick's coffee bar was filthy beyond belief and always full of steam, cigarette smoke and the smell of fried breakfasts, especially on winter mornings. Presley, Jim Reeves and Connie Francis entertained us from the ancient Wurlitzer in the corner.

Georgie and I sat next to the juke box, away from the big front window and downed several mugs of strong tea. The amphetamines were entering the chronic phase of the comedown period now and we were both gabbling like manic parrots and feeling very horny. "Who do you think that guy was who went for us outside the Limbo?" asked Georgie.

"Come to think of it. Did he go for us?" I remarked.

"I thought that he worked for the Krays and that he'd sussed you dealing," he explained, working his bottom jaw in a fascinating, rotating fashion.

"Perhaps we'd dropped a 10 bob note and he wanted to give it back to us."

"Christ!" And we whacked a poor, innocent, honest gangster," continued Georgie. We were giggling and comparing our tannin coated tongues when we were joined at our table by a smiling Gary Gardner.

Gardner, as he was known in Oxford, was a top hard man in the city. He was vicious, cunning and queer. His best friend was a mountain of a man called Steve Barr, also a poof, who delighted in beating up American servicemen in the Nag's Head Pub and then pitching their limp bodies into the canal outside. The Yanks came in for rest and relaxation from the nearby bases at Upper Heyford and Brize Norton. After a few of them had encountered Steve they preferred to live it up in nearby Witney instead. Oxford town was known for its hard men and rumour had it that Oxford was the one place in England where the travelling fairground boxing booths did not accept fights from the local lads – too risky, so they set up their own stooges to get knocked out.

Gardner sat down, pulled up a chair and looked at me with a smile on his round, impudent face. "Doing anything this morning?" he asked me.

"Coming down very nicely thank you Gary," I replied.

"Come up to my place for an hour, I've got something to show you," he said, sipping at his hot tea and continuing to smile.

"Right, I'm off for a wank etc," beamed Georgie, sensing that private business was now on the agenda between me and Gary. I didn't trust Gardner further than I could spit a piano but I wasn't going to pass up on any business.

Gardner's mother was at work when we arrived at his house in North Oxford. He continued to live at home, cared for by his mother who doted on her charming psychopath. "Right Joe. I'll give you a fiver for a couple of hours of fun," he offered, looking at me sideways on.

"Fun?" I asked sinking back into a soft, expensive sofa.

"Oh do fuck off," he smirked. "Won't be a tick." My body was tired from lack of sleep but my mind was working like a speeded up dirty porn movie. I lay back in comfort until I heard Gardner call me from upstairs, "Joe, I'm ready. Come up." I climbed the wide staircase and walked to an open door. The bedroom was huge and decorated in a very feminine style. The weak winter sunlight filtered through the net curtains on to the chintz, frills and pictures of roses. Obviously, this was his mother's bedroom. Gary Gardner stood next to the large double bed dressed in, what I assumed, was his ma's lingerie, plus extras. The Oxford hard man wore a long blonde wig, black nylon stockings, suspender belt, a black lacy bra and a transparent 'baby doll' nighty. His outfit was completed with black, shiny, high heeled shoes. He had made up his eyes and wore pink lipstick. Gardner stood, smiling coyly at me, with his left hand on his hip and his left leg slightly bent, fluttering his large false eyelashes. He wore no knickers and he was fully erect. I was shocked to discover that I quite fancied him.

Gary Gardner posed for me as I lay on his mother's perfumed bed and later, on that sunny morning, I fucked him from behind, eventually coming with a painful, rushing scream of release. After, smoking together on the rumpled bed in Mrs Gardner's boudoir, I said a prayer to myself, "It wasn't me God I swear it. It was the drugs. Dear Heavenly Father please don't let Sonia find out about my perverted activities and, for that matter, no one else either. Thank you very much. Amen."

6

A Cold December

It would not have been acceptable to call ourselves beatniks or hipsters. One simply defeated the object of trying to live without labels, outside society, if we had branded ourselves. But lying there in Tom's room, on that freezing December afternoon, listening to Allen Ginsberg reading Howl on the Dansette record player it was inescapable – we were just so.......so....... super cool.

The four of us: me, Sonia, Tom and Diana lay on the ancient, grimy, carpeted floor of the large room surrounded by Tom's oil paintings, some completed and some in the process of creation. The room, on the Iffley Road, stank of oil paint and Charas. We had spent the last four hours passing the joint and listening to James Brown 'Live at the Apollo,' a young Bob Dylan and now Ginsberg, whining through our smoke.

'I saw the best minds of my generation destroyed by madness, starving hysterical naked through the negro streets at dawn looking for an angry fix..........'

Pulling on the soggy spliff I said, "Some good guys have died this year you know: Kennedy, Huxley, it's a drag."

"You're going to die if you don't remove your foot from my right breast," giggled Diana. I shifted my position and for a while we listened to the poet crank on.

'who ate fire in paint hotels or drank turpentine in Paradise Alley, death, or purgatoried their torsos night after night, with dreams, with drugs, with waking nightmares, alcohol and cock and endless balls.......'

"God, this is cheerful," groaned Sonia slumped over my chest and stoned as a wazzer. "At least the Great Train Robbers made it. Two million quid they stole. Cool eh?" We were forever discussing, and inventing, our own anti-heroes. It was time for the young and the outsiders to rise up and wreck a few things. There were too many fat cats and too much privilege in our green and pleasant land.

"How much bread do you make now Joe?" Tom asked idly.

"Not much. I only deal to provide the poor with good drugs. A public service so to speak," I replied, transfixed by one of Tom's oils hanging on the crowded wall. It depicted a long, blue woman with a pot on her head. "Just a little bit of Charas for my friends that's all." It was a lie of course.

Earlier in the year, whilst I was working as a fireman in Oxford, I had made contact with a West Indian importer in Notting Hill. I called him Uncle Albert. I'd met him one night outside Wragg's Café and he had tried to sell me a good ounce of PG Tips. When he realised I wanted to score a lot regularly he never again tried to cheat me. He was a skinny fellow with bulging, brown eyes which made him appear perpetually surprised. I arrived every Friday night at his house and after he'd taken my order and cycled off to get the weed, I was entertained by his ancient wife and his grand children. Granny rolled the joints, knitted and hushed the kids during my hour long wait for Uncle Albert. The eldest of the children, a pretty girl called Dezrine often sat next to me and played with my hair. "You just like them Rolling Stones man!" she sang gleefully.

"Hush child, leave de man in peace, he workin'," commanded Granny watching Coronation Street on her tiny black and white television set. 'You're right Granny,' I thought. 'I am working. My dealing, in hearts and dope, took up most of my time and I could never afford to let my guard down.'

I had been scoring from Albert for nearly a year now and I was beginning to shift large quantities. I had decided to use the small business of supplying Charas to my friends as a cover for the real and more profitable business of supplying three Oxford dealers. They were acquaintances of mine who were new to the dealing game, largely because the dealing game was, in itself, new. Of course this arrangement was more lucrative and less risky for me. I knew that eventually someone close to me would blab to the fuzz, on some pretext or other, and so I played my cards close to my chest. Typically, every week, I would buy half to one kilo for my pals and then, on top of that, another two to four kilos which I would sell personally to my dealers. My close friends, including Sonia, knew nothing about this duel arrangement of mine.

Every Friday evening, after finishing work, Derek and Lorraine, two of the Randolph gang, would pick me and Sonia up from Iffley Road in their battered Mini. I gave them a quarter ounce of dope and paid for the petrol for a return trip to Notting Hill Gate. It was always an enjoyable journey to Uncle Albert's and fairly risk free until we returned to Oxford at around 11pm or so. This is when I implemented my cunning master plan to avoid capture and we followed the system religiously.

When we arrived back in our city Derek and Lorraine would drop me off, with the dope, a few streets away from a room that I rented in Divinity Road. Then, they would drive on to my pad and I would drop all the gear over a randomly selected garden wall and walk home empty handed. If the Drug Squad was watching my place in Divinity Road they had two opportunities to pounce: on Derek, Lorraine and Sonia or, ten minutes later, on me, and we were all clean. I figured that if plod was going to attempt a bust then it would either be in Divinity Road or Iffley Road.

The four of us would wait an hour in my room and then I would leave to pick up the dope. On my return I would dump my 'secret dealer's' Charas over another garden wall, to be picked up by me in the middle of the night. Back in Divinity Road I weighed up the deals for my pals and later Derek and Lorraine took the bag of stuff to Iffley Road where our customers waited patiently. Whilst Derek parked and waited around the corner, Lorraine walked into the studio carrying an empty paper bag. After ten minutes or so, when Derek was certain that he wasn't being watched, he took the Charas into our friends. Well, it seemed foolproof and sophisticated at the time! Indeed, the system worked well for two years or more, without a sniff from the police, although they knew

I was shifting cannabis and Drinamyl in fairly substantial quantities for that particular era.

I was very careful, but inevitably, being stoned most of the time, I said and did some pretty reckless and silly things. One night, at the beginning of December, I had stolen a Mini, just for a joy ride, and I was spotted driving erratically by the police. After a long car chase, from Woodstock to Oxford they finally overhauled me in St Giles after I skidded the car sideways into their overtaking police car. I was charged with 'taking and driving away without the owners consent' etc. I asked the police to take a further 28 stolen vehicles into consideration as these were the ones that I could remember taking but unsure if I had used gloves or wiped the car clean later. I wanted to tidy up the record there and then, in case the police bounced me later with a further list of nicked cars.

As the desk sergeant released me from my cell the following morning, after being charged and given bail to appear later in court, he handed back my belongings including a silver snuff box containing a couple of dozen Drinamyl. I could not believe they had missed them – but they had. "OK fucking Stirling Moss, sling your hook," commanded the cop. "Your boss, the Chief Fire Officer, Sidney Boulter, has been on the phone. He's disgusted with you. He says you have brought the brigade into disrepute and you should be ashamed of yourself. He really thought you were going to make a great officer apparently – he feels badly let down. Go on, fuck off, you should be ashamed." As I walked out into St Aldates that early, raw morning I felt hot, unsettled and vulnerable. I felt ashamed.

I never really understood how the hell I ever got into the Fire Service in the first place. I remember a dreadful day in the previous year when I had visited my mother. I was nursing a massive come down, feeling the fragility of hopelessness and paranoia that always came after days of amphetamine use. She pitched a copy of The Oxford Mail at me and said, "Look at the advert I've ringed." It was inviting men to apply for Oxford City Fire Service, offering excitement and some stability. In my terrible desperation and confusion I applied the following day and, to my huge surprise, I was accepted.

Three other chaps and I were duly dispatched, as fresh recruits, to London Road Fire Service Training School in Manchester. By this time we had all heard the rumours from the old timers at Oxford City Fire Station. "By fuck! Manchester's tough! The toughest training in the world. It'll take real men to survive their training course. Those instructors will eat you alive. They are all ex-marine commandos you know. Run you into the ground etc. etc." We all took this ribbing with a pinch of salt naturally, until that fateful night when we were eating our first supper in the college canteen. A small, red faced Sub Officer marched to the front of the mess hall, "Quiet," he shouted. "At the moment this intake of trainee recruits numbers 56 men. By the end of the week 26 of you will have packed your bags and gone home to your mummies. You won't be tough enough or intelligent enough, to take what we dish out and you'll run away. Well, that's good because the Fire Service does not want your type. Mark my words gentlemen." He marched out and left the canteen hushed and unsure. One week later only the valiant were left on the course......29 of us.

The next dismal morning at breakfast another Sub Officer marched into the dining room and yelled, "You.

You at the back." He was, unfortunately, pointing straight at me. "Stand up girly." I stood up slowly, dressed smartly in my Fire Service dress uniform. "What's your name?" he shouted.

"South, Sir."

"Turn around South," he commanded. "You've got two claims to fame already South. You're the youngest recruit here and you've got the longest hair ever seen at London Road. Get it cut by tomorrow you twat." I sat down and with a blush whispered to my neighbour, "I'm famous."

No doubt about it, I was proud to have survived that first freezing week in December 1962. The three training school instructors set about weeding the men from the boys. The rationale for their harsh tests was logical enough. The fire grounds were dangerous places and you needed to be certain that if you were in a life or death situation the men in your team were as brave and tough as they come. The selection tests were simple. Pick up your man in a fireman's lift and run with him to an escape ladder. Up the sixty foot ladder to a second floor balcony. Run round two balconies surrounding the parade ground, a total distance of three quarters of a mile, and down the stone steps to the drill yard. Still running, we ran around the large training area. At this point men began dropping their partners and this, invariably, was the end of their fire service career. No guts – too weak.

Those of us who survived the run were met by a Sub Officer who gently told us, "Top of the stairs and into the gym men. Then you can drop 'em." Legs wobbled and bodies shook as we gratefully entered the gymnasium, but inside the door stood another officer who shouted, "Run,

run, round the gym." When, finally, we were allowed to stop most of us felt so light and dizzy that our legs buckled and we saw stars. I, for one, quite enjoyed that bit and….. I was proud of myself.

One icy freezing afternoon, three weeks into the arduous training, a truly glorious, magnificent moment occurred. I had quickly developed a reputation for having the loudest voice on the course. It was training procedure for the No 1 in any drill team to yell, "Drill completed Sir," after they had completed a standard set of pump or ladder drills. During the first three weeks I was sometimes chosen, by a Sub Officer, to demonstrate how to holler properly to any whispering wimp who hadn't quite made the grade in the shouting stakes. "By 'eck South, you've got the loudest voice I've ever heard," remarked an officer one day early on.

On this marvellous, sub-zero afternoon my team had just completed a four man pump drill and as the No 1 it was my job to march smartly one pace forward and bellow, "Drill completed Sir," and then salute. At the end of this particular drill I realised that Sub Officer Soames, a loathsome creature, whom we all disliked, was standing barely three paces from my position. He was busy watching his own squad perform and oblivious to my team behind him. My own Sub Officer stood behind us and had a clear view of the following event. I calculated that if I took three steps forward, instead of the regulation one, it would bring me right up close to Soames' left ear. I decided in an instant to risk the wrath of my own officer because I knew that Soames could do nothing about me simply completing a drill properly. He would not have seen the two illegal paces forward. One, two, three quick, smart strides and I let rip, full blast into his small pink ear, "Drill completed Sir." I saluted and watched as Sub Officer Soames' shoulders lifted in order to defend his ear drums against the sonic boom. I turned in a regimental fashion and marched back to the squad. Behind me I heard Soames mutter, "You enjoyed that didn't you South," whilst in front of me, my own Sub Officer and squad battled to keep straight faces as they watched the red and fuming face of Sub Officer Soames.

Later, a few guys jacked the training in after failing to survive being shut in a smoke filled room for the regulation time and more quit when attempting the elegant and dangerous hook ladder drills. Very quickly I came to love and excel at using a hook ladder. Twelve weeks later I was selected to demonstrate this beautiful art to the assembled Fire Chiefs, from across Britain, and recruit's relatives at our passing out parade. Much later I was saddened to hear that our Sub Officer trainers were to be court martialled for 'cruel and inhuman' treatment of trainee firemen. I believe though, that the case was abandoned because of a lack of witnesses who were prepared to testify. I was glad, but perhaps, only because I had not only survived the tough training but positively thrived on it.

I was placed on probation for the car thefts and sacked from the Fire Service. I quickly got a job in a builder's merchants loading lorries with bricks, cement etc and I continued to deal. I had also moved in with Tom and we shared his artist's studio, co-existing amicably enough. Amongst all his paintings, rubble and discarded tubes of oil paint were our two beds. I had a single and Tom slept in the double. Sometimes I awoke in the middle of the night gagging on the strong odour of linseed oil. When

I was stoned I sometimes believed that that the oil had somehow permeated my body and was travelling around me internally via my blood supply. This explained the ever present taste of linseed oil in my mouth.

Lying there, on the floor, tangled up in warm, smelly bodies (no one bathed too frequently in those days, perhaps once each week if you were lucky and hardly anybody used deodorants) I wondered why I continued to smoke the reefer. I hated the effects of cannabis. I disliked, and was frightened by, the distorted images, time lapses and paranoia that accompanied my inhalation of the thick, pungent smoke. Although I presented to others as cool and in control I was, in fact, over sensitive and half mad. The dope just made my mental state even more difficult to endure. I became fragile and anxious. "Ooooh…..oooooh…I've got the horrors!" my pals would sometimes whimper after a couple of joints, like it only happened now and again. I used to think, 'fuck me man, get real. I live with the horrors on a daily basis….and long before dope came along.'

Sometimes I enjoyed the experience of smoking weed; when I was alone, safe, watching a film or listening to music but usually the holy smoke sent me to Double Bedlam. I suppose that I felt that I had to smoke because I sold the damn stuff and also because I didn't want to be considered odd. No, I needed a drug that calmed my frantic brain. There was some nembutal around at the time, coming from someone's leaky script, and I found these pleasant. Well, the first buzz anyway. The truth was that I hadn't yet found my perfect drug.

"So how much money are you making?" asked Diana, stubbing out a roach on her Levis.

"Don has already asked me that. Do keep up Di," I muttered, glaring at her.

"Oh sorry Joe missed it. So how much?" she persevered.

"Nothing is the answer. I give the little that I make to the poor," I teased.

"He's not going to tell you Di, please change the subject," suggested Tom.

"Good idea. What happened to your Amedeo Modigliani period," I asked Tom. "You liked those long, thin, skinny figures didn't you?"

"I am now officially entering my new Giacometti era," he chuckled.

"I like my women round, plump and voluptuous. Like this," I laughed, grabbing a large handful of Sonia's bottom. After this spell of chatter we lapsed back into our individual dream worlds, breathing in linseed oil and hash smoke. Together in a heap, we were all in different places, feeling and seeing different things. We were alone, each one of us, that afternoon on the Iffley Road.

"I heard that the Oxford fuzz set up this new drug squad because of you," whispered Diana after what seemed like months of silence. Tom had decided to replay a part of Howl and had flopped back down on to the floor to listen.

'who faded out in vast sordid movies, were shifted in dreams, woke on a sudden Manhattan, and picked themselves up out of basements hung-over with heartless Tokay and horrors of Third Avenue iron dreams & stumbled to unemployment offices, who walked all night with their shoes full of blood on the snowbank docks waiting for a door in the East River to open to a room full of steamheat and opium.......'

"They say it's the first drug squad in Britain," said Tom quietly.

"Congratulations," tittered Diana. I knew that I didn't have to respond. I knew that they wouldn't think that I was being difficult or rude. They'd think that I was being cool. That's the thing: don't smile, don't feel, don't let on, exude cool. God, I was so cool.

Later that evening we drifted down to the Swan and Castle. The tiny pub was situated next to Oxford Jail and had become very popular with our crew. Bob and Mary, the landlord and landlady, welcomed the fresh, young trade to their small saloon. Over time Bob replaced lots of records on his juke box with the Blue Beat sounds which we all loved so much. Both Bob and Mary had confided in me that they had hated the incessant, throbbing rhythm at first but now, after listening to 'Carolina' and 'The Lion Sleeps Tonight' several thousand times, they were beginning to dig it. When the four of us entered the bar 'Love Me Do' by the Beatles was playing. "This is pleasant enough you know," confided Tom, "but it won't last. This group will vanish without trace soon."

Slim was already in the saloon talking to Jeannie. He yelled across at me in his Texan drawl, "Josh was in here ten minutes ago. He was looking for you." Slim was referring to Josh Macmillan, the grandson of Harold Macmillan, the Prime Minister at the time, and a new addition to our crowd. Josh and I had met in The Crown some weeks before and I had instantly liked this charming but fragile young man. He was sensitive, hesitant and twitchy. "He looked like he was hungry," said Slim, nodding at me meaningfully. Josh had a desperate need for any kind of drug and the depth of his desire was alarming. We bought our drinks and plonked ourselves down besides Jeannie and Slim. "Well you're a sight for sore eyes. Welcome home," says I to Jeannie.

"Yeah thanks. Back on the scene man. Where I belong. Writing crap poetry and mixing with crap people." quipped Jeannie. She spent half her life touting for trade with the Yanks and the other half as an Oxford bum. "How can you say that girl? We are the brains behind the coming revolution – an intellectual elite," joked Sonia. Slim gave her the thumbs up and nodded his agreement.

Slim was a full blooded Cherokee Indian and he was stationed at the nearby American base of Brize Norton. Since I first met him, a year earlier, he had spent all his leave with the 'English Beatniks' and we had formed a strong friendship during that time. As an outsider himself maybe he felt at home with us. During last summer, drunk and stoned, Slim had decided to smuggle me back into the base for a couple of nights. When he first suggested the idea to me I asked him, "What for Slim? It's a crazy idea and it's too dangerous for both of us."

"That's why we should do it you son-of-a-bitch. I'll show you where they carry the atomic bombs," he argued persuasively. "I do declare Joey boy is a chicken."

"Come on then you Yankee bastard," I laughed. "Let's go."

Getting on to the base was not a problem as I was huddled, hidden amongst a dozen or more returning US airmen, in a special bus which transported the servicemen between the base and Oxford. We were on the late night run and the bus sailed through the checkpoint with a brief wave from the MP's guarding the gate. I was excited to be on enemy territory. I'd been on a couple of CND marches in the past but I'd never been entirely convinced by the idealistic arguments put out by the pacifists. Their philosophy, it seemed to me, was based on a naïve assumption that both parties in any dispute were good and rational human beings. Already, at 19 years of age, I knew that there were some bad and evil people around and the only thing that impressed them was superior strength. Nevertheless, it was a great buzz to be close to the atomic bombers with a CND badge pinned under my lapel. The first thing that Slim did, after we entered his neat and polished room, was to sit me down and chop off my flowing locks.

The next evening, after spending the day dressed in US fatigues and working alongside Slim at the motor pool, we decided to go to the airmen's club for a drink. Good time girls were bussed in from the nearby towns at the weekends so that they could drink and dance and entertain the servicemen. The buses were known as the 'trash wagons.' Back in Slim's room he kitted me out in a long drape jacket, wide shouldered, with a silver thread running through the black and grey pattern, a white shirt with a cowboy 'Slim Jim' tie, narrow black trousers and black leather, beetle crusher shoes. He smeared my newly shorn hair with Brylcream and drenched the entire ensemble with Old Spice. Slim stood back to admire his handiwork. "You look just fine," he purred.

We entered the club easily and sauntered over to the bar where Slim ordered a couple of Schlitz beers. It was sweet and tasted like something out of a cough medicine bottle. The club was crowded and the music was loud. Some couples were dancing but most were sitting drinking and talking. Slim and I were engaged in earnest conversation about his mothers long term interest in his penis when I noticed my friend Jeannie waddle past us on her very high heels. She was wearing a figure hugging, silver sparkly number and she had her hair piled up in a beehive style. Jeannie was as blind as a bat but much too vain to wear glasses. On her wobbly journey past me she glanced in my direction but continued on her mission towards the loo. I watched her stop, pause and then slowly turn around. Obviously she needed to check out what she thought she had just glimpsed. She clip-clopped back in our direction, beehive held proudly aloft by varnish-type hair spray. This time she walked closer to the bar so that she could get a better look at me.

A yard away I watched her start to narrow her eyes and stretch her neck forward to get a clearer view. Slim and I leaned against the bar fascinated by the show. Again Jeannie passed me by and then, two yards further on, she stopped, paused again, returned and stood brazenly in front of me. With my sparkly jacket and Yank hair do I leaned back against the bar, lifted my glass towards her and said, "Hi Jeannie." Neck craned forward and eyes narrowed into slits in order to improve her focus she recognised me at last. "Oh God! Oh fuck! I can't believe it's you," she howled. She began to laugh so much that she had to squat, in a very un-lady like posture, on the floor with one hand holding her lower stomach area. She laughed until her mascara ran small rivers of black goo down her cheeks and I really feared that she was about to wet herself. Finally her paroxysms of laughter subsided, but by that time Slim and I were long gone.

7

THE LOST THREE WEEKS

Mid-summer 1964

"It opened in the 1820s as The Oxford Lunatic Asylum,"
I declared. Sonia and I were sitting on a bench staring
at The Warneford Hospital. That afternoon the summer
sun was hot and the blue sky was cloudless. We were
breathing in the scent of freshly mowed grass and Sonia
looked pale and quiet, next to me, in the bright sunshine.
"Twenty years later they called it The Warneford, after the
benefactor. Apparently he wanted to create the ambience
of a rich country house," I went on.

"It's still like that today – gentile," murmured Sonia.
"It still feels grand and, sometimes, I feel privileged to be
here."

We were both patients at this hospital and the
extraordinary thing was that we had arrived, by our own
circuitous routes, completely independently of each other.
Drifting across the lawns, from occupational therapy, we
could hear a record playing; Henry Mancini's, 'The Days
of Wine and Roses.' Sonia looked close to tears and I
knew that she'd heard the soft melody. "They're playing

our song," she whispered, staring at the lovely building in front of us. Quietly I agreed with her as I already knew that I was dependent on one drug or another to cope with my stretched and shrieking sensitivity. The fear I felt inside was ever present and only disappeared after a drink or a pill.

Sonia had started to withdraw into a prolonged, dreamy kind of trance whilst I was working in London. Her psychiatrist called her condition 'insipient schizophrenia.' I told her that she'd simply 'temporarily vacated her premises.' She was admitted to The Warneford a couple of months after I was sectioned under the mental health act and sent there by Bow Street Magistrates Court. It was a cosy arrangement in a way. I lived on Ward M2, on the men's side, and she lived on F1, on the female side, so we were able to see each other nearly every day. We were enjoying the kudos that being a patient here brought. At the time, being slightly mad was very good for one's reputation on the mean streets of Oxford. Looking at Sonia's strained face I realised that I felt frightened and somehow guilty. Here she was, clearly genuinely mentally ill and here I was, acting the loony to avoid going to prison. I was perturbed........things were getting out of my control.

My slippery slide began in earnest about a year earlier, whilst I was grafting in the builder's merchants, after I had been drummed out of the fire service for car theft.

Along with three other guys I was busy unloading 15 tons of fresh cement into a large shed for future retail. Covered in sweat and cement dust I was surprised to see Oxford's Fire Chief, Sidney Boulter, walk into the hanger-like building. He was, as usual, immaculate in his dress uniform and it felt incongruous to see him here in this hot and dusty place. I jumped down from the loading bay and greeted my former chief, "This is a surprise Sir. Do you want some cement?"

"No, I came to see you South," he announced with a serious expression on his face. We walked together out of the shed and into the sun light. "I've spoken to the Chief Fire Officer at West Ham Fire Service and told him about you. Although he has major doubts, and I don't blame him for that, he's willing to take you on at Romford Road in East London and to give you a second chance."

"I don't know what to say Sir," I stuttered. I remembered what the police desk sergeant had said after my arrest and I was touched that the Chief had that much faith in me and my abilities. He was putting his reputation at risk by recommending me to another brigade.

The offer came completely out of the blue and I was amazed at his kindness. He handed me a sheet of paper, "This is the number to ring if you are interested. For God's sake don't let me down again South," he said, turning on his heel and walking off to his car, parked nearby. "Good luck son," he whispered without turning round.

I joined Red Watch at Romford Road Station in Stratford, East London and served under Sidney Boulter's fire chief friend. During my first interview with him he never once dropped his suspicious manner but he finally took me on board with a stern warning, "Let me and the fire service down again and I'll have your guts for garters."

After two weeks in London I'd moved in with a middle-aged homosexual called Willy and I had also resumed my dealing activities down the road in Soho. I'd met Willy in The Two Puddings, a pub in Stratford, and after some conversation he invited me to share his flat in Forest Gate, rent free. It was only after I arrived in his neat and highly polished flat that I realised that I was to share a bedroom with this Ford assembly line worker. We had twin beds, barely 2 feet apart. Oh well! Put it down to experience and it was rent free. Life in Forest Gate with Willy was largely uneventful and his expectations of me were fairly limited. He seemed content just to have a young man around the place, although I did wake up a few times, in the middle of the night, with a thin, bald man in pyjamas sucking on my penis. He once broke off from the job in hand to look up at me and say, "I do take my false teeth out you know. Do you like it?"

My colleagues in Red Watch absorbed me into their team quickly and were anxious to take care of me, in spite of the fact that they must have known about the bust in Oxford. Sonia came to visit me occasionally and once called in at the station while I was on night duty and the entire watch were in the mess room. When she walked in, and after I had introduced her, they sat around staring at this beautiful young woman, goggle-eyed. After she left that evening Mickey punched me playfully on the shoulder and said, "Christ you're a lucky bastard. She is one of the most gorgeous women I've ever seen." I was, once again, reminded of how fortunate I was, but everything that these fine men of Red Watch wanted: the love of a good woman, a secure job, children, maybe a house and a car, never ever entered my shopping list. All I really wanted was to stop the fear that lived inside of me, or to forget it for a while – nothing more. Excitement, alcohol, drugs, sex, secrets they all removed my trembling apprehension, albeit temporarily.

The day I was arrested in Trafalgar Square had been a nightmare. During that afternoon I had scored 2000 French Blues from a Greek in Rathbone Street and promptly swallowed a dozen or so. I hadn't used amphetamine for several weeks and my tolerance was very low so the overdose of Blues had an immediate and dramatic effect. I was high, very high, walking into Soho across Oxford Street. I was very, very, very high. I headed for a cellar bar in Frith Street where I was to meet a young hood who had previously ordered an ounce of Kif and a thousand Blues from me. Spike was sitting in a darkened alcove drinking and playing cards with two older blokes when I arrived. They were all wearing expensive dark, mohair suits. Sitting at the bar, on a high stool, perched a lady of the night downing her 'livener' gin and applying her lipstick with the aid of her compact mirror. As I bought my beer, she turned and smiled at me. In place of wrinkles her face wore dark criss-cross cracks in her make up, but like so many hookers, her eyes were kind. "Morning deary. Life goes on regardless doesn't it?" she sighed, patting her bright red lipstick dry with a paper napkin. "Bloody regardless." I gazed at her, spellbound, intrigued by her profound philosophical remark. "Spike's over there," she pointed, "in the dark where he belongs." Her street intuition had told her accurately why I was there.

I moved over to Spike's corner and after he had introduced me to the two gorilla gentlemen we exchanged drugs for cash. "Do you gamble Joe," asked one of the old timers.

"No never," I replied. "It's never appealed to me much man." He studied me for a bit, pointedly watching my agitated jaw. He reached into his jacket pocket and produced a small, chrome plated revolver. He placed it on the cluttered table. "There's one bullet in there. I'll give you a 'long 'un' if you play Russian Roulette."

"Now?" I asked incredulously.

"The game now, of course," he replied laconically, "and if you survive, I'll pay you immediately naturally." I was high, very, very high. No one spoke for a while and the bar was deathly quiet. I felt my jaw working an amphetamine beat and my pupils dilate to plate size. "Put the 100 quid on the table then," I croaked. Mr Baldy Gangster pulled out his roll of notes and counted out 100 one pound notes on to the table top.

It was pleasant to feel that I was the centre of attention as I picked up the small gun. I checked to make sure that there was only one bullet in the revolving chambers. A one in six chance of blowing myself to kingdom come I thought. No, just do it. I spun the chamber, placed the barrel against my temple and pulled the trigger......
..'click'........I replaced the shooter on the table, gathered my cash, stood up and said, "See you later Spike, give me a ring yeah?" I climbed the steps out into the traffic and daylight of Frith Street. Walking towards Charing Cross Road I was aware that I couldn't feel any sensation in my legs or arms. I needed to sit down for a while and reflect on a few things.

I sat in Trafalgar Square for the rest of the afternoon. I had trembled violently for a couple of hours after 'the event' but I was calming down as dusk fell over Nelson. I was alive and I was loaded.

Later that evening, dealing in pound deals of Kif in Gerrard Street I was approached by two scruffy guys, flashing CID ID cards. They had been watching me selling the cannabis for an hour and I was placed under arrest. The pavement was crowded with the night time crowd and as the smaller of the two policemen reached towards me to fit the handcuffs I hit him with an almighty right hook to his jaw. A lucky one and he went sprawling across the flagstones. Whizzing on the 'hurry up' tablets, I was off, running towards the Square. Although I had managed to put some distance between me and the pursuing officer, when I entered The Strand, I ran slap bang into three uniformed cops. They had come out of nowhere and I felt as if I'd run into a solid brick wall. Busted again. I felt sick and later in my cell in West End Central Police Station I had a quiet word with God and confessed that it was certainly time for a career change and if he had anything less upsetting in mind I'd like to hear from him please. Amen. On finishing my prayer four cops burst into the cell and, mob-handed, gave me a good drubbing in retaliation for my earlier assault on their colleague.

The following morning I was charged with possession of cannabis and amphetamines and remanded to Brixton Jail to appear at a later date at Bow Street Magistrates Court. This grimy prison smelled to me exactly like a zoo; a strong aroma of rotting fruit and manure permeated the atmosphere. Despite the filth it was fairly friendly. The convicts were of all ages and so the old timers brought some maturity and steadiness to this awful place.

After a day or two in Brixton I was shipped, in a meat wagon, to Ashford Remand Centre where I was to languish for some months awaiting my date with justice. Ashford was a different kettle of fish to Brixton. All of the inmates were young and the atmosphere bristled with hostility and aggression. Every young man, it seemed, wanted to prove something or other. I found their collective attitude boring and predictable. The wings were of modern design and they were very clean with none of the zoo smell of Brixton. Despite the presence of hundreds of young tearaways the place was eerily quiet. I wrote one letter to Sonia but didn't receive a reply. I figured that she was with one of my pals, cracking up or both. I was relieved in a way not to have any contact with her. I did not want to be responsible for anything. I was locked in my cell 23 hours a day and I was scared for a lot of that time. I began to sleep for most of the 23 hours. One of the trustees told me that was because the tea contained bromide, an old lust suppressant and tranquilizer, allegedly used by our troops in the First World War.

During my time in Ashford I wrote to my parents and told them where I was. Believing that I was looking at a long prison sentence I began to explore my options. I reasoned that it would probably be much more comfortable to spend time in a psychiatric hospital than a nick, so in a remorseful letter to my folks I mentioned that I was pretty convinced that I was mad and getting madder. Maybe I needed help.

One sleepy, sunny afternoon my cell door opened and a screw announced, "OK pack your things. You're bailed." A friend of mine from the Swan and Castle days had heard of my predicament and he had put up my bail. Red Eddie was waiting for me in the reception hall at Ashford, "You're free," he smiled.

"And you're my friend," I replied. We travelled back to East London where I packed my belongings, gathered my various stashes of drugs and cash and then we left for Oxford. I was ashamed and so I didn't return to Romford Road Fire Station. I knew that I'd let everybody down and I could never justify my behaviour in a month of Sundays. I was eventually admitted to The Warneford Hospital some weeks after I had been examined by Dr Roland Goffmann, a consultant psychiatrist there. He attended Bow Street Magistrates Court and persuaded the bench that I would benefit more from treatment than incarceration. Their worships all tut-tutted and looked doubtful but nevertheless sectioned me to stay in The Warneford for at least a year. I was very grateful and began to look forward to my holiday amongst the loony intellectuals of Oxford.

I was admitted to Ward M2 and Dr Goffmann informed me, looking at me over the top of his glasses, that the first job was to detoxify me. I was to have narcosis therapy and be put to sleep for three weeks. "After that, young man, we'll be able to see more clearly what the problem seems to be," he stuttered. Always in attendance, his entourage of young doctors nodded their agreement at him and at me. "Three weeks seems like a long time Doc and I haven't used much lately to warrant a detox. Bit of booze, bit of cannabis, bit of amphetamine that's all," I protested weakly.

"Never mind, never mind. Do you good. Bit of a rest what?" countered Goffmann. In truth, I was fascinated and quite looking forward to what I perceived as an exciting experience. Feel nothing, see nothing for 21 days eh? Let's have a go then. It may even remove my perpetual horrors.

In my corner bed, under a large window on M2, I was dosed with the evil smelling/tasting liquid paraldehyde, barbiturates and a variety of other colourful tablets. I remember snuggling down under the clean, starched sheets and thinking, 'This is very cosy – good bye world.' When I was roused by nurses out of my narcotic slumber to eat, go to the lavatory etc. I was very, very drunk on the effects of the paraldehyde and the barbs. I remember few things during my three weeks asleep.

When I was finally brought back to consciousness a night nurse told me, "Goodness I've never known anyone like you for the paraldehyde. You used to knock that foul stuff back in one and then ask for more. You used to hold up your empty medicine cup to me and say, 'more, more, please nurse.' Just like Oliver Twist you were." This object of my unconscious affections was one of the oldest known sedatives. It was crystal clear in appearance and smelt and tasted awful. An alcoholic brew of rotting vegetation and human body parts, but it got you there really fast. Five seconds after gulping the stuff down you were unconscious.....sliding down a short but delightful 100 proof alcohol high. The stuff was addictive all right.

I loved being a patient on M2. After a shaky couple of weeks following the big sleep I began to settle down and enjoy my sentence. Good food, barbiturates prescribed day and night, plus great stimulating company. The Warneford Hospital, set in its gracious surroundings was bliss to me. I shared a small dormitory with five other guys. Tim Sutton, an Oxford double first, who liked to sleep all day, Stephen Elliott, a young schizophrenic and kind person, Dr Jasper Franks, an Oxford professor who was also a paranoid schizophrenic and paraldehyde addict, Laurence Fletcher, an obsessive/compulsive cleaner who was awaiting a lobotomy and a young aristocrat, Rupert Seymour, a registered heroin addict taking the cure.

One lovely warm, late autumn afternoon we were all in the dorm idly chatting and reading when Dr Jasper got up from his bed and began to rearrange the pictures hanging on the walls. "Cezanne said that it was much better to look at pictures when they hung at 25 degrees and I think he's right. Don't you agree?" he asked in his gravelly voice.

"No I disagree. What does Mars say on the matter Stephen?" I asked.

"Nothing coming through at the moment I'm afraid, but I do prefer that particular still life on the horizontal plane please," protested Stephen. He regularly received important messages through the metal fillings in his teeth. There was also another young fellow in another dorm on M2 who got his instructions through the television set in the sitting room. It was sometimes difficult if the two boys received conflicting messages at the same time. The TV set secretly transmitting that God had just died and Stephen's teeth fillings announcing that God is arriving tomorrow in the occupational therapy department where he is going to make a speech about love and forgiveness. Because one patient always claimed priority over the other, the two differing messages often resulted in a violent fist fight between the two lads. Clearly, one of the two young chaps was tuned in to the 'left-hand path' and was being led up the 'heavenly garden path' with misleading messages. The ward had peace after the fights, but only for a few days, until the celestial telegrams started arriving again.

The lovely, relaxed days drifted by on M2. A comforting routine of medications, meals and camaraderie gave me a golden opportunity to stop and take stock of my perilous journey down hill, but I was once again flattered into criminality. George Ellwood was an ex lecturer from Christchurch College who had been in and out of M1 at The Warneford for years. I first met him at occupational therapy where he was moulding clay into a fine model of a lump of clay. "What are you doing?" I asked, genuinely puzzled. He looked up at me, startled, through his ancient horn-rimmed spectacles. He stared at me for several seconds and then continued to pummel the grey substance with more energy and resolve. "Do you know," he glared. "I don't sodding know." With that, the middle-aged, care worn academic sat down and burst into floods of tears. "I really don't sodding know," he howled. It upset me to see the old bugger distressed like this and I put my arm around his shoulders and tried to comfort him. A few heaving and sobbing moments later he dried his eyes and looked at me, "Thank you so much. I needed that. Thank you for being so kind." He wiped his eyes on the sleeve of his maroon coloured cardigan and scratched his greasy, thinning hair.

Several weeks later we had a further conversation in OT. "I hear that you sell drugs Joe," remarked George.

"Not any more George. I've taken early retirement in favour of an early crucifixion by the underworld," I replied.

"I used to take Drinamyl in the old days. They are the only thing that helps me with my depression," he continued sadly, shifting his weight from one foot to the other.

"They always fuck you up George. You can't take amphetamines for too long before you start to get seriously deranged," I countered.

"I'm already deranged," he said with a small, shy smile. "I'll give you £100 for two thousand." He looked apprehensive and in pain continually tugging at his old cardigan.

"Look George, no is the answer. In any case it's almost impossible to get Purple Hearts anymore. The only things around are French Blues."

"I know them. They are practically the same as Drinamyl," he argued. "I'll pay you £100 for two thousand."

"No George," I smiled at him and walked out of the prefabricated glass and asbestos building into The Warneford grounds.

One afternoon, several weeks later, I was discussing Nietzsche with Rupert in the dorm when two burly male nurses in long white coats appeared in the doorway. I recognised them as staff from the notorious Ward M3, a double locked part of the hospital for difficult and perhaps dangerous patients. Locked wards in psychiatric hospitals were heavily restricted by a 1958 Government Act but The Warneford continued to have one, arguing that they were protecting both their patients and the community at large. There was always discussion in the hospital as to whether it was legal or not. Ward M3 struck terror into the patient's hearts - it was the dreaded 'snake pit.' Once you were locked up in there, you'd had it, you'd never get out alive. "Pack your bags Joe. You're going to M3," commanded the larger nurse.

"Why?" I whispered. I was terrified.

"A patient says that you have been selling him drugs. The said patient is now experiencing a major amphetamine psychosis and is in a very poor way. Dr Goffmann wants you under lock and key," he explained.

"If the patient is psychotic, why do you believe him?" I asked.

"Because, Lucky Luciano, his mother saw you giving the tablets to her son and has made a statement to that effect. She said that you were such a nice young man and she made you a cup of tea at their house in Observatory Street."

"Very, very unreliable, relative's testimonies you know," I complained but I saw that there was no point in arguing. I was caught bang to rights with my pants down. No point in talking, or denying anything further I could see that. I'd just have to take what was coming but the thought of M3 scared me half to death.

The two large, male nurses marched me to my new ward. It was at the back of the hospital, out of the way. On our way down the main corridor I happened to see someone I vaguely recognised from the past. Sitting, huddled on a bench, was a small, grey figure staring at the wall opposite him with a fixed gaze. "Evening Professor," said Harry as we passed this rather pathetic patient. Only four years ago this gentleman had approached Pluto and me in the Gloucester Arms one night and asked us to beat his bottom for a generous fee. We accompanied this very dignified, upright and educated man to the deserted ox-pens in West Oxford. It was foggy and cold but nevertheless the chap lowered his trousers and pointed his thin, white bum at us both. "Take your belts off and begin striking me. Softly and slowly at first mind," he instructed. We did as we were told and started to bash his buttocks, first Pluto and then me. Of course, we daren't look at each other for fear of laughing out loud. After a while we had found a satisfying rhythm and 'The Professor's' penis was standing out in front of him like a flag pole. Suddenly, he shuddered and held up his hand to us indicating that we were to stop. Pluto and I, both curious, bent forward and saw that he had come.

Later, we discussed how amazing it was that he had not touched his dick once. "Clever that," remarked Pluto. As it turned out the grateful, old academic had no spare cash on him and so he paid us in Purple Hearts. This was the first time that we'd ever seen the drug. Obviously, now, 'The Prof' was paying a heavy price for his life of debauchery. Sitting there on the bench he looked empty of life and soul – he looked dead. We reached the main entrance of Ward M3 and big Harry withdrew his chain with its ring of heavy keys attached and unlocked the stout, old door.

8

CHINTZ, MANNERS AND MADNESS

Mid-winter 1965

David, immaculate after his morning ablutions, carefully and slowly lowered his large backside into the comfortable, winged armchair next to mine. I was half watching the state funeral of Sir Winston Churchill on the black and white TV. David had brought an atlas with him from the M3 library and he delicately opened the book at the continent of Africa. I watched him as he began to trace his pale, manicured index finger slowly across the Sahara Desert. After a moment or two, he quietly complained, "Christ its bloody hot here. Too much sand, too much sun." He stood up slowly and removed his sports jacket. He saw me watching him and he smiled at me, " I'm not going back there Joe, much too hot, look at me I'm dripping." The day had begun on the double-locked ward of M3 at The Warneford Hospital.

The fire blazed and crackled in the stone fireplace and the sitting room was fairly full as usual. The patients, mostly middle-aged, or elderly men, were sitting, reading, or simply gawping at an interesting spot ten feet in front of them. A few were occupied chatting to invisible friends, or enemies. Some were dozing and Francis Lightman was busy making his 1324th hearth rug. "I'm so happy here. I've been here for over 50 years and I don't regret one day of my stay. Marvellous, a wonderful place. I can't speak highly enough of this establishment. This rug, by the way, is for Dr Kane, such a kind young man. Yes, yes I'm quite sure that he wanted it in pink. Pretty what?" he enthused.

At first glance you could easily imagine that you were sitting in some exclusive gentlemen's club somewhere in the City. The rich, chintzy upholstery and the curtains, the oil paintings and the polished wooden floors, until you noticed the stout bars covering all the windows. You could only leave this place by passing through two locked doors which had a long corridor in between them. It was like an air lock and so it was very difficult to escape, although Edward Warwick tried everyday to leave. It was his duty to escape he said. Edward was admitted to M3 in 1937. Since his incarceration he had taught himself six languages and he was currently studying Russian chemistry.

From early morning Edward had his nose in some book or other. At medication time, when he was made to queue for his drugs, in a long line with the other patients, he would hold his book an inch or two in front of his face and continue to read. He was short, had a shiny bald head and piercing light blue eyes which lived behind his gold rimmed spectacles. There was fear and intelligence in his face but no violence or cruelty. His enormous drug regime was dispensed to him directly into his open mouth whilst a charge nurse held his nose to prevent any cheating.

Edward Warwick believed that he was the rightful King of England. He said that the impostor Edward VIII had replaced him by order of MI5, the domestic branch of our Secret Service. "I honestly do not know who he is or where he came from so he's a complete mystery," His Majesty confided in me, speaking of the impostor. He rarely spoke to anyone but I found that if I addressed him respectfully as "Your Majesty" he would deign to speak to me. I found him to be kind and gentle. "The doctors here are all MI5 stooges and long ago they locked me up saying that I was a danger to myself and others. What utter balderdash and nonsense! They say I'm paranoid schizophrenic….what twaddle!"

Edward felt that it was his Royal duty to escape from The Warneford and return to either Buckingham Palace or Windsor Castle in order to reclaim his throne. Although he did not get out while I was there, occasionally, in the years after I had left M3, I would read in the papers about a man being arrested at the gates of the palace or at the castle

In his presence I always half-believed that he was the King but after I'd left his company I knew that he was ill. Dr Roland Goffmann, on his flying visits to the ward would say to Edward, in his squeaky voice, "Still keeping up the act are we Edward, such nonsense." His travelling circus entourage of adoring young doctors would look embarrassed by this confrontational approach to Edward and some would blush whilst others shuffled awkwardly and Edward would sink deeper into his armchair.

Edward always had one ear cocked for the sound of the inner sanctum door opening but not being relocked. Sometimes a member of staff would quietly slip through the door to fetch something and couldn't be bothered to lock the door behind them, perhaps because of the shortness of their visit. It was a risky thing to do with Edward in residence.

Edward, alert as a ferret, would quickly travel the length of the polished wooden corridor, book held in front of his face, and slip through the open door. A few more yards up another wide corridor, ducking down past the office window, and he arrives at his destination. Pushing himself flat against the wall, under a print of The Scream, he waited patiently until a visitor pushed open the heavy door from the outside. As soon as it was open 12 inches Edward would duck under the incoming arm holding the key in the lock and flee to freedom and his throne.

Back in the sitting room Ernie, a nurse, arrived in the doorway. He leaned against the door frame, opened his battered, yellow book and announced to the room in general, "Bowels, gentlemen please." He would read through his list of patients and expect either a yes or a no in reply to the name he called. Yes indicated that you had had a successful evacuation of the bowels that morning and a no meant the opposite. David Woodman, sitting in the chair next to me, always answered, 'no.'

David was once a captain in the British army with a very distinguished career behind him. Now he was imprisoned in M3 and unlikely ever to leave. He was diagnosed, amongst other things, as a coprophiliac – someone who eats their own excrement. I always doubted this assessment of his condition because, after a little digging around in the office bookcase, I discovered that there is usually, but not always, a sexual or enjoyment factor associated with this diagnosis and this was certainly not the case with David. He simply believed that his body was a temple, belonging to God, and it was chock-a-block full of good, pure and Godly things. If he lost anything from his holy interior, including the odd turd, he would be in his maker's bad books.

Ellie, the homely, middle aged Yorkshire nurse, once giggled as she told me that David had eaten one of his droppings in front of a very respectable lady visitor years before. Apparently Lady Sidmouth had arrived one Sunday afternoon to visit her nephew Reggie who had recently been sectioned for stealing ladies knickers off their washing lines. As Lady Sidmouth entered M3 sitting room searching with her eyes to locate Reggie, David stood up, like the gentleman he was, shook her hand and then seemed to freeze. David looked down, and so did Lady Sidmouth, as the small hard turd rolled out of his trouser leg onto the lovely Persian carpet. With a gentle smile at her Ladyship, David bent down with a sigh and stuffed the brown object in his mouth and began to chew. Lucy told me that her Ladyship promptly fainted and never, ever returned to The Warneford.

On Thursdays I always felt sorry for David because that was the day the staff jumped him, mob-handed to give him his enema. Sometimes, his back against the wall, he'd fight the white coated nurses. Brave like a lion; swearing and cursing at his persecutors. The problem was that he was swinging lethal punches and the male nurses had to restrain him as gently as they could without hurting him. Sheer staff numbers was their solution. Smother the bugger; cover him in bodies until his resistance had gone. Of course they always won and David would emerge later from the secure bathroom looking angry, upset and marginally thinner.

Today, he was quiet and together we studied the other patients in the sitting room. Willy was in his usual corner, under the standard lamp, staring through the window at the cedars and the lawns outside. He always reminded me of an old, dying dormouse. He never spoke, he just stared. Willy was placed in The Warneford in 1907 by his clergyman father who suspected that his son was an evil homosexual. As an undergraduate at Oxford, Willy kept mainly male company and was known for his rather shocking soprano voice. Apparently, a scout on Willy's staircase at his college had interrupted him buggering a young, town boy in his room. His father was notified and poor Willy was sent to The Warneford and declared insane. I often tried to engage him in conversation but it wasn't much use. There was no intelligence or humanity left in his heavily doped eyes. Willy was a vegetable and he'd been turning into one for fifty eight years.

Dr Lipman, another long term madman, approached me and stood beside my armchair. With a shaky finger he pointed at the TV screen and asked about the occasion. "They are burying Winston Churchill," I said.

"Ahh, the hero of the free world, what a pity. Do you think the government will send a gun carriage to my funeral when I die?" He mused.

"Of course they will. That's the least they can do for you. Follow your corpse with cannon."

"Enough of your wit young fellow, you know full well that all I want, here and now, is to be called Sambo and to do odd jobs for people. It's not too much to ask is it? An errand here, a chore there," complained Dr Lipman. "Just call me Sambo."

Dr Lipman was an Oxford Don who had resided at The Warneford for some years, since his madness had first gripped him. A long time ago, one sunny, summer Oxford morning, he left his house on the Woodstock Road to go to his college for the day. His habit was to turn at his garden gate and wave goodbye to his beloved wife who was at an open upstairs window. On this particular day and for no explicable reason, she fell out of her window and crashed to her death on the stone flags below. Lipman never recovered from the accident and shortly after his wife's untimely death he became Sambo, the Jewish errand boy.

As Dr Lipman shuffled off in his over large carpet slippers Ron eased himself into the room. Ron was a London Jew and a professional villain. He had been a patient on the ward for some time and he had now earned the right, with good behaviour, to go out unaccompanied, therefore he was as indispensable to me as a gopher. He was short, handsome in a Mediterranean sort of way, flashy, perfumed and he was my friend. Rather than face a lengthy prison term Ron had managed to convince a Warneford consultant that he was mentally ill and that he would benefit more from treatment in a psychiatric unit than from jail on the Isle of Wight. "You don't have to convince me that you're sick Ron," I'd joke, "you're a fucking psychopath that's for sure."

"No, please no, you're dead wrong there. I'm neurotic, very anxious. I have an anxiety neurosis. Note the hand wringing Joe," replied a laconic Ron. "Heads up anyway because Warnie is in the office, I've just spotted him as I walked through. Back again, in a wheelchair this time and he's got that Myra Hindley monster of a housekeeper with him," he reported. "I don't think that she has had him out of his bed for days. The office reeks of alcohol and shit, it is truly horrible. Go and have a dekko, he's your friend isn't he?"

I quietly sloped up to the nursing station and sure enough it was Warnie. Slumped in his wheelchair; my bedraggled, drunken, stinking pal, Major Lewis. He'd only just been discharged from the ward seven days before and he was back, worse than ever. I was sad to see him like this and angry with his useless housekeeper but glad to see him again. We had talked a lot about things, Warnie and me.

Warnie was the brother of a famous children's author who wrote stories with highly moral messages, CS Lewis. His books, although profoundly Christian were, nonetheless, very popular with children. His other adult publications on religious themes were also best sellers. Warnie however had, by his own admission, no special talents bar drinking. He was diagnosed as chronic alcoholic and during the past several years he would regularly enter the hospital to dry out. Sometimes under his own steam and at other times he was captured and pushed in by wheelchair. During his alcohol withdrawal period Warnie was allowed one Guinness at lunch time and one sherry at dinner time. One of The Warneford's many idiosyncratic contradictions at this time.

Three months previously I was eating dinner one evening at a table with Warnie and Ron when we were attracted to a commotion on the next table. The raised angry voice belonged to Phillip Renfrew, an aristocratic paranoid schizophrenic. The outburst was nothing new as Phillip erupted in loud fury at least 3 or 4 times every day. On this occasion it sounded as if he was accusing Timmy Goad, his dining companion, of stealing his bread roll. "I saw you do it you thieving hound, don't deny it," he remonstrated. "It's in your pocket - give it back or......" At which point Timmy picked up his bowl of vegetable soup and smashed it into Phillip's raging face. "That Sir was a Goaded missile," muttered a satisfied Timmy Goad as he got up and left his table. A quiet, soup drenched and humbled Phillip staring after him. Needless to say for sometime after that hilarious incident the term 'Goaded Missile' became very popular with the staff and with Warnie, Ron and me.

Back in the sitting room, André, the charge nurse on M3, came in and gestured at me to follow him. Outside the room Andre told me that Dr Goffmann had asked to see me. I was puzzled because it wasn't his usual day for a consultation. There was a tiny private visitor's room off M3 main corridor and this is where we found the distinguished psychiatrist, lounging on a chaise long with a whole bunch of untidy reports on his knees. As usual his half lenses glasses were perched on the end of his nose and he appeared to be asleep when we knocked on the open door and entered. Dozing in company was fairly normal for the good doctor and you simply had to wait patiently until he stirred, opened his eyes, acknowledged your presence with a 'Humph' and then began his inquisition in his high, reedy voice. He stared at me over the top of his specs with bleary eyes. I wondered how far away he was from his last Dexedrine tablet. A couple of hours by the look of him; a bad come-down was what I was looking at.

He cleared his throat and began, "Still writing your poetry, hmmm? Very Ginbergian I seem to recall. How is Sonia, is she still on F4?" F4 was the female locked ward.

"Yes, still there. Another narcosis unfortunately Doc," I replied.

"Perhaps, if one might *dare* to suggest to you, it might be more appropriate to say another narcosis *fortunately*."

"Hmmm, not too sure about that Dr Goffmann," I said.

"Three weeks asleep seemed to help you I remember," he countered.

"It gave me a mad craving for more paraldehyde," I mumbled. He peered at me and delivered his famous 'I will not be bamboozled by a young psychopath' look. "I have decided to lift your section as of the end of this month. Two weeks time in fact," he announced.

"I'll be free to leave?" I spluttered, hardly daring to believe what I thought I was hearing.

"We have done all we can for you, what? Gave it our best shot, ehh? Time to strike out on your own again, what?" I couldn't take the information in, it just wasn't possible. Freedom at last! I was also now conscious of a growing fear of the outside and all that it implied.

I had been happy on M3 and learned so much from my lunatic teachers. Probably, for the first time in my life, here was a place where I felt safe and I didn't wake each morning with the horrors. Andre smiled at me and gave a little nod. "I won't be arrested if I leave?" I ventured.

"Only if you leave before the 2 weeks is up," he replied. As I stood to leave Goffmann quietly asked, "There is something I've been meaning to ask you for sometime. Did you sell George Ellwood those purple hearts, the 1000 Drinamyl?"

"Of course not Doctor. I've told you all along that I'm completely innocent of the charge."

"In that case you must have felt very misjudged and hard done by over these last few months on M3," teased the psychiatrist. "Although I must say the opposite appears to be true. Indeed, you have fairly blossomed here on the ward, so perhaps I didn't get it so wrong after all."

"Perhaps not Dr Goffmann and I'm grateful for all your help," I smiled at him. As Andre and I walked back along the corridor I turned to him and said, "He's a crafty old sod that one, very sneaky."

I walked back to the sitting room and felt very lonely. I really did not want to leave this madhouse. I would miss the brilliant, sparking, free-fall conversations, the hilarious fantasies, the companionship, the comforting routine and structure of this marvellous asylum. It had become my first real home and now I had to leave and survive the best way that I could.

I sat down between Ron and David and told them my news. "You jammy bastard, how did you manage a discharge date this early?" asked Ron.

"Lies, charm, lies and charm," I told him. "I'll go back to the builder's yard for a bit and load some lorries. Get fit and save some money." Ron leaned closer, "Will you open up shop again?" he whispered.

"Maybe, I don't know. There will be pressure to deal, but I hate the weed personally. I get so paranoid when I smoke. I prefer 'hurry up tablets' or barbs any old time," I replied. Some of the Kray's crew got too close for my peace of mind last time. It felt dangerous to me, I had too many customers who knew too much about me and I began to take stupid risks when I was stoned. I really don't fancy getting bashed up and buggered by Ronnie Kray in a Wardour Street back alley. But there's money in it, that's for sure."

"Well if you do decide to start up again and you need a driver and a minder just let me know and I'll be there," offered Ron.

"You're too small to be a minder and you are also a Jew which means that eventually you'll steal all my profits," I said. Ron threw a cushion at me and giggled.

Two weeks later I left M3 and moved in with Tom, my artist friend, on the Iffley Road. Away from my pleasant institutional life it took a few days to become accustomed to freedom. Smells 'on the out' were too strong, people moved too quickly, colours were too bright and everyone talked too fast. The outside appeared frenetic, furious and confusing and it frightened me. I felt like a small, vulnerable boy who had suddenly been expelled from a loving family with no explanation. I was alone.

9

SOMETHING MUCH BIGGER THAN ME

Late autumn 1965

I'd injected my first heroin into my arm about an hour before. Beethoven's Late Quartet, Op 131, was playing quietly in the background and I knew then that things would never be the same again.

The year was 1965, Malcolm X had been assassinated in New York, the Yankee/Vietnam war was raging, a woman called Mary Quant had invented something called the mini-skirt and everywhere you went you heard Marianne Faithful singing 'As Tears Go By.' Quite frankly, at that moment, post fix, I didn't give a shit about any of it.

I'd scored the heroin from Wilbur Driesen. I first met Wilbur at Tom's Iffley Road pad six months previously. He was fairly famous in the bohemian underworld of the city on several counts: he held a double first class honours degree, he was a Rhodes Scholar, he was a flamboyant old queen and he was a registered heroin addict at a time when there were only a few hundred in England. I loved Wilbur from the first moment I set eyes on him. I loved his ridiculous, aristocratic English accent and the way that he flapped his arms about in helpless gestures. He came from a wealthy Canadian Mennonite family and obviously had found his calling in Oxford. Always deathly pale, from the narcotic I suspected, he wore horn-rimmed specs and a grubby Harris Tweed sports jacket. There was no doubt that he had a powerful intellect and I had no doubt that Wilbur was fixing to die. He knew too much about himself, people and life, and he didn't like any of it one bit. He was too fragile and sensitive to survive this awful life for too long. We came to spend lots of time together, Wilbur and me. One evening amidst Tom's oil paintings he warned me about a young Welshman at Balliol called Howard Marks. Wilbur told me that he was mad for cannabis and he had been asking his dealer where his dope came from. Wilbur was quite emphatic and warned me not to talk to him. "Don't trust him, he's big trouble." On reflection it was sound advice and I'm glad I heeded it.

I'd pestered Wilbur for months to lay some jacks of heroin on me but he always refused. He was obeying an old junky code which said that you never gave 'horse' to someone who wasn't addicted. Fair enough if he had an established habit but not if they were clean. Various medical articles on addiction proclaimed that there was nothing to fear from heroin for the wider public as it was only the more intellectual who were susceptible to its charms. The bulk of registered addicts at this time were GP's, writers, painters, poets, jazz musicians and other oddball misfits. Wilbur once confided in me a great fear that he had. "If the proletariat ever get hold of this stuff, society, as we know it, will be fucked forever. God forbid that the common man turns on to horse."

Wilbur got his heroin and cocaine from Lady Isabella Frankau. She was one of a handful of so called 'renegade doctors' prescribing junk at that time and she was known to advertise her services to Canadian heroin addicts through the medium of newspaper articles etc. where she advocated treating addicts as patients, not criminals. Some American and Canadian addicts arriving in London for the first time died taking their first fix. These junkies were simply not used to 98% pure English heroin and could not believe that these tiny, saccharine sized, sixth grain hypodermic tablets would do the trick for them. They were accustomed to using their street powder cut to between 3 or 5% purity. There was no doubt that I was attracted to this mysterious, exclusive junky world and found the underlying philosophy of nihilism and lengthy suicide seductive.

Earlier on this day I'd caught Wilbur depressed and off guard in the Cape of Good Hope pub. He'd just received a savage letter of goodbye from a previous boyfriend and he was upset and angry. "I suppose you still want the gear don't you? That's the only reason you're here talking to me. I'm such a miserable cunt you know," moaned an unhappy Wilbur. "Come out to the bogs and I'll give you a grain. I know you only too well Joe, you'll get the stuff somewhere, sometime eventually." He was right of course. I was like an obsessive terrier when I wanted something; I never rested until I had my prize. In the pub's lavatory he counted out six small white tablets into my hand. "You won't be able to control this stuff," he cautioned. "It's too nice and it will defeat you." He looked sad and exasperated as we left the Cape of Good Hope. I wanted to be alone when I took my first fix and so I was relieved when Wilbur said he was going home to sleep.

In my flat, in Divinity Road, I had already accumulated some paraphernalia especially for this moment. I always knew that one day I was going to try heroin. As a small boy I saw a TV play about a black woman in Harlem during the fifties. She was a heroin addict and somehow, the way she was, her demeanour, her attitude, stuck in my mind. I wanted to be like her. I put Beethoven's Opus 131 on my record player and cut a jack of H in half using a razor blade. I carefully placed the hypodermic pill in a teaspoon and covered it with tap water from the syringe. I cooked the liquid until the tablet dissolved using my Zippo lighter. When the solution was clear I sucked it up into the works. It was years later before I realised that there was no need to cook the gear. Of course the pills were water soluble; it was a hang-over ritual from American beat literature I suppose.

I slipped my leather belt around my upper arm and pulled it tight, keeping the tourniquet secure by pressing it against my knee. My veins stood out on my inner arm, fat with trapped blood. I pushed the needle into the most prominent one and felt its wall yield easily. I pulled back the plunger and watched as a red, marble twist of my blood crept beautifully into the transparent barrel. I had a hit. It was easy, not difficult at all. I pushed the liquid slowly into the pulsating, red highway.

The warmth filled my arms first, then my legs and then........I was home..... safe. I felt no fear, no pain. God was here in my room, in my brain, I was reassured, and everything was going to be alright. I was a fine, good and talented person. Through the sadness of the Beethoven counterpoint I heard God say, "You are a favourite son and I love you." I needed nothing, I wanted nothing, I was complete and untouchable. Sublimely melancholic, impossibly content, at last I belonged to something. At last I was in from the brittle cold, away from the despair and discomfort that had been stalking me all my short life.

In the last few months I had been thinking and writing poetry about my suicide a lot. It seemed that everything conspired to hurt me. The cold winter mornings, the suffocating apprehension I experienced every morning on waking, what I believed people thought about me, the self-centredness of my fellow human beings, famine in Africa, Vietnam and my present conviction that I was never, ever, good enough. Unlovable, worthless. At times death was an attractive prospect and H gave me this 'death state' without the bother of having to do something to myself which required courage. I could see a pattern emerging within me. I chose behaviours or substances to take away, or mask my fear. Alcohol, drugs, sex, heroin but first of all, back when I was a child, I used manipulation and my imagination as my chosen painkillers.

I recalled clearly, listening to Beethoven's sweet, interweaving harmonies, an incident that had occurred when I was about 6 or 7 years old. I had a terror of going to school and I was convinced that one day I would go to this wicked primary school and never ever return to my mother. My sister dragged me screaming to St Michael and All Angels on more than one occasion. However, one morning, before leaving for school, I went to our outside lavatory. My mother was washing the breakfast dishes in the kitchen sink not far away. I left the bog door open and proceeded to make loud vomiting sounds into the toilet pan. After a minute or two I re-entered the kitchen looking, I really hoped, pale and wan. My mother broke off from her washing up and looked down at me, "What's wrong son?" she asked, looking concerned. She'd heard my sick noises all right then. "Dunno mum, but I think that I've got cancer," I replied, looking up at her in my best begging, pathetic manner. I knew that she wouldn't believe me of course, how could I possibly know if I had cancer or not. But the important thing was that she thought I was a little odd - a strange child. 'How could he say such a thing? Cancer indeed!' I calculated that if she was worried that I was a barm-pot then she would be off guard, wrong footed and easy to manipulate. "You'd better stay off school today," she said with a sigh. "Go and lie down and read your books." Mission accomplished!

The Budapest String Quartet played its melancholy way towards its finale. Wilbur had given me this record for my birthday and he had said, "I hope you like this, it's my favourite." And now it was my favourite too. As I sat slumped in the armchair the heroin continued to feed me answers and I felt at peace. I knew that the word heroin came from the German 'heroisch' or hero. When Bayer, the drug company, was first testing the new drug in the late 1800s volunteer guinea pigs reported that the powerful analgesic made them feel like heroes. Curious, but I had an inkling of what they meant. In my sleepy, impregnable state I knew that I could tell Sonia, heroically, that I was not going to get married to her after all. The wedding was planned for next month but we'd just have to call everything off. I was going to be married to heroin instead because I had fallen in love with her and I had no doubt about my love. Yes, I felt heroic, nodding there in my chair with blood on my arm and peace in my heart. My parents would be pleased that I was cancelling the wedding. They had a strange notion that Sonia was too beautiful and too sensual to be wholesome. 'Too sexy for her own good that girl!'

My parents had not been pleased about something else earlier in that year; in May I think it was. Some plainclothes gentlemen arrived with an ordinary uniformed policeman at our house in Henry Street. The cop explained to my mother that they were 'special policemen' from London and they wanted to search my bedroom. "But he doesn't live here anymore," protested my mother.

"He stayed here for 5 days two weeks ago," answered one of the plainclothes men. "We have a warrant, so if you'd be so kind, we'll have a look in his bedroom."

"Why are you interested in my son," asked my worried mother.

"The Prime Minister's grandson, Joshua, died yesterday at Balliol and Joe was an associate of his. That's all I can tell you at the moment," he explained, upending the mattress on my bed.

"Why aren't you going to his room in town to see him?" persevered my mother.

"Maybe we will, maybe we won't," he replied in an enigmatic fashion. They found nothing but if they had gone out into the back garden and dug down six inches under the apple tree they would have found several dozen empty, crushed Drinamyl tins.

My mother never told me about the raid until years later and the fuzz never came to see me. Not officially anyway, but about this particular time, I seemed to inherit an uninvited minder or two, or three, who stayed on my tail for a few months. I was terribly sad about Josh, it was a shock. I hadn't seen him for ages and the last time I did see him he told me that he was going to Switzerland to take the cure. I understood that he was free of H when he died in Balliol. Probably taking something else to get by in the first few months after heroin withdrawal. He was the first of my pals to go and I missed him. I wasn't too bothered by the surveillance because I was now committed to my new wife, heroin, and I would be leaving the dealing well alone. Special Branch would have no reason to capture me in the future.

In a way heroin rescued me from myself. Two months before my first fix Gilbert, Sonia and I had made a suicide pact. The agreement to kill ourselves came after a heavy weekend of drug taking. Sonia and I were on an almighty amphetamine come-down and Wilbur had had two speedball (heroin and cocaine) overdoses in quick succession and he was hell-bent on ending it 'once and for all.' It was a Sunday afternoon when we met up at Wilbur's place on the Cowley Road having managed to harvest a hundred or so nembutal, seconal and amytal. The decision to do away with ourselves seemed to have no more importance to us, at the time, than planning a day trip to Brighton.

We sat on the floor in Wilbur's flat and shared out the brightly coloured spansules. "Around 30 each," said Wilbur. "More than enough I should have thought. Can't wait. Ta-ta everyone. No wait, I think that we should make our departure with something from Bartok. What do you think? Very appropriate eh?" Sonia started to swallow the capsules one after another, sipping cider between each one. "The balance of their minds was seriously disturbed," I said. "That's what the coroner will say in the Oxford Mail. The headline will run 'The mystery suicide pact of three young Oxford troublemakers.'"

"Should we leave notes?" asked Sonia.

"Yes, mine is going to say, Good fucking bye. I hate you all," smirked Wilbur chewing on a nembutal.

"Mine's going to say please make sure I'm dead before you chuck the earth in," I laughed.

"Bollocks," said Sonia.

"Yes bollocks is good, very good in fact. Bollocks, yes," mused Wilbur. Bartok played on as we became drunk on the massive doses of barbiturates. Then…..nothing.

When I woke up I was horrified to find myself alive. Still intoxicated, but desperately afraid and shocked at my survival. This was not what I wanted at all. Where in Gods name was Sonia? There was no sign of her in the flat. The kitchen clock said midnight and Wilbur was snoring in a laboured way on his sofa. He was a funny bluey, greeny colour and his breathing sounded like a dozen tropical frogs croaking in the heat of the night. He didn't sound healthy but he was still alive. He is going to be most pissed off about this I thought. I was cold and my whole body began to shake. I was going into shock. On the kitchen table Sonia had left a drunken scrawled note, 'Gone home to mothers. It didn't work. What were we doing? We should all be dead by now with the amount that we took. I feel awful. We are all deranged…..mad, mad, mad! How could we do this to each another? I've got to sleep now.' She scratched her name underneath the sad message.

With the heroin there was no need for me ever again to resort to that kind of desperate act. There was a new pleasant taste in my mouth I noticed. I smiled and luxuriated in this body-smell of my new lover. I started the Beethoven again and nodded and dreamed into the night.

10

A DIAMOND, SOME DREAMS AND BEING A DOG

Late summer 1966

There were eight of us crammed into that second-class train carriage compartment and I could smell every last one of 'em. 'This is how a dog must live all the time,' I thought. It was truly bewildering, all these aromas. Sonia and I were on the 8am Oxford to Paddington train. We were making our weekly visit to our croaker, Doctor Diamond in Parsons Green, to pick up our weekly prescription for heroin, cocaine and methedrine.

As usual we had run out of heroin a couple of days early, over-using our script on the first five days. So we were always junk deprived on that regular trip to London, which accounted for my super heightened sense of smell. When I was junk sick I could smell faint aromas at 200 yards. Of course it wasn't just the sense of smell that returned in a magnified form as the heroin left your body. Everything came back in a mighty rush. What had been dead, under the rule of the poppy, came to life again with a painful intensity. Every ache and pain in my body sprang into frantic activity. I'd come in my pants for no reason at all, several times in the past twelve hours. Colours were impossibly bright and beautiful, sounds were too loud and paranoia was rampant – 'No one likes you Joe. Keep your head down or they'll get you.' Every cell in my body and mind was stretched out of shape until they screamed at me, 'Make it better please boss. Give us some H.'

The motherly woman, by the window, was wearing Chanel No 5. The man next to her, possibly her husband, had a whiff of St Julien's Flake pipe tobacco coming off him. The business man opposite me, in spite of his white shirt and pinstripe suit, had not washed under his arms for days. The undergraduate near to the corridor had some feminine hygiene problem, in a most intimate area, I reckoned. Sonia, next to me, smelled of stale sweat covered with lashings of Johnson's Baby Powder. The elderly woman next to me had the unmistakable scent of kippers on her breath and the boy in the corner, near the window, smelt of Lifebuoy. Good boy! I was the most odious of all of us smelling of a mixture of sulphur and methane.

I felt like I was going to faint when Sonia nudged me and whispered, "Why are you pointing your nose at people? Can you smell something?" I looked into her smiling green eyes and began to giggle, and then laugh, and then hysteria set in and I gulped for air and cried until the tears flowed down my cheeks. She'd caught me out sniffing other folk and it was funny. Sonia became infected by my great, heaving guffaws and went red in the face with mirth. I knew from long experience, with my wife, that she was in danger of wetting her knickers if this kept up. After a minute or two she upped and left the compartment heading for the loo. That left me alone with six sets of curious, embarrassed and hostile eyes aimed squarely at me. I stopped laughing under the glares. "Sorry, very sorry," I muttered.

Sonia came back from the loo and sat down next to me, all our previous hilarity forgotten with the discomfort of cold turkey. Now we just had to endure another 30 minutes of train journey, trying to minimise our withdrawal symptoms so as not to alarm our fellow passengers. We had been at least 36 hours without junk and our muscles were often in painful spasm. We both had diarrhoea and were screamingly alert from lack of sleep. I tried to forget the sickness for a bit by remembering our wedding last September. It was awful.

Although I'd firmly made up my mind that I was not going to be married to Sonia, when it came to the tears and recriminations, I relented. On a grey September day, last year, we were brought together as man and wife in Sonia's old, local church, close to her parent's house, a stone's throw from the Isis. She looked radiant, like a film star in her beautiful white wedding dress. Naturally, I was stoned and so were all our friends. I'd wanted Wilbur as my best man but I knew that this would upset both sets of parents. Christ, he could have said anything in his speech and even if his speech was fairly innocuous, his camp delivery would have given the older generation mass, multiple heart attacks. So I chose Phillip, a newly arrived on the scene Welshman. He was a slimy, devious bastard but I liked him well enough. He'd managed to borrow a suit and tie that was the main thing, but he was incoherent and wobbly after celebrating the stag night on booze, nembutal, dope and two Benzedrex inhalers.

The whole of the Swan and Castle, Cape of Good Hope and Randolph crews were there. A veritable platoon of fuck heads. Even then, I felt desperately sad for my mum and dad who looked lost and angry throughout the whole day. As Sonia and I exchanged vows, I saw Phillip, to my right, swaying back and forth. I thought that he was perilously close to falling over and so I put out my hand to steady him. The vicar droned on and Phillip swung nicely back and forth and smiled. Suddenly, in spite of my support, he went over. He crashed forward, pole axed and rigid, catching his forehead on an altar step with that distinctive, hollow, head thump sound. The vicar stopped his ceremonial speech, the congregation became as still as the grave and there was a complete silence. Phil laid there for a while, obviously having a wee rest, and then clambered back on to his feet, blood trickling from his forehead. Still smiling and in a quiet, humble voice he said, "Sorry" to the vicar, "Sorry" to Sonia and me and then he wobble-turned towards the congregation and said "Sorry, very sorry."

As the vicar recommenced the service again I remember thinking that it was appropriate somehow that my best man fell over at my wedding and that most of our guests probably had some difficulty knowing exactly where they were. A pity about the parents though.

Sonia and I got off our train at Paddington and raced for the tube, making our way to Dr Diamond's surgery in Parsons Green. The small, dingy waiting room was packed when we arrived; mostly guys, but a few chicks, all pale, thin and twitching frantically. Danny Halliday, the Canadian, was there, shooting his silly gob off about needing a 'fix bad.' We all needed a 'fix bad' for fucks sake. Danny was an infamous addict in London. His script was reputed to be thirty grains of heroin, thirty grains of cocaine and dozens of amps of methedrine and that was just from Lady Frankau! He boasted that he picked up the same from Dr Cohen and now from Dr Diamond also. I resented this drama queen being here, with my doctor, he'd spoil everything with his thuggish behaviour that was for sure.

Months before, when Sonia and I first registered our habits with Dr Diamond he had very few addicts on his books and the ones that he did have were 'old school' civilised patients who bore their sickness well. During those early months Mrs Diamond used to bring us tea and chocolate biscuits down to the waiting room making soothing noises as she poured our tea. Not now. I hadn't seen her in the waiting room for weeks and I couldn't say that I blamed her. "Fuck it, gimme a fix. I need a fix bad," shouted the out of control Canadian, waving his thin, track-tattooed arms about. "Fucking shut it Danny," bellowed a young girl next to me. "What the fuck is that idiot croaker doing? Making the fucking stuff?" ranted Danny, unperturbed by the brave chick's intervention.

"What's the best horse you ever tasted Danny?" she persevered.

"What do you mean babe?"

"Where in the world did you score the best H?" she asked him, leaning towards the old timer.

"Here of course, London."

"That's fucking right you big Canadian Wally, here and it's called dia-morphine hydrochloride BP.......British Pharmaceutical. 98% pure heroin. You get it here in England you crap head. Wise up Danny, act cool and be grateful to the nice, kind doctor and don't fuck a good thing up for the rest of us. OK?" she fumed. Danny looked suitably chastised and he calmed down. He'd seen her wisdom and decided to adopt the English model of quietly waiting, without complaint – just allowing himself a quiet squeak, cough or spasm now and again.

That tranquil Saturday morning when we came for our first appointment with Dr Diamond, after our tea and biscuits, I met him in his surgery, opposite the grass and trees of Parsons Green, and in a high, reedy voice he trilled at me, "I charge thirty shillings a consultancy," and, "how much do you want?" Almost as an afterthought he asked me, "Let me see your arms please. If you need me urgently and I'm not here you can reach me on this number." He handed me a blank prescription with a number on it. "I'm a police doctor and so you can contact me via the police radio." It was so easy to score from him. I walked out of his surgery after 10 minutes holding a script for heroin, cocaine and methedrine. The daily allocation of heroin for me was enough to kill ten healthy people. I was ecstatic and so was Sonia as we both had a regular supply of wonder dust. We were registered addicts.

We went in to the surgery straight after Danny and left five minutes later clutching our prescriptions. We decided to cash it at Calder's in Notting Hill Gate as this pharmacy was always fairly quick in dispensing stuff. As usual, as we got nearer to the horse and 'getting well', we both began to fall apart a bit. On the tube to Notting Hill my arms and legs started to kick and jump out. Very sodding alarming this was. I watched Sonia's pale, strained, ageless face and could have cried to see her in this awful pain.

We met Jan in Calder's pharmacy and we all went back to his pad, nearby, at the bottom of Clanricarde Gardens. His street was a cul-de-sac of elegant four storey London town houses and he rented a large flat on the third floor of one of them. Jan was a Dutch heroin addict and a fine artist who specialised in beautiful, detailed ink drawings. He was a freelance book illustrator. Carlos, an Australian addict, was already in the jointly shared flat when we arrived. This large sitting room, cluttered with Carlos' oil paintings and tubes of paint and Jan's inks stank just like Don's place on the Iffley Road in Oxford but with the added seasoning of TCP topping the pungent aroma.

Jan, Sonia and I quickly prepared our fixes and injected ourselves. The relief I felt was so great that I almost fainted. Indeed, most of the H buzz these days came not from a euphoric opiate high but simply from relief from the withdrawal pains. "Alex has just left," reported Carlos. "He's always so angry that man. He's got it made, he's a famous author for God's sake, why doesn't he just cool it?" Carlos was talking about Alex Trocchi, the high priest of British beatdom and a heroin addict of many years standing. "What do you expect Carlos? He's a Scot and they all have fury, resentment and inferiority lurking somewhere beneath their kilts, especially the Glaswegians!" said Jan.

"He's getting to be a bore," complained Carlos. The H felt good. I'd fixed a grain of heroin, a grain of cocaine and an amp of meth and I felt warm, dislocated and easy. Sonia began to smile and nod, leaning against the leg of Jan's bed.

"What is your dream Jan?" Sonia asked out of nowhere in a murmuring hum.

"Ah, a good question my angel……..to paint the Mona Lisa I think," smiled Jan. His dark brown eyes and his floppy, schoolboy hair made him look so innocent; pure like a child.

"But it's already painted Jan and hanging in the Louvre. Do you mean you want to paint over the top of it?" I asked.

"You know exactly what I mean clever bollocks. I want to paint something that people will value for ever and flock to see. Something that will keep my name alive for eternity," declared Jan.

"That's beautiful," sighed Sonia. "What's your dream Carlos?"

"To quit this shit, fall in love with someone just like you and have children and live happily ever after," muttered Carlos, eyeing me up with one, half open eye and a thumbs up gesture.

"and you husband?"

"To rob a bank, or, to con a rich man out of millions of pounds. I want to commit the perfect crime. My rationale would be Robin Hoodesque in that I'd give two thirds to a deserving cause of my choice," I answered promptly and with conviction.

"Interesting," whispered Jan.

"You'll get caught and go to jail for ever and a day," said Carlos. "They've just given James White 18 years for his part in The Great Train Robbery and that gang was pretty noble in that they didn't want to use violence."

"But they did and they bashed the poor old train driver over the bonce and they intended to keep all the bread to themselves," I replied.

"They've caught up with the Kray Twins at last," said Jan.

"Yeh, I'm glad about that," I said. "Thieves get caught mainly because they talk too much to all the wrong people. They also involve too many weak links prior to the heist and then they boast and brag in pubs and clubs afterwards. It's always been the same. The fact is that if you plan a job, using only a minimum of trusted buddies you will have a 90% chance of getting away with it."

"Interesting," said Jan again, nodding his head, eyes half closed.

"Don't tell him that Jan. He'll be so flattered and I've seen him turn these crazy fantasies into reality a few times now. Not a pretty sight especially for the relatives of those involved," giggled Sonia.

"You can't polish a turd," muttered Carlos wisely and then he fell asleep. He looked like a skeleton covered with a white skin. I searched but could not find a single ounce of fat on Carlos. I began to panic internally as I studied him. 'What were we doing to ourselves?' I thought.

"What about the perfect con Joe," asked Jan, still interested in my dreams and bringing me back from my frightening meanderings.

"OK. First you pick your victim. Preferably a rich, obnoxious bastard who's clawed his way to the top by pissing on lots of people. Someone with a huge ego and someone who, as the confidence trickster, you despise but like at the same time."

"Like the personality but hate what he does to make money?" offered Sonia.

"Exactly."

"Sounds good, go on," encouraged Jan.

"Oh please Jan, don't gee him along. You'll both be in Buck House next week chatting up the Queen to buy a dodgy masterpiece by Carlos," sighed a long suffering Sonia. "OK we've chosen a victim. He's an arms dealer, selling guns in Africa. A hugely rich, psychopathic, Dutch guy," postulated Jan.

"Yes, he's just the kind of guy that we want," I replied, "but here things tend to get intellectually challenging, because there are so many complicating factors in the relationship between hunter and victim. Personal chemistry, a similar sense of humour, the value of the conman's proposal, unforeseen events, the number and quality of the people on the conman's team, and then, above all else, a very strong nerve, especially during the closing stages of the rip-off. Of course, to make the crime perfect the victim never has to discover that he's actually been fleeced. He has to remain oblivious throughout and that's what makes it so juicy."

"You've thought about this a lot," said Jan reaching for his pen and artist's pad.

"Hmm.....it's kind of a hobby I suppose."

"Until we all read in the newspapers next week that the Duke of Edinburgh bought the Statue of Liberty from someone who looks remarkably like Joe," put in Sonia from behind a thick cloud of cigarette smoke.

"Ah, they are just poppy dreams then?" teased Jan.

"Not really. I've always had day dreams and fantasies long before I tasted junk. When I was very young, maybe five or so, I day-dreamed this scene where I was being eaten by a whole bunch of naked ladies. The mind pictures used to give me a hard on. I didn't know then what that signified of course, but it did feel nice and I wasn't frightened at all by my penis doubling in size. I began to look forward to the dream every night before I fell asleep," I told Jan and Sonia.

"Interesting."

"A group of naked middle-aged women were sitting around a long table set with a white table cloth and silver cutlery. They were holding their knives and forks upright on the table in front of them waiting for me to be brought in…..the main dish. I used to appear from nowhere lying naked on a large silver platter with sprigs of parsley and stuff scattered over me."

"Were you cooked?" asked Sonia looking worried.

"No. Uncooked and alive with a hard on."

"Holy shit Joe, you're fucking deranged," cackled Jan.

"The dream always ran out of steam before the eating stage I'm glad to say. I just remember that it was very erotic and I liked it giving me a funny, stiff thingy."

"Nothing's changed in that department then," remarked Sonia.

"I have had loads more………."

"No, no please spare us," protested Sonia.

"Interesting," said Jan.

"Stop fucking saying 'interesting' you moron, he'll get going again."

We all nodded for a while listening to Mingus. The afternoon in Notting Hill was pleasant and the company was good. We cranked up again after an hour or so. "What do you think of the fuss about Dylan going electric at the Royal Albert Hall," asked Carlos to nobody in particular. "I love his music whatever he does and I'm glad that he's kicked those appalling folksy types into touch. Someone called him a traitor for God's sake. They said that he'd betrayed his roots," raged Jan quietly in that distinctive, cool, Dutch way. "The only roots that he's got are his own. The minute an artist stands still he stops the process of creating."

"Oh dear God! Two opinionated cunts together in the same room," said my wife. "Let's go home Joe, we can go through the Dilly on the way to Paddington and see if we can find Tommy." Tommy owed me money from a loan I made him six months before. It was £10 so it was worth getting back but I didn't hold out much hope.

It was dusk at Piccadilly underground station when we arrived and it was busy with homeward bound commuters. I entered the men's lavatory and looked around for Tommy. There were four junkies fixing openly over the hand basins. Pale skin, skeletal bodies, shell shocked eyes, black tracked arms, tourniquets, curses, the smell of Jeyes fluid, the smell of stale, male sweat, the smell of shit and blood but the brains were probably in Paradise. Jabbing, probing, needle fucking, interested only in their ticket out of here, they indulged their habits. "Anyone seen Tommy?" I yelled.

"He's dead man," said a frail tranny with long, dirty, blonde hair. "He died last week in the bog over there." He pointed with his works to a cubicle door with a cross painted on it and the words RIP Tommy written above it in magic marker. "He owed me £10, the bastard. He can't just die without paying me back," I complained.

"Take the matter up with the filth," smirked the young TV.

"Poor Tommy, God bless you mate," I said.

Sonia and I caught the train back to Oxford, nodding and cosy, content with the drugs in our pockets; we had no worries, just dreams.

11

FLORRIE'S HOUSE

Mid-summer 1967

I felt my eyelids flicker once or twice and then slam open. My heart was racing and my mind was full of the certain horrors to come on this day. The familiar heroin withdrawals had also started. It was dark but I knew what the time was without looking at the alarm clock - it was 4 am. I reached over and switched on the bedside lamp. Sonia was also waking as I shifted into a sitting position on the edge of the bed where I could cook my fix.

Our bedroom window was wide open and the air was still warm from the hot day before. Sonia was lying naked on the grubby sheet, her pale, thin body already showing the characteristic muscular spasms of early junk deprivation. In this state my arms had a tendency to both shoot forward simultaneously and so I had to be careful when I prepared my fix in case I spilt any of the precious fluid. My nose was running, I felt like my stomach had been surgically removed and my eyes were wide with the onset of my morning horrors.

Arranged carefully on the floor, near the gas fire, was our paraphernalia: a glass jar, full of alcohol, containing two French syringes, a small wooden laboratory rack of test tubes, a bottle of TCP, ampoules of apyrogen, a bag of cotton wool, leather belts for tourniquets, a neat stack of empty methedrine boxes and rows of empty heroin and cocaine bottles. I put the last three jacks of heroin in my syringe and filled up with a mil of sterile water. This half grain was all I had left from the previous day's script and was only enough to remove some of the withdrawal pain, temporarily, until the morning when I'd fetch a fresh script from the pharmacy. With any luck we'd both sleep for another few hours. I shook my works a couple of times and the H dissolved obligingly. I slipped my arm through a belt and pulled it tight. It took me a while to find a vein but eventually the plunger eased back and admitted a little curl of blood into the liquid opiate inside the glass syringe. I had a hit and I could send the drug into my vein. Although this morning dose was small it removed the pain instantly and I lay back to watch Sonia moving in the gloom.

I found it almost unbearable to watch her fix these days. Her veins were either thrombosed or retreating far from the surface and, as a solution; she had taken to injecting in her feet. When she injected herself she managed to get her blood everywhere in her desperate and impatient attempts to get a hit. I watched this pale, skinny, blood splattered woman hunched on the side of the bed. She had been so beautiful once and I felt ashamed that I had led her to this. At last, she found a vein in her left foot and she lay back with a long sigh, leaving her gun in the vein. We both slept until around eight o'clock when our withdrawal pains woke us again.

At half past eight I would walk a couple of hundred yards to Archie Lyles Pharmacy so I could pick up our daily scripts. Not so long to wait now and I pulled on my leather overcoat in anticipation. I lay down on our bed and listened to Sonia's mother, Florrie, pottering about, downstairs in the kitchen, as I waited for the minutes to pass. As the opiate left my blood my senses awoke, sometimes violently, and I began to smell the acrid, bad cabbage smell of our unwashed bodies. Normally we couldn't smell ourselves so we only washed now and again; a wipe with a damp flannel here and there. We listened for the front door to bang and that told us that Florrie had gone across the road to open up her small knitting and wool shop for the day. Her husband Ralph had already left for work earlier at Morris Motors and the house was empty except for two, half dead drug addicts.

We had moved in with Sonia's parents a few months previously as we could never raise the cash to pay the rent on our flat. To explain our awful appearance to her parents Sonia had told them that we were both getting over Hepatitis B and that our recovery would be a long job. I'm convinced the Florrie never bought this story but I don't know what she believed. If I had been her I would have hated me with a rage and a passion for not protecting her lovely daughter better, but instead, she was kind and loving with me the whole time we lived there.

"I'm really sick Joe, when are you going to pick up?" pleaded Sonia.

"I'll go now, don't worry and I'll get back as quickly as I can," I replied. Despite my withdrawal pain I quite enjoyed parts of this early morning walk to the chemist. The fresh morning air, a bonfire smoking somewhere, cheap perfume coming from a lady at the bus stop, the scent of the Thames on the breeze. All these smells triggered memories from my childhood evoking strong emotions within me, some sad and some happy. William Burroughs once wrote that someone ought to bottle and market this marvellous side effect of heroin withdrawal. All my senses were alert and heightened for part of each awful day.

I usually arrived at the shop before Archie or his lady assistants. To others I must have looked a pathetic sight pacing up and down outside his pharmacy every morning. Long, greasy hair and a white, sometimes blue, face. My clothes hung loose on my skinny frame and were now several sizes too big for me. Grimy, grey plimsolls, blood splattered Levis: a shirt peppered with nod burns and buttoned up unequally, so that one shirt tail hung 6 inches below the other outside my jeans. My brown, Belgian leather overcoat topped this ensemble, old, scratched and scuffed. A sad sight to others maybe, but I felt as if I was at the pinnacle of cool. My hip, dramatic protest at a cruel, harsh and unfair world. Waiting there, shivering, sniffing and shaking I was Jean Genet, Coleridge, Byron and Trocchi all in one……but much more radical. I was deliberately killing myself…….that is…. until it got too painful. Come on, come on, the waiting is getting tedious now, hurry up Archie, for fucks sake hurry up, I thought.

At last, 5 minutes later, Archie arrived and with a brief nod in my direction he unlocked the shop where all the nice drugs lived. Without taking off his coat or trilby he unlocked the DDA cupboard and placed our prescriptions on his small dispensary counter. He checked them over before he put them into a large paper bag. "OK. Sonia first. 5 grains of diamorphine hydrochloride, 5 grains cocaine hydrochloride and 5 ampoules of methyl amphetamine hydrochloride," he reported as he stacked her boxes.

"Yup," I said.

"You next. 7 grains diamorphine hydrochloride, 7 grains cocaine and 7 ampoules of 1.5 ml meth. All correct?" he asked.

"You can give me a bit more if you like," I sniffed.

"Do you want any syringes, needles, sterile water or anything?" he added ignoring my request.

"Just some 26g by half inch please Archie. Give me a dozen."

Archie chucked the needles into the open bag and smiled his goofy smile. He had a lovely smile did Archie. Red faced, eyes wide apart like a frog, and a broad thin lipped mouth that took up half his face when he smiled. I loved Archie; he took away the pain and gave me so much pleasure. I wonder if he ever guessed how much he meant to me.

I had no 'holy mescaline recall' experiences of childhood on my return journey. I was, as usual, in an almighty hurry to get back to Florrie's and to get well for a few hours. In spite of the summer warmth Sonia was huddled, naked and shivering in front of the lit gas fire. She already had a leather belt around her left ankle. "Give me, give me, gimme, gimme," she squeaked. "Lovely heroin, lovely coke, lovely meth. It's going to be alright after all." She snapped open a meth ampoule and filled her syringe with the clear amphetamine. She put 4 jacks of heroin and a grain of coke into a test tube and squirted the meth on top of the tiny tablets and the crystals. The speedball dissolved as soon as the liquid amphetamine hit it and Sonia drew the one and a half mil into her works. After another ghastly, blood splattered 10 minutes of poking and probing she found a vein, pushed home the precision made glass plunger and gently lay back on the bed, a soft smile playing on her face. Yesterday's mascara had run during the night and left black stains on her cheeks.

I used a grain, a grain and an amp. The concoction hit my brain instantly and the pleasure was intense for some minutes. My aches and pains had all gone. The fear and anxiety replaced by peace and an illusion of hope. Trocchi called this heroin high 'inviolable'. A sense of being 'intact and unbrittle.' We both nodded for a couple of hours.

We came to with the sound of 'She's Leaving Home,' drifting in through our open window. Obviously our neighbour, Sam, had just bought the recently released Sgt Pepper's Lonely Hearts Club Band and we listened, with interest and pleasure for awhile. The songs were lovely it was true, but it wouldn't have been too cool to admit to liking anything by the Beatles, no matter how long they grew their hair. My mad suspicious, anarchistic mind saw them, even then, as a tool of the establishment. If we had to have pop music then the Stones would just about fit the bill.

I took another fix, nodded for a while longer, and then announced to Sonia that I had to go into town. "Charley wants a selection of men's trousers so I'll get my bag and go and get 'em." Charley was my fence on the Cowley Road and if I popped into his second-hand shop he would tell me what he needed. He gave me only a fraction of the true value of the stolen clobber but we almost always needed the money so badly I seldom refused his paltry offers. "Take care," she said, sipping her first cup of tea of the day. Sonia was an expert shoplifter. A couple of weeks previously she came into the basement kitchen of her mother's house and told me to 'hush' by pressing her finger against her lips. She was wearing her short, shiny, black plastic mac and she had something big inside it which she was supporting with both hands held in front of her. Her mother was busy at the kitchen sink and quietly talking to Ralph who was sitting at the kitchen table reading The Oxford Mail. Sonia pointed to the stairs and we slipped by the pair without them giving us a second glance.

Inside our bedroom she unbuttoned her coat and out tumbled a large pile of LPs. There were twenty Music for Pleasure albums which she had just pinched from WH Smith. Beethoven, Mozart, Delius, Tchaikovsky, Bach - a lovely, marvellous haul of beautiful music. I was impressed. "So many. How did you manage to lift them all?" I asked. "There's loads and they must have been so heavy."

"I chose them, one at a time, carefully from the display counter until I had what I wanted and then I walked out of the shop," she said matter of factly.

"So why did you arrive with them under your mac?"

"Oh! I didn't want mum to see them," she explained." I didn't want her to think that I'm a thief."

"A cultured thief though, with good taste," I reassured her.

On one occasion during a very cold spell, when we were living in Divinity Road, Sonia walked to the local hardware store on the Cowley Road. Inside, she chose a large paraffin heater and walked out of the shop with it. She always told me that the trick was simply to believe that you already own the goods that you were liberating. Leave the store with confidence, head held high, clutching your four hair dryers, say, and you'd be OK. Of course, it would be impossible today to leave a shop without getting electronically busted with an alarm going off, but then, if you had the nerve, you could get away with almost anything. You didn't need cash at all.

Feeling good and confident from a recent fix I headed off into the city centre and Marks and Spencer. As I approached Carfax I was praying that I wouldn't bump into Dick Webb. I was getting really bored with the game that we compulsively played out every time that we saw each other. Dick was a junky and a thief just like me and he sometimes liked to parade his junk thin frame inside a Wyatt Earp frock coat, wearing a smart, black Stetson and carrying a magnificent replica Colt 45 in a gun belt at his waist. I always knew when I saw him dressed this way that he was flush with horse and probably money too.

I don't know how, or why, or when the Dada started, but over those Oxford heroin years we dropped into a habit of acting out an imaginary gunfight whenever we saw one another, whether he was kitted up or not. We would spy one another, across a busy street say, and then slowly adopt a gunfighter's stance, facing each other until one of us drew his 'two fingers' gun. The stand off could take minutes, confusing passing shoppers with the frozen tension that they sensed between us. After the draw, one of us would obligingly drop dead on the pavement, or in the shop, or wherever. We never spoke to each other during these encounters and at first, when we were both young in our habits and our tolerance to H was low, our performances were hilarious and enjoyable. Over time though they became a nuisance. They wasted precious time when we were both engaged in important junky business and we didn't have the patience anymore to act out this compulsive theatre. But we were locked into the game and we were powerless to stop it.

The last time that I had seen Dick was about two weeks earlier. I was skint as usual and I had decided to visit Marks and Spencer to relieve them of a few shirts to sell to Charley later. With my grey, grimy heisting mac on, concealing my thin body and laundry bag, I entered the famous store. I quickly located the shirts that I wanted and I was getting ready to transfer 10 or 12 into my bag when I noticed, behind me, a whole line of men's trousers moving with some rustling sounds coming from the same location. I moved closer to the trembling rack of pants and peered behind to see Dick, on his knees and ramming strides into his big poacher's bag. Precisely at this moment, he saw me and then, simultaneously, we both glanced over to the left where we saw a store detective standing about 25 feet away and apparently studying something interesting in the opposite direction. We couldn't tell if he was aware of us or not. There was a look of panic on Dick's face as he stood up slowly. We had only two choices: gunfight at the M&S corral, or leg it fast. We chose to fight, clearly the show must go on, whether we were in horrible danger or not. We paused ready to draw, waiting, staring flinty eyed at each other. Dick drew and I fell down dead. We left the store very quickly, Dick clutching his huge bag and I, empty handed. For some unfathomable reason the detective had not seen, or heard us and had moved off down the shop floor.

Leaving M&S I almost collided with Wilbur Driesen. We embraced, delighted to see each other again. He was thinner than ever and parchment white, "Christ Wilbur you old tart how great to see you," I yelled.

"Ah, my only true love, such a delight," sang Wilbur. "Come on, let's go to the Cadena. We'll go upstairs and have ice cream sundaes. My treat." We sat in our usual corner and Wilbur ordered two Knickerbocker Glories, four fresh cream meringues and two pots of tea. We smoked and jabbered as we waited. "My pater's cheque has just arrived so I can afford it," smiled Wilbur.

"Where have you been?" I asked. "I was worried about you."

"Why, for Gods sake. The worst thing that can happen to me is that I die and death, my dear, still appeals to me," he screeched. "I've been in town. Isabella died so I had to get a new croaker. Now I have a young buck in Harley Street. He's OK I guess, he's even increased my script a wee bit. But I do miss dear Lady Frankau it's true."

"The American and Canadian narcs won't miss her," I said seriously.

"No, it's true; she was an aristocratic thorn in their arses that's for sure."

"You look fucking awful Wilbur," I giggled.

"You look fucking worse Joe," he laughed, beginning to cough on his meringue. Sometimes when he laughed this way, semi hysterically, he used to suck in more air than he could handle and end up choking. He was a peculiar blue colour now, but his coughing stopped as abruptly as it started. His nose and mouth were covered in cream and I laughed at him again, pointing at the daubs of cream on his face with a nicotine stained finger. "You do cheer me up," he said. "What an awful, dreadful life it's been and heroin doesn't help that much any more don't you agree?" I nodded my agreement.

"How's Sonia these days, still using I presume?" he asked.

"She's still using," I said.

"You never loved her did you?" he said, taking one of my cigarettes. I wasn't surprised by his question; it had been an unspoken fact for years.

"No, never. It's funny you know because she was beautiful, funny, talented and kind but I never felt deeply for her," I replied. "I can recognise the feeling of being in love because I've had it with others but never with Sonia."

"I knew all along. You loved your Aunty Wilbur more than you loved her I reckon," he teased. He still had a daub of cream on the end of his nose but I didn't tell him. I didn't want to wreck the romance of the moment.

"You're right of course, you outrageous old queen." I said sadly. We sat quietly: licking bits of cream, smoking and complaining, when the thought occurred to me that we must have looked like Belsen inmates, sitting there in the Cadena, let out on a day's pass for rest and recreation. "Everything is so fucking grotesque Wilbur and the horse doesn't really do it these days. I feel desperate," I whined.

"Another fine mess you've got me in to Stanley," he chuckled, but his eyes were wet with tears.

"Here is a couple of pounds, come and see me soon. I'm back in Paradise Square," said Wilbur chucking the notes on top of the white tablecloth.

"Why are you going so soon," I asked, scared to lose his company.

"I need a big fix and some Beethoven," he replied quietly.

"Oh, that reminds me, is your favourite poet still Houseman?" I asked.

"Of course, who else is there for the likes of me?"

"John Betjemen, try him. I love him. You do understand though, that as the cutting edge, hip intellectuals of our generation we should appreciate Ferlinghetti, Ginsberg, Corso and the like," I said.

"Dull fuckwits," muttered Wilbur as he got up from the table leaving a tip under a plate. We parted company in Cornmarket and I caught a whiff of paraldehyde coming off his sports jacket as we hugged goodbye. "Don't forget to pop around to Paradise sometime," he shouted.

I never saw my friend again. He died, a few days later, from an overdose in a public lavatory, near Leicester Square.

That evening I spent two hours in the lavatory. I hadn't crapped for at least five days and things were getting dire to say the least. Laxatives had proven useless in the past and so I had taken my bicycle pump and some Vaseline with me into the loo. This particular crapping aid was my very own invention and, as such, it had seldom worked. I lowered my pants and greased my anus with the petroleum jelly. I drew back the plunger and introduced the cut-off rubber adaptor into my arse and blasted a few strokes of the pump into my rectum. I sat and waited. Nothing, so I blasted again and waited for perhaps 2 or 3 minutes before I was rewarded with one huge, loud fart followed by one tiny hard turd dropping into the water with a minute splash. Oh God, how frustrating. Still it was a start. I kept repeating the process for another one and a half hours but never really achieved much apart from a thick, oily, foul smelling sweat covering my body.

Ralph was waiting in the kitchen, looking very angry, when I emerged from the lavatory. "I've been waiting an hour for you, you inconsiderate bastard. You know that is the only toilet in the house. What in God's name were you doing in there?" he raged.

"Oh sorry, I fell asleep," I muttered meekly.

That evening, lying in bed, after Sonia and I had swallowed our Mandrax and had our last fix of the day I turned to Sonia. "It's no good you know. We have to clean up soon. This is too awful, let's take the cure."

She stared at me, searching my face for something. "OK," she said.

12

THE CURE IN THE
SUMMER OF LOVE

Late summer 1967

It was late afternoon on Ward B7, at Littlemore Hospital, Oxford and I was sitting with Sister Jones in the ward day room. The large, pleasant room was empty of other patients who were probably outside in the sun. It had been a hot, sultry, August day and the mood on the ward was tranquil. I was in love with Sister Jones and I was very content to watch her knitting a heavy, cream sweater for her husband. She was Spanish and she was beautiful. I wanted her as my mother and lover at the same time. She had dark, olive skin, rich, brown, doe eyes, a round face and a soft, voluptuous figure. I loved Sister Jones. She wore a starched, lacy sister's cap on her short, shiny, curly black hair and a navy blue sister's uniform with a silver buckled belt. Oh, I did love Sister Jones as I watched her working with her big needles.

Sonia and I had been patients on B7 for two and a half weeks and we were withdrawing gradually from our heroin habits using a reducing regime of methadone. On admission, our psychiatrist Dr Tony Willems, warned us to expect a period of ultra, high sensitivity and awareness, "For about a month you will experience something like an LSD trip. It's a long time to have a distorted perception of things but it will pass eventually. You'll probably enjoy most of it I reckon. All your senses have been asleep for some years now and they are about to come alive again. Sounds, scents, touch; everything will be magnified hugely for a few weeks. Try and ride it if you can - accept it and enjoy it." I trusted this Anglo/Dutch doctor and liked him instantly at our first meeting. One week into our cure he introduced us to his colleague, Dr Fernando Arroyave, who had just arrived from Colombia, South America and he could barely speak any English. I came to love and respect this small, podgy, handsome, laughing South American.

"You're staring at me Joe," said Sister Jones, putting down her long knitting needles.

"Yes, I like to stare at you," I whispered.

"I think you love everybody don't you?" she asked, giggling wonderfully. "I heard that you told Fernando that you loved him too?"

"I do, I love you both." She picked up her knitting and continued to smile as she worked. "I love Maria as well you know," I said.

"The new patient from Madrid?" she asked.

"Yes, she's magnificent. I don't understand a word she says but already I'm in love," I explained.

"Is this the withdrawal talking or is this a normal Joe we are seeing?" enquired Sister Jones.

"Normal, I'm afraid."

"Well, that's a pity because I can't very well say, 'never mind, you'll be better soon can I?'" We both chuckled and then settled into a comfortable silence with the golden evening light coming through the large windows "Oh well, they call it 'The Summer of Love'," she said quietly into her knitting.

Littlemore Hospital, formerly the Oxford County Lunatic Asylum, was built in 1846. Following the well intentioned Victorian pattern, the vast building was set amidst its own sprawling grounds and was situated away from the public view, behind walls and trees. It was a place that, for over a hundred years, had offered sanctuary, asylum, for troubled minds. When I first arrived at Littlemore I would stare out of the windows of B7 at the long term schizophrenic patients who were brought out every morning and afternoon for exercise in the yard outside. Most of these patients were burned-out and functioned like unthinking zombies; not so much wasted by their terrible psychotic condition but brain damaged by the enormous amounts of anti-psychotic medications they had consumed through the years. The main offending drug was chlorpromazine, or Largactil, to call it by its popular trade name. Even if these early prescribing doctors had known, in advance, of the consequences of the long term prescription of Largactil they would probably still have dished it out because the illness of schizophrenia can be so hideously cruel to its host, relentlessly taunting the sufferer with threatening and frightening voices 24 hours a day. The doctors were between the devil and the deep blue sea. The cause of the illness was not known so it was a case of managing the terrifying symptoms until a cure came along and the only thing that made life more tolerable for the patients was also something that slowly destroyed their brains.

When Sonia and I were taking the cure on B7 there appeared to be some kind of power struggle going on within the hospital. The two leading consultants, Dr Felix Letemendia and Dr Bertram Mandelbrote, were having a major difference of opinion on treatment methods for the mentally ill and one could easily see manifestations of this simply by walking between the two wings of the large building.

Enter the Littlemore and turn left and you were in Letemendia's territory: clean, tidy, nicely decorated, well furnished and with the nursing staff wearing starched uniforms. Turn right, on entry to the hospital, and you would walk into 'Bertie' Mandelbrote's principality. Paint peeling off the walls, litter, unmade beds, staff in sweaters and jeans. This was the 'progressive' side. Minimum medication, lots of group therapy, a philosophy of 'the patient is responsible and is in charge.' Sometimes very large groups were called of perhaps 20 to 30 patients.

The discipline used by Mandelbrote's team was difficult to identify. I felt that it pretended to be a lot of things, Gestalt, Encounter Group Therapy maybe, but it didn't quite know where it was going in those days. In the main, to the outsider, these groups looked and felt intimidating and without guidance. I watched secretly as doctors and nurses sat and said, or did, nothing as these sessions collapsed into noisy chaos or sullen indifference. The guys who walked out smiling were invariably the bullies and the psychopaths. I used to think watching these groups in action, 'If I could do it myself, without help, I wouldn't be here in the first place would I?' I felt that Gestalt and similar therapies were misguided in that they seemed to be saying, 'Suit yourself, and do what you feel comfortable doing and fuck everybody else.' It denied the inter-dependency that every human being has on another. The 'new' therapy supported the individual and not the community. Dead dodgy stuff I thought and I was reminded of The Great Beast 666, Alisteir Crowley the Satanist and heroin addict, whose basic tenet was 'Do what thou wilt shall be the whole of the law.'

Letemendia believed in conserving any structure worth preserving that remained in a patient's life and guiding his patients back to sanity using medication and one-to-one counselling. Of course he used group therapy for the alcoholics and addicts he treated but these groups followed a time tested and effective 12 Step approach based on the Alcoholics Anonymous programme. I felt safe in the clean, well decorated wards and I trusted Dr Willems and Fernando Arroyave.........and Sister Jones.

"Do you love Sonia?" asked Sister Jones gently.

"No, not anymore.......if ever. I love her as a friend but not as a lover. I never have really," I replied. "She sneaks off now and again for a night with a lover and she thinks that I don't notice."

"Do you care?" she asked.

"How can I? I do exactly the same myself, so why should I care?" I answered and then, a minute later, "I do get jealous, but I have no right, I don't love her you see."

Sister Jones looked sad and then suddenly smiled, "I have been married for ten years and my heart still thumps when my husband walks into the room. It's lovely, I'm lucky I know."

"Yes you are lucky. What does your heart do when I walk into the room?" I laughed.

"When I see you my heart giggles," she said. I was so touched by this remark that I couldn't speak and tears filled my eyes. After a minute or two I realised that this was the first time that I'd shed tears for several years. I started to sob and heave, there in the armchair for loonies, next to Sister Jones. She leaned across and gave me a tissue, "That's good, you are coming back to life," she purred, smiling her Spanish, dimpled smile, gentle and soft. 'I don't know if I really want to come back to life,' I thought.

"Dr Willems phoned me this morning to say he had seen you and Sonia sitting outside the main entrance staring at the Magnolia there for at least half an hour. What were you doing?" asked Sister Jones.

"Oh that. It was a strange experience for us. We just couldn't believe how beautiful those Magnolia blooms were. We were on our way to the hospital shop to buy some fags and I suddenly caught sight of the tree up against the wall."

"I know it well. It's to the left of the main entrance," said Sister Jones.

"The flowers took my breath away, so exotic and the depth of the colours was difficult to understand. I could have drowned in their beauty and we couldn't take our eyes off them. It was as if I was seeing flowers for the first time ever. They were sacred and I felt that we were worshiping the damn things after a bit. This is some trip," I enthused. "I got locked on to Maria's lovely, big breasts yesterday and followed her around the ward like her pet dog just so I could look at her tits. They were sacred too."

"You really ought to write these experiences up for Dr Willems so that he has a patient's subjective account of heroin withdrawal," she suggested.

"Hmm, I can't concentrate for long enough that's the problem. Oh! and smells are the worst thing. Nice perfumes knock me out cold and bad smells, like lavatorial stuff, make me want to vomit on the spot."

"Did you know someone called Dave Edney," asked Sister Jones, still knitting contentedly.

"Yes I did. It was very sad." Dave Edney, a local Oxford boy had killed himself a few years earlier. He'd taken just one jack of heroin but the experience had been so pleasurable for him that he killed himself soon after, using rat poison. It took him days to die apparently and he told his girl friend that he knew in his heart that he'd never ever again experience that marvellous feeling so it was best if he ended it there and then. "It was all over the national press because it was so shocking. Of course Dave was right in his way, he'd never ever repeat that first heroin high but whether that is a reason to kill yourself........," I mused. "Mick Strutt, a cop from Oxford Drug Squad, accused me one day of supplying Dave with the fateful jack, but I hadn't. I tried, like Wilbur, to follow 'the code' when it came to horse. There's quite a few of my friends who have popped their clogs now. It's horrible."

"When you two first came into B7 we were all worried about you because you were so thin, just like skeletons. What must your parents think when they see you like this?" she asked, looking fierce.

"I don't know what I look like. I know Sonia looks so awful and I worry about her but I have had no self awareness until a few days ago when I looked in the mirror. I saw a scary, white, thin stranger staring back at me. I've already had Hepatitis B twice," I said.

"I thought that you could only get it once."

"That's what I thought. I almost died with the jaundice. I was bright yellow for weeks: eyeballs, skin, semen, piss like coca-cola and I ate nothing because I'd puke it all up straight away. Just a dirty fix I guess." The other patients started to drift into the sitting room in dribs and drabs and our pleasant afternoon was coming to an end. I caught a whiff of Sister Jones's scent as she got up and I suddenly remembered something from my childhood. I was ill in bed, reading a Rupert Bear book, and my mother came into my bedroom after a visit to the shops. It was cold outside and she was wearing a pink woollen scarf wrapped around her neck. She bent down to kiss me and her cheek was cold and I could smell her scented powder. Suddenly I was frightened and I wanted my mum.

13

THIRD TIME LUCKY

Spring 1970

I had been sweating in this prison cell for 5 weeks and I was a weary, hopeless 25 year old. The good thing was that I did have the 'peter' to myself because it was a designated hospital cell. I was almost off opiates now, five weeks without heroin and just taking a tab of methadone every couple of days. For the first four weeks of my incarceration I hadn't slept at all and had to endure almost a cold turkey regime. I'd lost everything: habit, money, friends and now I was losing my wife and child.

I could feel myself turning into a dangerous predator that would do anything for a fix. What kind of person was I that, hand on my heart, could say that my greatest loss through the years was heroin. Above all and more than my loved ones, heroin was the most important thing in my life. Even more important than my new best friend Henry, a young addict, whom I'd known for a couple of years and we had become inseparable.

I'd been arrested in the middle of the night in East Oxford Health Centre. I was living with Sonia and our daughter, Annie, in a damp cave of a flat off the Cowley Road. Sonia had managed, with great courage, to stay clean after our cure at Littlemore but I had relapsed almost immediately. I had been turkeying for a day and a half and I couldn't take any more. It was another two days before I was due to pick up my week's script and I knew that I'd have to break into a chemist, or a doctor's surgery somewhere, to stop the pain; both physical and mental. It was around midnight and Sonia and Jo were both fast asleep.

I went to the kitchen to fetch some tools. Christ this place stank of damp. I was screaming for some relief from the pain and I needed to think clearly for the job in hand. I put a large screwdriver, a hammer, a small jemmy, a sharp knife, torch and some gloves into a plastic shopping bag and stepped out on to the Cowley Road. There was a new GP's health centre just up the road in front of the Cowley Road Hospital where I had been born. The surgeries would have a little bit of something nice, I was certain of that.

Luckily the window I chose to enter by was screened from the main road by some bushes. It was already half open and it was simply a matter of sliding my knife in and pushing the catch off the fastener. Easy, but when I hauled myself inside, the window crashed back into position with an almighty bang. Incredibly it hadn't smashed but my heart almost stopped with the frightening din. After a while I got up from the floor and took a peep through the Venetian blinds. Nothing happening out there, quiet as the grave.

My eyes got used to the gloom and I could see that I was in a waiting room. Very intelligent I must say. Of all the windows accessing surgeries I had chosen a waiting room. The surgery doors were bound to be locked. The first two doors I tried were locked but the third was open. Oh joy! It was situated at the back of the centre and had a drug cabinet fixed to the wall. I opened the steel box with my jemmy and was delighted to see the smaller, locked cupboard inside marked DDA (Dangerous Drugs Act) The DDA opened easily with a yank of my large screwdriver.

I'd opened an Aladdin's Cave. Boxes of heroin, morphine, methadone, methedrine and some big bottles of tuinal and seconal. I filled my bag with the goodies and I felt so happy. There was a box of 2 mil syringes on a side table and I chucked a few dozen of these in with the junk. That was enough. I wasn't going to get greedy and push my luck. I decided to leave without forcing the other doors. I moved to the window in the waiting room and peeped through the slatted blinds. A blue light was flashing outside. The police were here and they were on to me. I was too sick to make a run for it. I knew that they would have the place surrounded and so I swiftly found a lavatory and luckily it had no windows, so I was able to turn on the lights without giving away my position to the fuzz outside. I quickly filled my syringe with two amps of dia-morphine and, Hallelujah, I hit a vein straight away. Such a rush, such a relief. Rapidly I filled another works with a further two amps of heroin and sent these home also. I could hear the cops in the building and so I thought, rather melodramatically, 'I won't be taken alive.' I up-ended the tuinal bottle into my mouth, washing them down with water from the loo, and repeated the procedure with the seconal. I was singing something when the cops finally bust open the door. Someone said, "Oh God Joe, so it's come to this has it?" and I dropped into blackness.

I woke up in the Radcliffe Infirmary the next day, handcuffed to the bed and with a cop sitting by my side. The cop was an old friend who had been in Oxford City Fire Service with me seven years before. He'd obviously changed jobs. "You've woken up then Joe?" he said. "You had us worried during the night. We thought we were going to lose you boy." He had tears in his eyes and he went on to say, "You were singing 'Love is Strange' when we found you. When I saw that it was my old pal I didn't know whether to laugh or cry. You're a fucking mystery you are," he said. I was charged with 'burglary and possession' and remanded to Oxford Jail to await my court appearance.

My cell was on the 'twos' on A wing, which was on the ground floor of this ancient establishment. My 'peter' was about 9' by 12' and painted in a dark brown gloss colour. I had a pisspot in the corner and a metal, framed bed with a thin, horse hair mattress. There was a window, but it was high above my head and very small. The basement floor, the 'ones', housed the isolation, punishment and choky cells, rule 43 etc. Sex offenders were put down there along with other prisoners who felt their lives would be threatened if they were placed in the main body of the nick. The fourth floor was mainly for remand prisoners awaiting trial and the third was for convicted prisoners.

During 'slop out' I peered up at the surrounding balconies of the 'threes' and 'fours' of A wing. This place was like a vast, satanic cathedral and it struck me as very otherworldly. Every sound was magnified and echoed a couple of times before being eaten up by the thick stone walls. At night I could hear clearly the clink of a screw's keys, or the sad crying of an imprisoned Gipsy, or the savage taunting of a 'nonce' from the 'threes,' although they were far from my cell. The smell of the place was unforgettable. My probation officer once told me that he was astonished to discover, on visiting other jails in the USA and Germany, that they had exactly the same odour as British prisons. A heady mixture of male sweat, Brasso, piss, detergent and boiled cabbage.

This old 'goal' was built in the 1100s and renovated in the early 19th century. The cells were originally designed for one convict a piece but nowadays they often housed three prisoners. Two bunk beds and a single crammed into each small room was normal. Oxford nick was still hanging its inmates up until the 1950s and the last public execution to occur at the jail was in 1863. A condemned old lag called Webb was put to death on March 26th 1827 and he wrote in his exercise book prior to his death,

Within these gloomy cells confined
A weeping wretch I lie
Oppressed with care and hurt in mind
To think I soon must die.

One of the most unpopular old hospital screws often used to threaten us loudly with, 'I would have enjoyed taking you on the 8 o'clock walk my boy!' He obviously regretted the abolition of capital punishment in Britain. This place was grey, utterly grey.

Sonia visited me once a week bringing little Annie with her. As I stared at them through the toughened, wired glass in the visiting room I felt guilty that Annie should be seeing her father here. "Do you have to bring her?" I once asked Sonia.

"Don't be silly Joe, she wants to see you."

"This is a horrible place for a two year old," I persisted, squirming with shame.

"She doesn't see the nick, she just sees you," she said. Annie's birth, in 1968, was a surprise to me and a shock. I didn't want a child and Sonia knew it. I wasn't cut out to be a father, for fuck's sake, I couldn't take responsibility for myself let alone a child. Sonia and I were on the rocks and we both knew it. Sonia was clean and I was dirty. I had teamed up with my using pal, Henry, and it must have made life unbearable for Sonia. My presence wasn't conducive to a healthy recovery for her and certainly not good for little Annie who had been born addicted to methadone. I was guilty then and I'm guilty today of handicapping my child with such an awful start to her life. Although I was getting supplies of heroin and cocaine from Dr Arroyave it was never enough to satisfy my constant need and I had spent the previous year breaking into chemist's shops, doctor's surgeries and carrying out elaborate con tricks to get more junk.

In the May of the previous year something extraordinary happened. I was sitting in Soho Square, in London's West End, with Phil Seamen, the famous drummer and friend of Ginger Baker. Phil was a registered heroin addict and when I came to town I often used to see him in the Square, shooting the breeze with his adoring fans, or just nodding alone on a bench. We'd originally met some years previously in Boots Piccadilly where we were both picking up our scripts on the stroke of midnight. We got on well and I enjoyed talking to him.

Lately though Phil had really begun to deteriorate. He was swallowing great gob fulls of barbiturates in order to supplement his increasingly ineffective heroin habit which was no longer giving him any pleasure or pain relief. On this lovely, fresh, sunny spring day I looked at Phil's tired face and felt so sad for him, even though he managed his goofy smile now and again. He was a great musician and one of the world's leading drummers and he still chose the living death of heroin.

"Oh...oh! See this guy walking towards us," said Phil quietly. "The Pakistani in the smart suit?"

"Yup."

"He's looking for major quantities of H and needs a supplier," Phil informed me. "I'd stay away from him if I were you." Sure enough the dapper chappie with his flashing, white teeth smile and his sparkly, black eyes came up to our bench and sat down after brushing the seat carefully with a white handkerchief.

"Morning Phil. Indeed it is a beautiful day. Very, very delightful to be alive isn't it?" said the smiling Asian hood. Aged around forty, his face was pitted with the deep cavities left by smallpox but his face radiated happiness and confidence.

"Morning Azam. How are you? This is a friend of mine, name of Joe," said Phil.

"Joe from the Limbo?" asked a curious Azam.

"No, no, I don't think so," I replied.

He stared at me unconvinced and then said, "Please come to my hotel I need to talk to you," he announced.

"Hmmm.......well......I dunno man....."

"I'm at the Ritz and this is my room number. I have an interesting and lucrative proposition for you," he said handing me a small blue card on which he'd scribbled his name and room number at the great hotel. "See you at three o'clock this afternoon," he said, leaning towards me persuasively and shaking my hand. "He has more 'bottles' than you Phil my friend," he laughed as he walked out of the square.

"I hate him already," I moaned at Phil. "Heroin for vast profit is not my idea of fun."

"Too much death......too much heartache.....but you'll go anyway," smirked Phil.

"Hmm. I've got an idea," I muttered.

At five minutes past three I was in Azam's room at the Ritz. We were drinking tea and smoking his Sobranie Black Russians. I hated him more with each passing minute. Ostentatious, pretentious, successful villain that he was. "I need a kilo of pure heroin immediately," he began settling back into his soft armchair. "I can unload it in one week and then I shall want more." I couldn't quite believe his naiveté. He must have been completely new to the heroin scene to not know there was very little powdered H in England at that time. A little bit of brown coming from Chinese sources in Gerrard Street but most of the junk on the street was legitimate, prescribed diamorphine hydrochloride BP. This was a great business opportunity for me and I planned to take Mr Azam for a ride. What the hell.

"I will pay you £12,000 per kilo," declared Azam,"for quality stuff."

"Hmm." I needed time to think. "How are you going to test it if I get you a sample?"

"I have a tame junky friend who will test it for me. I trust his judgement," he replied confidently shooting his cuffs and reaching for his cup of tea. I was tempted to say, 'You must be stark raving mad to trust a junky,' but I stayed in my role and didn't comment. "OK. Have him here at six tonight. I'll bring a sample for you. If he approves the quality, and it will be first rate I promise, I'll need £6,000 on the spot and the remaining six grand when I deliver the kilo," I asserted.

"Very good. I'll see you tonight at six." As I walked out of the Ritz I couldn't believe that he was actually going for the deal, but I had a strong, certain feeling that he was going to fall for it. I didn't even have any way of checking whether twelve grand was the going rate or not but it must have been close. Hateful, murdering bugger, it would be a pleasure to take his money and maybe save some lives along the way.

I went to Piccadilly Underground Station and entered the men's lavatories. As soon as I closed the door to the cubicle I knew that this place would not suit my purpose. I needed somewhere with a clean table top and something to crush my heroin jacks with. Lyons Corner House, that's just the job, but before I went I decided to have a fix. Steady me up a bit for the risky job in hand. I injected a mixture of heroin and methedrine and slumped back, needle still in my arm, to enjoy the buzz. When I finally woke up, I panicked. Fuck! How long had I been on the nod? I shouted out loud as I gathered my paraphernalia together, "What's the time man?" The answer came back immediately from another cubicle.

"Half four man." I was late but I still had time. I headed for Lyons.

I got myself a cup of tea and sat down at a table away from the crowd. I spread a napkin on the Formica top and counted 14 tablets of heroin on to the clean surface. I figured that 16 tablets was roughly a gram and so I could easily get away with 14. Anyway this was just his sample, albeit an expensive one. I folded the paper napkin over the tabs and started to bash them with the heavy glass sugar dispenser. It took no time at all and when I lifted a corner of the soft paper to inspect the H it was already lovely white powder. I wrapped it neatly in another napkin and sat back to enjoy my tea. Should I keep him waiting? Make him nervous? After all, the 'man' is always late, it's a junky tradition. No, afraid not, my nerves wouldn't take it. I'd be there at five to six on the dot.

"That was quick Joe," said Azam, ushering me into the plush hotel suite. "This is my expert taster Alan."

"'Azam and Alan Buy Some Heroin' by Enid Blyton," I quipped, but it fell on stony ground I'm afraid. I'd never seen Alan before anywhere but he looked like a junky: thin, pale, sensitive poet's face. "I've brought a gram for you to test. If you like it I want £6,000 now and the remainder when I come back at 8 o'clock with the K. Azam nodded at Alan and the addict rolled up his sleeve and produced his works. It was a nice French job just like the ones that I used. I wondered where he got it. "What is the strength Joe?" he asked.

"95%, very pure," I replied. It was actually 98% but I felt that if I told Alan that, he'd smell a rat. Too good to be true, kind of thing.

"That's hot," he whistled. "So how much do I need?"

"I don't know what your tolerance is Alan. You'll have to work it out yourself bearing in mind that the powder is not cut. With that he chucked about five tabs worth into a spoon. "You don't need to cook it, it's so pure," I commented.

I could see Azam getting excited and shifting in his chair. Alan got a vein and pushed home. The look that came over his face said it all. He looked blissful. If his mother could have seen his face at that moment she would probably have said something like, 'Oooh, aahh, look at Alan! Just like when he was a contented little baby,' or something like that. I could not believe that they were falling for this blatant con but Alan gave Azam a sleepy thumbs up.

Azam handed me a brown paper shopping bag and said, "That's £6,000 there, the other half at 8 o'clock."

"OK it's a deal. I won't be long, so is it OK if I come back before 8 if I get the gear early?"

"No problem, we'll be waiting," smiled Mr Azam.

"See you later." I left the Ritz and made straight for Paddington Station. I was going home with £6,000 in a brown carrier bag. It was a small fortune in those days.

The train was just pulling out of Paddington as I ambled through First Class on my way to a Second Class compartment. The train was moving slowly and I was happy. The carriages were almost empty and I was tempted to just flop in First Class but then I saw something that interested me. In one of the empty compartments was an old leather brief case, lying flat down on the seat. I knew, instinctively, that the bag contained money. A lot of money. I just knew it and don't ask me how I knew, but I did. I looked up and down the corridor and after I was sure I was alone I dived into the compartment and picked up the mysterious brief case.

Humming; no quietly singing, a song from South Pacific, 'Some Enchanted Evening' I think it was, I quickly located a vacant toilet in the swaying carriage. I sat down and opened the case and could not believe my eyes. It was full of ten bob notes, pound notes and fivers. All used notes, plus there were some half crowns and two bobs at the bottom. It must be a week's takings from somewhere I guessed. What a day! I was so happy. I'd buy Sonia a new dress and new clothes for Jo. No, fuck it; I'd buy us a palace in India. I was too excited to start counting but I knew that there were several thousand pounds in the brief case.

I left the loo after stuffing the money into my brown carrier bag. I lobbed the old case out of the window and strolled down the carriage. Ahh perfect, two nuns sitting together. Just the ticket. I'd sit with them until we got to Oxford and try and look as holy as I could for half an hour. During this pleasant journey home I decided to put the money into a left luggage locker on Oxford Station and reclaim it in a few days in case anyone started to look for me. On the platform I had some difficulty squashing the bag in the locker because it was so fat with cash, but eventually I managed it. I was rich!

I waited five days before I returned to the station and told no one of my lucky day during that time. It was difficult not to share my amazing good fortune but I managed it and there was no sign of Mr Azam anywhere in Oxford. I was home and dry......and wealthy. It was raining hard when I opened my box and it seemed like months since I'd stuffed the fat sack into this confined space. What a giggle! The door swung open easily and the square, steel box was empty. Stupidly I put my hand inside to check, not believing the evidence before my eyes. Black clouds of doom and despair descended on me. 'Someone has stolen my money,' I thought. 'Obviously it must be a member of the railway staff, someone who saw me stuffing the swag into the left luggage box. Dishonest bastards!' I was furious and waited as all my marvellous dreams of the past five days evaporated in the rain. I went to the enquiries office and handed the overweight, piggy faced, thieving porter my key. "My property has been stolen," I told him.

"Anything valuable? It's very unusual for this kind of thing to happen you know," he chuckled happily. The fact that he was laughing almost tipped me over the edge into a hideous assault on the fat cretin. "Anything valuable?" he repeated with a sly smile.

"Hmm," I said biting my bottom lip and bunching my hands into fists. 'I swear I'll kill him,' I thought.

"Well Sir, I don't know where you got that key from because there is no record of that particular box being hired out. See for yourself, there's no record," he said, showing me his stupid, well thumbed, grimy receipt book. I'd had enough. I knew when I'd been done. I turned and walked out of the station, back to a life of poverty. Just outside the main entrance I spied a five pound note lying on the floor, wet from the rain. Fuck.....fuck.....fuck....

Walking around the exercise yard in Oxford Prison I remembered that terrible day when I made and lost a fortune. I was feeling depressed. "Joe, sell us some dope," yelled one of the cons from across the yard. "Cheer up boy. Not long now." A lot of the inmates had been my customers on the 'out' and the banter between us was pretty persistent. "I heard that you turned the Governor on yesterday Joe," or shouting at one of the screws, "That one over there boss, South that's right, he's got half a K of Kif in his cell. I'd turn him over if I were you." Very funny, but also inevitable now that my cell would be searched thoroughly and it was. Another piece of rumour doing the rounds in the nick was that I'd just sold some junk to Keith Richards of the Rolling Stones. It happened to be true but I wasn't letting on to anybody.

Young Freddy Smith had knocked on my door last August. I liked Freddy a lot; in fact, I liked his whole outlaw family. They were notorious Oxford crooks and infamous for their open hatred of the filth. Mrs Smith, the mother, had helped me out many times in the past, stashing gear for me etc., until the heat died down. I also had a close friendship with Freddy's elder brother Dave. None of them were junkies but they used plenty of cannabis and amphetamines when they were available. Young Freddy was a cool guy who barely moved his lips when he spoke and his movements were slow and easy. "Joe, my darlin'. I need some 'elp," he announced from the doorstep. We moved inside and Freddie accepted a cup of tea and sat down.

He talked slow, with a local Oxford accent, and he had an earnest way of talking which always made me want to take him seriously but laugh at the same time. One smooth gangster was Freddie. "I 'ave a colleague, oo I 'appened to meet in the boob, oo 'as a large quantity of stolen intoxicants about his person," Freddy informed me in his laconic way. "Morphine, barbs and amphetamines. In fact, Brother Joe, you could say ee's got the entire contents of several chemists' shops in the Leeds area."

"So?"

"Roight, I knew you wuz gunna say that. We could sell it in dribs and drabs but we don't really know the dope market like you do and we want to try and unload it in one or two drops."

"Hmm."

"I knew you wuz gunna say that. I told my colleague Stuart that Joe will say, 'Hmm.' You're very 'elpful I must say," drawled Freddy.

"OK. Will do. Be ready at 10 in the morning. We'll go to the smoke and see about dropping it all off. Still got the Minivan?"

"Yeh."

"Good, very nondescript. What's my cut?"

"15%," answered Freddy.

"OK. See you in the morning then."

By midday on the following day Young Freddy, Stuart, the Leeds chemist robber and I were in Notting Hill Gate talking to my old aristocratic friend, Rupert Seymour. "OK. I've had a word and he'll take all your morphine and also the methadone tablets. Maybe the physeptone linctus too," said Rupert.

"Oo is ee?" asked Young Freddy.

"Keith Richards," answered Rups.

"Keith Richards?" asked Stuart, looking like someone who had just had live electric wires attached to his testicles.

"Of the Rolling Stones?" whispered Freddy.

"Yah, that's right, the Stones," said Rupert. "You're to be at Olympia Studios, with the gear at midnight tonight."

"I'll take everything else that you have. Barbs and the amphets at the agreed price. Agreed?" We began unloading cardboard boxes filled with large glass sweet jars containing what looked like the entire drugs supply for the City of Leeds for at least a year. It took us sometime, up and down Rupert's stairs, but we finished eventually and the money was handed over to Freddy. "You can stay here this afternoon if you want, until it's time to go to the studio," offered Rupert.

Midnight arrived and found us outside the recording studios of the most famous rock and roll group in the world. The bouncer checked us over and led us through to a large room close to the sound-proofed studio. After a few minutes Keith shambled in with a cigarette dangling from his lips and wearing a terrified expression on his face. He was so scared that he was shaking. It was either fear of us or heroin withdrawal, but I could see that his pupils were pinned so it must have been us he was scared of. I recall that we did look pretty ugly. Years on the streets had turned us into low-life, criminal predators and I suppose that it showed. Keith had built his career on wanting to look like a cool, wasted street dude and we were the kind that he aspired to. He had never known the street ever: protected by his minders 24 hours a day, how could he live on the street? He lived in luxury and in the best hotels. Life was strange eh?

"Can I try a bit of morphine?" he asked.

"Sure you can. Stuart, give the man the morphine," I ordered. Keith sauntered off with the bottle of M and came back soon after shaking his head and smiling. "Nice stuff. How much for everything?"

"£300 to you mate," I replied.

"Done. But I haven't got any cash, will you take a cheque?"

"No problem," I answered knowing that the cheque would be good. At which point Mick Jagger sailed in, put his arm around my shoulder and kissed my cheek. "Got any coke boys?" asked Mick.

"Get you some if you like. Next week?"

"Write me a cheque for 300 quid Mick. I've not got any cash on me," Keith asked him. Moments later Mick came back and handed me a cheque for £300 and we left the studio with hugs and kisses. We were almost in Oxford before Freddy and Stuart started to speak again. "It's no fucking good me telling anybody because they just won't fucking believe it," complained an embittered Stuart.

"Fucking 'ell," commented Young Freddy.

The following day we visited the allotment shed where Stuart had a few pills left from his once large stash and we all walked slap-bang into an ambush. The drugs squad clambered all over us in a matter of seconds and we were ceremoniously busted for 'possession' of half a dozen diet pills and some Vitamin C tablets known to have come from a number of successful drug burglaries in Leeds. We spent the night in police custody and Freddy and I were released on bail the following morning after being charged. Stuart, however, was returned to Leeds and charged with the break-ins. While the desk sergeant was handing back our confiscated property I watched as he handed a bank cheque to Freddy. I closed my eyes and prayed hard until we had left the station. Outside, on St Aldate's, near Christchurch College, Freddy showed me the cheque. "Look," he said. The cheque was clearly signed 'Mick Jagger' and our drug squad had missed it completely, "The day is ours," shouted a jubilant Freddy as Old Tom struck 12 noon.

The marvellous memory made me smile as I slid between the coarse prison sheets and tried to get comfortable for the night. I was still freakishly thin but almost clean now, thanks to Her Majesty's Prison Service.

14

LOVE AND COCK UPS
IN JERICHO

Mid-summer 1973

I didn't know why she wanted me. For the life of me I couldn't fathom out why she needed to stay with me. The early morning sun was filtering through her grimy, dormer window and I watched her as she slept. Although it was only dawn I was drinking cider and I was drunk.

Emma was pretty and she looked like a little angel with her blonde, wavy hair strewn over her pillow. She was a nurse and she had got to bed late the previous evening after a long, hard shift at the Radcliffe Infirmary. It was the summer of 1973 and I was lying beside my lover at her flat in Jericho, Oxford. I had met her the year before and she had rescued me from a slow suicide, reclusivity and certain death. I had just been released from another spell on remand in prison and I was living on the Cowley Road in a decrepit, large, three storey house near the Plain. Six months earlier I had been placed on a withdrawal regime of methadone and as the dose got lower and lower I began to drink alcohol again. As my opiate blindfolds slipped off and the pain of living started again, I turned to booze after a period of abstinence from alcohol of about ten years. It was metabolically impossible for me to drink and use heroin at the same time because I would vomit uncontrollably. So one drug had to go and, for me, there was no choice between the two because heroin was my one true love.

I was sitting in Jim's room, drinking cider and listening to him play flamenco guitar when Mick, another Oxford junky, came in with a beautiful girl. She was tiny, no more than 5 feet tall, and she looked scared as she followed Mick into the mock-up of a city dump that was Jim's room. This girl was Emma Soames.

Jim and I had spent the evening drinking and listening to his singing and guitar playing. Jim told me that it was a 'welcome home from jail' party for me but I knew that we would have been drinking and drunk anyway, no matter what the occasion. I had been hanging on to life by a thread for some time now. I had reluctantly quit the heroin as it was impossible to obtain enough through the new methadone clinics to satisfy me and I'd turned to drink. I was drunk and inappropriate almost all of the time these days. In and out of jail for petty thefts and getting involved in hideous, drunken brawls on a regular basis. I was confused, malnourished and I was losing the will to live. The grief I felt for the loss of heroin was profound and influenced my every waking thought. It was only a matter of time before I achieved my death wish during some drunken fight or dare.

Most of my original addict friends were now dead and so was my reputation as a cool, smart dealer. I was a seven and half stone bum who trusted no one and was trusted by nobody. I was now divorced and saw nothing of Sonia or Annie anymore. At long last Sonia had grown tired of my unrelenting pursuit of drugs and she had left me. I felt no anger, no blame; I had no time for Sonia or my daughter and they deserved a better life. I lived mainly on yogurt and Ambrosia Creamed Rice and because I had no money, I stole everything I needed. I drank like I used to fix, 24 hours a day, and sometimes I would be visited by delirium tremens in the form of halucinosis even though I had a brain and belly full of alcohol. I sat and stared at Emma crouched beside Mick on the dusty floor.

"So where did you meet Emma, Mick?" I asked. She had been watching me closely ever since they had arrived at Jim's pad. God knows what Mick had told her about me. "I met her in 'Casualty' at the Radcliffe. I had overdosed and woke up with this angel looking after me," he replied shyly. She glanced at me with her large grey eyes and then looked down at the floor. The drink and the flamenco flowed during that night and I found that I could not take my eyes off this girl for very long.

I was awoken the next day by a frantic tapping at my window. It was Emma gesturing for me to let her in and giving me that strange half smile, half pleading, look I had seen the previous evening. I let her in to my filthy room and she sat on the bed without taking off her navy-blue duffle coat. "Would you like some tea," I asked. "What's the problem?"

"I fell in love with you last night. I haven't slept all night," she said breathlessly without looking at me. Emma was the product of a 'nuevo-riche' family from Virginia Waters: private school educated, she was beautiful and she drove a Triumph Spitfire. And she wanted me? It was beyond me, I thought as I made the tea. I was fixing to die and along comes Emma. "I don't know what to say," I whispered. "I'm honoured, but you don't know anything about me."

"But I do know lots about you," she looked up at me. "You're famous in Oxford you know. Everybody knows who you are and I've heard all about your mad escapades, so I do know who you are."

"A bum," I said.

"Yes, I can see that you're a bum, but I love you," said Emma. I felt sorry for her in that moment: there's something wrong with this woman to want me like this. We kissed and made slow, gentle, sweet love. On this sunny morning I was glad that Emma had chosen me. She was determined that I would stop the drink at some point and then maybe we would be set for domestic bliss in Esher or somewhere like that. I watched her sleeping and felt a great fondness for this little angel.

The last time that I had shared a bed with a woman was 18 months previously when Henry and I were shacked up with Delia. I had just robbed a chemist in Headington and I got away with a fairly large amount of heroin and durophet so we needed somewhere to hole up for awhile, to enjoy the gear but also to let the police get bored with the case. Delia was a young girl who worked in a greengrocer on the Cowley Road and I got to know her when I popped in to buy the occasional bunch of grapes. She was pretty and scatty with a deliciously, infectious giggle. She wasn't too bright intellectually but she was a sensual, sexual creature and very kind. So, she was the obvious choice as a place to stay for a few days after the job.

"Oh go on Joe, again, again!" pleaded Delia, naked and covered in an oily perspiration. She was bashing my leg and trying to mount me at the same time. She had large, full breasts, a tiny waist and a full, delightful bottom and she appeared to be insatiable. We had been screwing for over two hours and I was having a fag and thinking about a fix before the next assault. Henry was pretending to be on the nod on Delia's single bed. "Henry, Henry, Delia wants to accommodate your member straight away," I yelled, thinking that it would give me a nice break.

"I can't," replied Henry.

"Why not?" asked a petulant Delia, kneeling, with her hands on her splendid hips.

"I'm in love with Mary," he said. Mary was Henry's first, and only love. The day that she discovered that Henry had a registered heroin habit she signed herself into a convent as a novice nun. My pal Henry immediately committed himself to a long term plan of cleaning up and then going to Mary's convent and asking for her hand in marriage. In the meantime he needed to stay pure for her. "She's a nun," I explained to Delia.

"Ooooh, how sweet! I wish I had a boyfriend like that," she cooed. "Come on you, I can't let that big thing go to waste." She mounted me and soon we were bucking furiously on her linoleum floor. I caught Henry peeping at us and I thought that I saw temptation knock on his door a couple of times, but he held out.

We fornicated until well past midnight and then, after a final mighty orgasm, we collapsed on to her pink, nylon, 'sheepskin' rug to smoke and rest. After a while Delia asked me, "Do you believe in God Joe?"

"Of course, it's religion I have problems with, not God," I answered, pulling on my cigarette.

"Henry, do you believe in God?"

"Naturally, but I don't think he believes in us right now," muttered Henry.

"Oh that's really nice because I can say a big 'thank you' prayer before we go to sleep," chirruped Delia. "No wait boys. I'll read the 23rd Psalm, 'The Lord is my shepherd,' and then I'll say a goodnight, 'thank you' prayer."

"Fine, but let us take a fix first Delia," suggested Henry moving off the bed towards his paraphernalia which was on Delia's dressing table. We both prepared our fixes and shot up. "OK boys," said Delia standing up naked in the middle of her bedroom clutching her bible, her lovely body glistening in the flickering candle light. She gave a shy snigger and began to read, "The Lord is my shepherd; I shall not want. He maketh me to lie down in green pastures: he leadeth me beside the still waters. He restoreth my soul…….."

Later, after Delia's prayer and after we had turned out the lights, Henry whispered from the bed, "Delia."

"Yes Henry."

"You were fucking magnificent saying that prayer tonight."

"Thank you Henry. Good night boys," murmured Delia snuggling up to me on the hard floor.

Back in Jericho, at around 11am Emma began to stir. She opened her eyes and looked at me, "How long have you been looking at me like that?" she asked in a sleepy voice.

"Hours," I said.

"You should be sleeping, not drinking Joe. You have to stop you know. Remember what good old Dr Pepe told you?" Emma was referring to the last time that I'd been admitted to the Radcliffe. I had returned to consciousness very early in the morning on a large ward in the hospital. A night nurse was busy scratching away at her report on her desk, near the main door, and the patients were sleeping. I scanned the place and it looked like a heavy duty, serious problems ward. Loads of flashing monitors and tubes going into veins. I had two tubes myself. I hadn't a clue how I got there. As I came to I looked down at my body and I was shocked to see that I was covered in blue and yellow bruises. There was hardly any pink flesh to be seen, I was all blue or yellow. I knew that I'd had yet another alcoholic seizure and I was scared.

God, I needed a drink badly. At that moment a small, Latin looking, white coated doctor entered the ward and marched up to my bed. "You are Joe South, the recovering heroin addict? You were picked up in Cornmarket yesterday suffering from a massive alcoholic fit. I understand from my friend Fernando that this sort of thing has happened to you many times and he doesn't understand why you are still alive," he said slowly in a nasal Spanish accent. "From now on you must consider yourself to be alcoholic, which means that you can never ever drink again. Nothing, ever. You have to learn to live without alcohol as well as the heroin." With that Dr Pepe turned on his heel and walked out, briefly nodding at the nurse as he passed her.

I lay there fuming with this midget doctor. Who was he to come in here and tell me that I can never drink again? It wasn't right. I had come through years of junk hell just to be told that I couldn't even use alcohol safely? Nothing to take the edge of this hurting life, it was a nightmare thought. But as I watched him disappear I knew that he was right. The problem had never been the alcohol or the heroin; it was me and my inability to co-exist with my sensitivity. It was inside me. The penny had dropped another millimetre in the slot. What motivated Pepe to tell me that? It was plain that he had made a special trip to see me and so early in the morning too. He wasn't getting his rocks off on any good counselling shit. He just wanted to deliver his message and then he had done his duty as a human being and the rest was up to me. Plain, simple and true. He was right and I was grateful for his courage. That's it then: no more booze, no more junk, ever again. With that commitment to a life of sobriety I gathered my belongings, unplugged my tubes and checked out, pushing aside the frantic, whispered objections from the night nurse.

Outside the Radcliffe I took a deep breath and started my new sober life. I headed straight for the High Street because I knew that the International Stores opened at 8.30 am. I walked into the quiet store and headed for the end of the second aisle where there were pyramids of Old English cider stacked up. I was wearing my old thieving mac with the large poaching pockets sewn inside and I carefully placed two bottles in one side and two in the other. I then clink-clinked over to the chill cabinet and selected a strawberry yogurt. I had just enough to pay for this one item - 10p. I approached the lone check-out girl trying not to bash my bottles together too much as I walked. I placed the tub of yogurt on her stainless steel table and produced my 10p piece. As I gave her the coin she took my hand and looked up into my face. She was so pretty and she looked worried when she asked, "Why are you shaking love?" She held my hand and gently stroked my fingers.

"It's because I've just stolen four bottles of cider and I'm frightened you'll catch me," I stuttered. She looked at me with her soft, concerned eyes and smiled. She handed me a penny change and whispered, "Take care. You don't look so good." Drinking my cider in Blue Boar Street public lavatories I tried to make sense of all that had occurred in the previous hour. I was completely confused by my compulsion to drink. I had seen the light, courtesy of Dr Pepe, and committed to a life of sobriety. I had confessed my crime to a young girl and then I had relapsed. I drank heavily from the green bottle. Things change fast.

Emma glanced at my glass as she got out of bed. "I love you Joe. I want you to stop before you kill yourself and break my heart."

"I will stop Emma."

"When we met I had heard about your reputation everywhere I went. The cops coming into 'Casualty' told me about your dealing and your activities. I met some of the Randolph crowd and they also told me about you. They thought that you were very colourful," she said sadly, slowly brushing her long blonde hair. "But when I finally met the 'legend' I couldn't believe it. You were nothing like the tales I'd heard. You were a dirty, undernourished, repetitive, boring has-been. I was shocked to finally meet you." She continued brushing her hair as I slumped back into the bed, sinking under the weight of her truths. "I love you and you have to stop." Of course she was right. I must stop or die, but how?

Since I'd begun to drink my life was becoming much more bizarre and sometimes violent. Under the rule of heroin I was quiet...... but when I drank, I lost control and when I woke I had no recollection of my actions. I was covered in scars from knife fights. My throat had been slashed and my face cut many times, especially around the eyes. Stitch Fisher, a detective with Oxford City Drugs Squad, told me that he'd once watched me pull a flick knife on someone in White's Bar and that he'd enjoyed watching the other guy pull a blade also. "Why didn't you stop it you fucker, I might have been killed," I protested.

"That's what I was hoping for," said Stitch.

One night I planned to break into a doctor's surgery on St Giles. It was around 10.30pm and it was a clear night. I liked to do my break-ins at this time because the pubs were turning out and it was a ready made diversion for the cops to look at. I figured that the only way in was from the rear, but because I was drunk it was difficult to identify the house I wanted from the back. I reckoned that the surgery must be in the fourth house, north of a small tobacconists shop. I counted four houses along and then climbed over the wall. At the top of the wall I seemed to lose my grip and I fell head first into an old flower bed. I stood up and shook the soil out of my hair.

The house was in darkness and felt deserted as I put my elbow through a rear window. There was little noise, as usual, and I was soon inside. I searched the ground floor but it soon became apparent to me that I was not in a doctor's surgery but in a house of small offices of some kind. Never mind, I could be flexible, there was lots of office equipment that I could get a good price for. I wrenched down a curtain from a rear window and spread it out on the floor. Carefully I loaded in two electric typewriters, three adding machines, one portable TV, a couple of radios and a petty cash tin containing about £20. I tied the lot up in the curtain and sat down in the boss' chair to have a fag. I was out of condition, no doubt about it.

After a few relaxing moments I decided that it was too much of a task to boost this large bundle round the back and over the wall so I opted to exit by the front window which opened directly on to St Giles, one of Oxford's main arteries. I drew the curtains and slowly opened the large, elegant window. A nice breeze greeted me and the pavement outside was quiet. I clambered out and pulled the bag of swag after me. I had decided to stash the gear in Jericho until the morning. Ten yards up the road with the huge bag over my shoulder I suddenly realised that I'd left the window open and so I had to go back to close it. I parked my jumbo sized curtain bag and scampered back. I closed the window and silently berated myself for my stupidity. I trotted back to my bag, swung it over my shoulder and continued up St Giles towards Little Clarendon Street and my ultimate destination, Jericho.

Just as I was approaching my turn-off, three men came out of Little Clarendon Street and they were walking towards me. They were three Oxford City Drugs Squad officers. "Evening Joe. She kicked you out then?" one of them laughed as they passed. "Sensible girl."

"That's all your worldly possessions is it?" commented a younger plainclothes officer. "Crime pays then?" They were chuckling as they walked past me towards the city centre. I felt jubilation, blind panic and relief all within four seconds. Too many enormous feelings for a broken down old junky. I found my way to Jericho and stashed all the precious gear behind a church, under a pile of corrugated sheeting surrounded by stinging nettles, and went home to Emma.

The next day I was back with my fence. "Fuck me I could have sworn it was here. I tell you Charley, it was definitely St Barnabas' Church," I hissed at my fence as we rooted through the stingers and discarded metal behind the old building.

"Well I don't see any corrugated iron sheets my boy. You're wasting my time. There's nothing here," glared Charley. "You need to clean up fella and start to operate in the real world. You fucking dreamt this little lot." With that supportive remark Charley got into his large Humber and drove out of Jericho.

Quite soon after this balls-up I decided to rob a chemist on Walton Street. It was a spur of the moment idea, spontaneous and graceful. It was another physical act which showed that my higher mind had been short circuited by too many intoxicants over too long a period. However, an analyst might have told you, 'Well it's obvious isn't it? He wanted to be caught.' I could not reconcile any part of my present violent or erratic behaviour to my personality and this made me frightened. I was watching someone else act out in crazy ways; he certainly looked like me but it wasn't me.

The front door of the pharmacy was a glass panel set into a wooden frame and I decided to simply walk through it 'Hulk' style. And I did just that; I walked through the door and once inside I ransacked the DDA cupboard and then escaped with the alarm screaming bloody murder.

Needless to say that I lost practically all my medicines in my drunken dash home to Emma's place.

I ceased my remembering and started to make Emma a cup of coffee as she was getting ready for work. She liked it black and strong. She was putting on her blue uniform and Demis Roussos was trilling 'Forever and Ever' on her stereo. She was a romantic and believed that life could be super and loving. Her tiny, neat and tidy flat was above a workmen's café on Walton Street and I could smell the bacon and eggs wafting in through the open window. I watched her preparing for work and I fervently wished that I'd obeyed Wilbur and not used heroin. I had seen my life through different eyes now and I feared that it was too late to adapt to normality. Emma finished preparing for work and sat down to drink her coffee. She smiled at me. "Don't worry, everything is going to be fine," she said.

15

BRANSTON PICKLES

If this was reality I didn't like it one bit.

I had believed for some time that I was losing my mind; that my brain had been irreparably damaged by the meth and the coke. I had been shaking and trembling for months now and I was suspicious and paranoid. So sensitive at times, I felt that my nervous system would just give up the ghost and go into melt-down. I felt like a little baby with no protective skin. I was double-wired and hyper-alert. I couldn't do this life without heroin; I had to go back to it. Every God damn thing hurt me: waking up, chilly weather, talking to people, crossing the road. Naturally, it was a part of me to be sensitive. When I was a small boy I overheard a neighbour tell my mother, "Never misses a thing that lad, he watches everything and feels every thing." Of course I still had that hungry, frantic awareness but now it was all busted up somehow. It felt like buckets of adrenaline were being poured directly into my bloodstream non-stop. It was unpleasant and I needed to rest.

I lay there in the January morning gloom and tried to make sense of things. I was in Branston House in Esher and I had been there for 9 months. This small community for recovering addicts had been open for 18 months and I had been its third resident. Branston House came to be a house of horrors for me. I wasn't a blamer; it wasn't in my nature to whine on about what I imagined people had done to me. I automatically believed that everything was my fault anyway. But I knew that there was something amiss with this awful place. I looked at the Dylan poster, stuck on my bedroom wall, and I wanted out.

Branston House was the idea of a local Esher GP who wanted to provide a therapeutic and rehabilitative environment in which addicts could get well. It was a kind and laudable aim for sure and the Branston House Trust already owned the house, a large grey, pebble-dashed house close to the race track, but it did not have the expertise and experience necessary to handle the devious disease of addiction. The therapists were all untrained, but with glamorous ambitions to work on the 'drug scene.' Of a left or liberal persuasion they practised the hippy philosophy of 'love conquers all' but were slightly lost when it came to the details of how to provide the treatment that would re-equip the addict to take part in some kind of a life again. To Zeke Goldblatt and his Branston team though, it was a 'far out' and worthy idea.

There were only five bedrooms in the place and so the number of residents were limited to below the minimum number of eight required to create a constructive therapeutic group. You can get away with it for a week or two, but not for months on end. The most I ever saw at a Branston group was five. Not enough to be therapeutically viable. We received no guidance, but were asked to make our own decisions and we were also allowed to drink? On admission I knew that I could not use any drugs, or alcohol, but suddenly I was confronted with a concept that said I could drink. Well, that's marvellous, such a relief, I'll just have a wee drink then. They obviously believed that drugs and alcohol were separate problems. The blind were trying to lead the blind. When I think of Branston now, I'm in turns furious and then incredulous that the place existed at all.

Emma had disappeared from my life, she had had enough. I was either drunk or unconscious and giving her absolutely nothing at all except sorrow. She was waiting for me to just throw in the towel and clean up, but instead, I continued to thieve and drink. My parents had moved away from Oxford and left no forwarding address. They were terrified of what I had become and they had given up on me. Sonia and Annie had left for India to find God. Lying in my Branston bedroom I remembered little Annie in her pretty, pink nightdress and her pouty, little duck lips and I was sad that we would never have a proper father and daughter relationship. I was alone in Branston House and most of my Oxford pals were dead. I had checked into St Mary's Hospital in Paddington for a detox and, from there, made an application to go to this new 'hip' rehab in Esher. I was accepted and moved in as its third resident.

A few days after I arrived at Branston a pretty girl called at the house and we spent the afternoon chatting and listening to music. She was the daughter of one of the 'friends' of Branston House and she was anxious to help the residents. Her name was Minnie and she was fun. For days during the summer months we talked and walked and fucked. She sang 'Dark Side of the Moon' to me, naked, and perched on the end of my bed. She clung to me like a baby chimp and gazed, seriously, earnestly into my eyes at point-blank range. Eventually Minnie said that she loved me. Her mother and sister were frequent visitors to the house and they especially used to like the Friday night parties that we held. "Let's go to your room and play mummies and daddies," whispered Minnie one Friday evening and off we'd go for yet another session of passionate lovemaking. "I'm going to take you to Africa," said Minnie, lying beside me, smoking a cigarette.

"And what would I do there?" I asked her.

"Fan me with ostrich feathers and fuck me in a luxury mud hut, with chickens pecking grain from the floor," giggled Minnie. The muscles in her white stomach contracting into an undulating, cobbled surface when she laughed. Stroking her long, wavy, brown hair, she looked slim and sparkly and naughty. She was a delightful young English woman. "Fags over, fuck me again Tarzan," cried Minnie. There was a knock at the door and her mother quietly whispered from outside the door, "Time to go Minnie. Come on, be quick darling."

The dreamy, Minnie days wore on and I was beginning to drink more and score codeine linctus cough syrup and Dr Collis Brown's opiated mixture from the local chemists. Minnie would push her face close to mine and tease me. I felt strangely oppressed, persecuted and almost crushed by this lovely girl. Without H I was often unable to say anything in her company. "I've got something to tell you Joe," Minnie said when we were sitting outside the local pub, drinking beer.

"OK," I said.

"I'm pregnant," she beamed. I fainted. The first fucking time in my life, but I fainted. Gone.......out cold.

John, another addict resident, was shaking me as I came to. I didn't know where I was at first until I saw the Mexican tapestry hanging on the wall and the Branston French windows open into the garden. Minnie came in from the kitchen, "Joe, are you all right? You frightened me. Here, have some water."

"Minnie, I'm frozen, nip up to my room and get me a jacket," I asked. When she left the room John leaned across to me and whispered, "You know you have to cool it man."

"You're telling me."

"You know that Minnie is only thirteen?" he said quietly. I fainted again. This time I landed face down, off the sofa and on to the floor.

"No fucker told me," I screamed. It was an 'emergency group' and I was using it. Boy was I using it. All the residents and most of the staff were present and we were sitting in the usual 'group' circle. "I've been frantically copulating with Minnie for a month and not one of you bastards said a fucking thing. Not the staff or my, so called, friends. No one said a bastard thing and now I'm looking at jail and Rule 43."

"We thought that you knew," countered John twisting his face into a pathetically, helpless expression.

"You think I'd fuck an under-age girl? That says more about you than me pal."

"It's your responsibility to find out," asserted Zeke, the boss therapist. I swear I could have wrapped his stupid beard around his neck and strangled him at that moment, but instead I just.........fainted.

Poor me and poor Minnie. The next day she called to say that she had 'come on' and she wasn't pregnant. "I'm glad Minnie," I said. "We have to cool it now you know. I truly did not know your age and I'm sorry I let it go this far, so please forgive me Minnie. You must forget me now." I eventually put the phone down after several minutes of sobbing and 'Joe, Joes' down the wire. I felt guilty and I missed Emma madly at that moment and wondered if I could ever clean up enough to share my life with her.

I continued to drink Collis Brown and drink when I could steal the money for it. I slept with a local guy for a couple of quid now and again. He would come to my room, after closing time, at the weekends and spend the night. His name was Kenny and he always brought his bag of frilly, feminine clothes with him. I watched him in the candle half-light from my bed. He was tall, slim and wore his hair long. He was a daytime hippy electrician and a Saturday night tart. Kenny took hours getting ready but I liked to watch him so it was not a problem for me. It was a part of the erotic experience, maybe the best bit. Stockings, suspender belt, no knickers, bra and hair in bunches.

He sat in front of my dressing table mirror and applied his bright red lipstick and eye shadow with his penis stuck up in front of him like a gear stick. A rather large gear stick. Kenny was lucky enough to have one of those huge dicks that most men hanker after. It was very fat and at least ten inches long with an attractive, smooth, pink foreskin scarf hugging the base of the swollen glans. His testicles also were large and hung down like two ping pong balls in a sack. He was pretty hairless too, and

I didn't think that it was because he used any creams or anything. He was just a natural, feminine, baldy baby. His equipment looked formidable and warrior scary though. But, Kenny wasn't about to frighten any virgins with this bazooka, he just wanted to be loved by a good man, do the housework, read Woman's Own and put on his make-up. Is it me you want, or this?" I asked indicating his 'dressing up' ritual.

"Both," he answered, sniggering and poking his pointy tongue out at me. He stood, wobbling slightly on his high heels, bending forward, he pulled the cheeks of his bottom apart, and said, "Make love to me darling Joe."

Such was my re-entry into real life. No different from stuff that went before really, except that my heart was perpetually on over-drive. I was still out of control, lost. I wanted someone to tell me how to get well. I wanted someone to tell me what I should do, but I was left to figure it all out myself. With a broken thinker that was impossible.

One of the other therapists at Branston became a friend. Her name was Sally and she hiked in from London a few nights each week to do night duties. She was kind and sympathetic. She had a loud, raucous laugh and she offered me some comfort amidst the madness, but I suspected that she too, was a part of the moral nightmare that I was waking up in to. We kissed lots and spent time together during my Branston days. She had a boyfriend who she lived with, but obviously, I was allowed to kiss her…..lots. I think I was half in love with Sally but, even then, I knew that she, and the rest of the Branston House crew, were naïve in their belief that they were helping us guys. Their whole attempt at rehabilitation for the addict was just silly. Based on liberal, middle-class sentiments and not much else, they clearly lacked any understanding of the addict mind.

A local lady often used to visit the house during the afternoons. Her aging mother brought her in the Daimler and pushed her into our house in her wheelchair. She was paralysed from her neck down; a horse riding accident a long time ago apparently. The family was stupidly rich but Lucy, the daughter, wanted to help the addicts at Branston. At the end of one of our afternoon sessions of tea and buns Lucy made an announcement from her chrome chariot. "I'd be most honoured gentlemen if you would come to my house next week for tea. You can use the pool if you like, it's huge you know."

The following Wednesday afternoon found me, John and Wally strolling up the long gravelled drive to Lucy's mansion. "Elton John lives near here you know," said Wally.

"Well, I hope he doesn't start singing because I've got a headache," answered John. We were admitted to the beautiful house by the butler and shown to some cane chairs next to the pool. "Lucy was right, it's huge. It must be Olympic sized I reckon," sighed Wally.

"If she asks one of us to marry her, will you do it?" asked John, picking at the salted nuts on the glass table.

"Only if I fall in love with her," I answered, trying to keep a straight face.

"You will go straight to hell with all your lies," said Wally. We could hear Lucy's mother coming into the pool area, she was pushing her daughter. "There's never enough gin in this house," she shouted at the butler.

"Order double what you normally order please Dobson," and then directly to us, "What can you expect really, the man's a Methodist for God's sake." She parked Lucy next to Wally and sighed resignedly. She gave us all a very emphatic and unmistakable 'don't stay in my house too long please boys' look as she turned and left the pool.

Surprisingly, the four of us fell into an easy and entertaining chat about music and I was interested in her love for Mozart when Dobson came in with the tea and cream cakes. We were happily munching on our sweet goodies and sipping our tea by the emerald green pool when Lucy asked us, out of the blue, if we'd like a drink. "We can really relax then. Perhaps I already drink too much but I find life difficult and it helps." We looked at each other, hardly believing our luck. Free booze, yippee! "I'd love a drink," said John. "Thank you very much." Lucy hollered for Dobson and asked him to bring in the drinks trolley. The dignified and stiff old codger answered in a weary and resigned way. He'd seen Lucy and the afternoon drinks syndrome before I thought. The trolley was wheeled in and Lucy instructed us to help ourselves. "Get me a gin and tonic John please," she commanded. We sat back down with our drinks and for some strange reason I'd chosen rum. I'd never been a great fan of this sweet spirit but I just fancied it at that moment. I remember taking a hefty gulp and watching Dobson turn on the pool filter and then........nothing......blackness.

I came to, back at Branston House, in my bed and it felt like the middle of the night. John and Wally were sitting on my bed staring at me. They didn't look happy, they looked furious. "What's happened?" said I.

"You smashed the whole place up, that's what happened," yelled John. "You smashed all the drink bottles and then caved in the front of the china cabinet with your fists."

"You were swearing and foaming at the mouth," continued Wally. "You were like a fucking mad man."

"I don't remember a thing," I replied hesitantly. I knew that they weren't joking. I could see by their bemused and angry expressions that I was guilty but I had no re-call at all. I raised myself up on the bed and felt fear again. What was happening to me? "You are a cunt and a prize bastard. You scared Lucy and her mother to death and we can kiss their goodwill goodbye forever," glared John.

"It took both of us to wrestle you to the floor before you smashed the whole sodding house up. I've never seen you like that before. You looked insane," said Wally quietly. I fell back on the bed. Fuck it, I knew it. I knew it before I came to this shit hole. I can't drink. "I'm not drinking, ever again. That's enough, I can't do it. No more," I declared seriously, staring at my ceiling and wondering exactly how many brain cells were still firing in my cranial cavity.

After Wally and John left my bedroom I exited the house and walked to a nearby pub. It was the middle of the night and dark. I climbed over the pub's garden wall and head butted the window of an outhouse. It was full of bottles of spirits and I picked up half a dozen, and then headed back to Branston.

Two nights after the dreadful happening at Lucy's the Branston staff threw a grand party. It was someone's birthday but I couldn't remember who. I was lying on the floor, sucking at a half bottle of vodka disguised as an orange juice and listening to Roberta Flack singing 'Killing Me Softly,' when Effie knelt down beside me and said, "Wally and I would like you to join us upstairs." Effie was a young, attractive staff member who had taken a 'special' interest in Wally. Much like my relationship with Sally, it was very close, in fact I suspected that Wally and Effie actually had sexual relations as a part of their 'therapeutic programme.'

I entered Wally's bedroom and the lights were dim, as someone had chucked their knickers over the lamp. Effie began to undress and Wally was already naked. He was long, thin and white. He was lying on his bed smoking a joint and watching my reaction to the unfolding scene. "We thought we'd cheer you up a bit," smiled Effie, kneeling in front of me and unbuckling my Levis.

"Great, I'm feeling better already," I replied. Effie began to lick me and Wally moved behind me and began to caress my bum. "I've been wanting to stroke this arse for ages," he murmured. The perfumed candles began to lose their hypnotic attraction as I fondled Effie's large, hanging breasts and jerked Wally's dick. Hmm, this was good, very good. No pain, no anxiety.

There was a freedom from fear after all. Things were OK. Slow, sensual, caresses, kisses, penises, fannies and arseholes. Losing myself into the drug of sex, we fucked for a couple of hours until Wally got either tired, or jealous of my perpetually erect cock, and called it a day. I left the bedroom and Effie was watching me, cuddled in Wally's arms, as I left. On my way down the stairs to the party I decided to grass Effie up in the next group therapy session. Let's see how she'd handle that in the cold light of day and with her bosses there. I wanted revenge and felt abused by them all. Zeke, Sally and Effie they were all riding on the exciting 'drug scene' ticket and they were all definitely fucking with my head.

I was cold in my bed on this January morning. I continued to stare at my Dylan poster and wondered what to do. I had grassed Effie up in group and had had a good blast at the lot of 'em. Middle-class, do-gooding perverts. "You're supposed to be looking after me and showing me a way out and you're all fucking lost yourselves. Why do you pretend? Is it that you all want to be real junkies and you simply haven't got the bottle? Is working with us addicts the next best thing to satisfying your vicarious desires? In fact, you are more lost than I am. Branston House is a lie and you are all living a lie."

Needless to say the group got pretty quiet after that. Poor Effie said nothing and when she did raise her pretty head she was crying. Wally stared at me like he wanted to kill me, so I mouthed an 'Anytime' at him across the circle of chairs. The doctor and Zeke spent some time studying their nails and John looked as if he was watching a favourite movie. Finally Zeke said, "Do you want to go Joe?" He stroked his long, straggly black and grey beard and looked thoughtful. I knew that this old hippy couldn't wait to get rid of me but he could never admit it in a million years. It was difficult to be honest in that idealistic era.

"Of course I want to fucking go. I'm getting worse, not better. I'm going back on junk." The group went quiet again and I walked out.

I was leaving today, back to junk and some quiet moments, away from the terror of reality. I'd find a kind croaker, and a room, and calm myself with my poppy dreams.

16

I AM A RAFFLE PRIZE

Summer 1976

I woke up to see Dennis peeping at me over the top of Hannah's sleeping body.

He was studying me intently but as he watched my eyes slowly focus, with my increasing consciousness, he turned over with a grunt. Dennis was Hannah's long-term partner and the night before she had won me as a prize in a raffle. It was a sticky, hot night and we were crashing in a large tent at the Walcot Sunshine Festival in Bath. Hannah and I had made love twice during the night and I reckoned that Dennis must have been out of his mind with jealousy. Of course, he couldn't admit to that because we were still in the era of 'free love' and you fucked who you damn well pleased regardless of the hurt caused to others. Let me explain how I came to be in that tent in Bath.

After leaving Branston house I stayed with my sister in London for a bit. I started using again very quickly and thoroughly abused her hospitality. I left her house after a couple of months, headed back to Oxford and after sleeping in public lavatories for a couple of nights, I eventually found Emma. She was delighted to see me again but worried as to what lay ahead for us both. She invited me to move in with her and I made money by conning and thieving.

During this period at Emma's I managed to make a fair mount of bread selling tap water as Lysergic Acid. The con relied heavily on my gift of the gab but it seemed to work well. I sold lots of tap water on small blotting paper squares to Alex Trocchi who was still hanging on to life by a thread despite his enormous habit. He swore by my acid and said that it was the best quality LSD he'd ever taken and bought more through the following weeks. Please, please don't ask me why he bought it because I do not know. That particular con remains one of life's mysteries. I must confess though that it felt very good to fool this great, underground writer. He was a cruel man at times and extraordinarily self-centred so I had no problem in rationalizing my crime. Like many of the 'Beat Scene' great poets and authors it was hard to see past their dazzling self belief and talents to the devastation of their personal lives beyond. Often I muttered my appreciative 'cool, cool' at their work but secretly prayed that I wasn't like them.

Another hustle that I particularly enjoyed involved Frankie, an old junky friend, and I posing as undercover drug squad officers. We would prey on undergrads, especially those from the USA. They seemed the most gullible of all the nationalities available to the likes of me and Frankie on the Oxford city streets. Frankie was especially proud of the fact that he was educated at Oxford High School and often boasted that he sat at the desk of

Lawrence of Arabia from time to time during his school years. "Which probably explains why I hate Turks but love it up the bum," he used to joke. He had short blond hair and piercing, almost black eyes. He had an agitated, jerky way of expressing himself and after making a point he would often collapse in hysterical, manic chuckles. I was always infected by the sound of his laughter and when we were together, after an hour or two, we would end up nursing very sore stomach muscles, torn and stretched by our merriment.

Anyway, Frankie and I would approach likely 'Furry Freak Brothers' dope customers in pubs and offer to sell them high quality cannabis. We'd escort the nervous gringos to a convenient alley, hand them the packet of blow, and then the theatre would commence. "You're busted gentlemen. Oxford City Drug Squad at your service," I announced to the terrified young men and women.

"Turn around, and put your arms up on the wall and spread your legs wide apart," commanded Frankie. "Now listen carefully folks, you are under arrest for suspected possession of cannabis........." Frankie then went on to tell them their rights and he was very professional. I often told him that he would have made a good cop. "Yeh, good bad cop," he'd laugh.

I spread a large handkerchief on the cobbles and asked them to empty their pockets on to the cotton surface: keys, wallets, cash, change and if we were really lucky, more cannabis. But we'd planted 'em anyway so it wasn't a problem, it just eased our consciences that's all. After we'd searched them and they were nicely quaking and vulnerable we'd give them the set-piece schpiel. "You're all from the USA are you?" I asked pleasantly, fiddling with their belongings with the toe of my shoe.

"Yes sir."

'Well, you are well and truly in the shit then," laughed Detective Sergeant Frankie. "The American Government and the Oxford University Authorities will show you no mercy for this offence, bringing them both into disrepute like this. Yup, you're fucked." Frankie sauntered across to me and we had a swift, well rehearsed, whispered discussion, occasionally looking up at the shivering future of America. "It's not just this offence, it'll be the repercussions and effect on your careers after," he said earnestly.

"What he's trying to say is that we feel sorry for you and we could be willing to overlook the matter this time and let you go," I said calmly and reasonably.

"OK. Pick up your stuff and leave all your cash and dope. You can go," instructed Frankie.

"Oh my gosh! Thank you sir," spluttered one of the girls, hurling herself at her belongings parked on my handkerchief. Sometimes we made almost £100 and once we cleared $500 from two guys and we also had their undying gratitude. It was good to help the young folk along in their hazardous journey through this life.

However, one dark night, a small, pale American student, tumbled instantly to the ruse and flatly refused to co-operate. "Put your hands against the wall and spread 'em brother."

"Fuck you."

"You can't speak to British police officers like that," I said.

"I can and I just did," he shouted, poking out his chin in a provocative manner.

"You are under arrest."

"So are you jerk-head." This was getting difficult and Frankie and I glanced at each other briefly. The boy was being troublesome to say the least. "You're no more the fuzz than my Great Aunt Petunia," sneered the Yank. "Goodnight. I'm going to the pub to drink your warm, English beer." With that the brave American sauntered off up the Chequers alley and out on to the High. "John 'fucking' Wayne," remarked Frankie.

"I liked him. Bags of bottle what?" I laughed, clapping my pal around the shoulders.

I was scripted for an insufficient amount of methadone and living with my lovely Emma, trying not to annoy her too much, but I had to survive and I was constantly breaking and entering, conning, dealing and thieving, driving my seven and a half frame to its limit. One night I passed out cold, very drunk, into my Chinese meal in the Shanghai Nights Restaurant. I woke up later in a police cell and was remanded in custody the following day. The Oxford City Magistrates, on this occasion, refused me bail. Although my offence was trivial they spotted that I'd been on probation for fourteen years, since 1962, and I had never served a prison sentence, despite a long, long record of convictions. I had served time on remand but never as a convicted prisoner. Gordon, my solicitor, made it a point of honour to keep me out of the nick and the magistrates were truly appalled. The lady magistrate addressed Gordon and said, very strictly, "We think there is something very wrong here Mr Colman. This young man seems to have evaded the consequences of his anti-social behaviour for far too long and you appear to have supported him throughout his sorry, criminal career. I will not grant bail and he is remanded to Oxford Crown Court. Take him down." I was devastated and Gordon was blushing furiously as I went down the miserable stone steps to the holding cell. I was sent to Winchester Prison to await my trial for several breaches of probation as well as not paying for the Chinese grub.

I waited for my trial at Oxford Crown Court for six long months in Winchester. I shared a remand cell with three other guys. Wayne was a young thief and member of the notorious Oxford Friar gang. Eric was a small time thief and suspected rapist and Jock was a red haired lion tamer, from Glasgow. As soon as I moved into their peter Jock attempted to assert his dominance over the seven stone junky weakling that had suddenly appeared in his life. "What I say goes in this peter, do ya understand ya skinny fucking article?" hissed Jock stabbing me in the chest with his index finger.

I continued to make my bed and put stuff into my drawer. "Hi Wayne, how are you doing these days?" I asked, ignoring the embittered Scot and addressing the young man sitting on his bed. We recognised each other from the street and Wayne had been present one night at a very drunken, violent party in Kennington, years before. I had beaten his 'boss', William Friar, in a bout of arm wrestling, much to the surprise of everybody and to the great delight of my good friend Freddie Smith who hated the rival Friar gang with a passion. I was very strong in those days thanks to the years of exercising but I never used to flaunt it until I had to. "Are you fucking listening to me South," screeched the red faced 'lady from hell.'

"Nope and I probably never will if you talk to me like that. Back off, sit down and shut your trap," I said quietly.

"Best do like he says," said Wayne lying back on his bed with a small smile playing over his lips. Maybe he'd been waiting for someone to come along and tame this tedious moron I thought. Jock sat down, puffing and muttering threats, as he rolled himself a fag.

Everywhere I've travelled throughout the world I've seen examples of the 'Jock' phenomena. The small, lone figure wandering along El Malecon in Havana, or in the Parque Central in San Jose, Costa Rica, or in the West End of London. Pale, often overweight, blue eyed, ferociously angry men yelling, "Scotland Forever," at the bemused and frightened citizens of foreign places. "I'm frae Glasgow," they proudly proclaim, as if anybody gives a toss where they are from, especially anyone this ugly. They like to holler vengeance against the English in pubs and bars, but they rarely fight. They just threaten and shout. Of course, this belligerence has little to do with the history of English persecution but everything to do with a particular, unpleasant personality that occurs everywhere, in every country. It just seems to be more common in Scotland that's all. They exude inferiority and take comfort from praising their homeland lavishly to boost their tiny egos. "I wish they'd just go and fucking stay there," I once heard a disgruntled Dutch traveller say.

Anyway, Jock quietened down after a day or two when he understood that I wasn't going to be intimidated by him. I suspect also that Wayne had told him about the night of the arm wrestling competition. Secretly, I was scared of Jock but it would have been the end of a comfortable life in Winchester Jail to admit to that.

There were four of us in one cell, originally designed for one occupant and we had to share one tin pisspot in the corner. This was normally emptied once in the morning during 'slop out' so you would imagine that the place reeked. Just one shower a week each could have added to the malodour but, in fact, our cell didn't smell too bad and the time passed fairly quickly. I got friendly with a coke head and dealer called Phil who was doing five years for 'dishonestly handling large quantities' etc. and he was philosophical about his jail term. "It's a game Joe. Cops and robbers that's all it is. Sometimes you get caught and you have to serve your time like a good girl."

We soaped each other down in the weekly shower and fondled one another under the cover of the thick steam. "A guy got his cock caught in the bed springs last week on 'A' wing. The screws had to chop him free with bolt cutters," reported Phil. "He had a hole in his mattress and he was busy fucking it when the end of his knob got jammed in the springs on the bed frame underneath."

"Embarrassing eh?"

"It's better than this 'swallowing' lark that's getting popular," said Phil.

"What's that?" I enquired.

"Guys gradually eat all their bed springs off their beds and cutlery too, if they can get hold of any. Apparently it's an acknowledged psychiatric condition that's well recognised," he went on.

"I'll stick with wanking thanks," I said.

"Me too."

At last I came up before the judge at Oxford Crown Court. Gordon told me beforehand that I was very unlucky as Judge Minette was a well known 'hanging' judge. Of course I pleaded guilty to everything and relied on Gordon's QC to blather on about mitigating circumstances: 'helpless, he's lost everything, very intelligent, suicidal addict victim etc.' I found that it was always the best policy to plead guilty to everything. At the end of the case the Judge stared at me over the top of his gold rimmed specs and declared, "You have the most appalling record. You will go to the Ley Community for 18 months so that you may attempt some rehabilitation from your addiction one last time. If you leave the community before you complete the treatment you will be brought back before me and I shall have no alternative but to send you to prison for five years. I shall leave this instruction on your record so that you do not escape me."

Emma drove me to the Ley Community, just outside the city centre in Oxford, in her Spitfire and we said goodbye on the gravelled drive in front of the large house. I was sad and didn't want to leave her and she was weeping when we kissed. "Bye Joe," she whispered and got into her car. Here I was again, just one small suitcase to show for my lifetimes work. I entered the front door and was asked to sit on a wooden bench in the hall until I could be admitted.

The Ley Community was run by a recovering addict from New York's Bronx district called John McCabe and he was supported and sponsored by Dr Bertie Mandelbrote of Littlemore Hospital. The Ley was seen as offering a new radical approach to addiction treatment. It was supposedly run by addicts for addicts and it was called a 'hierarchical concept house.' The programme had evolved from the American Synanon rehabilitation system and was very tough. Some said that it was cruel and ruthless.

Many years previously, in the States, a fellow called Charles 'Chuck' Diederich, disillusioned with his own recovery from alcoholism in Alcoholics Anonymous, started to develop his own programme for addicts. He constructed it without the spiritual element that he had so objected to in AA. A whole host of different treatment philosophies sprang up from the original Synanon which went on to a final collapse and disgrace in 1991 when they went bankrupt. The Synanon method had evolved into a 'cult' under the leadership of an increasingly paranoid and nutty Chuck and they began to use coercive and threatening methods with its members to keep them within the community.

These hierarchical concept houses developed further in the UK and were fairly popular with psychiatrists during the 70s and 80s. Phoenix, Alpha and the Ley Community were examples of these tough, highly confrontational 12 to 18 month rehabilitation programmes. Most addicts, sent there on court orders, left quickly when they found out that they were unable to con and manipulate anyone any longer. They were rapidly brought face to face with themselves and needless to say they didn't like it. Around 98% 'split' from the communities before completing their treatment.

After I entered the house John McCabe called me into his office and shook my hand. "Sit down Joe. It's good to finally meet you I've heard a lot about you through the years," he said.

I crossed my legs and tapped my fingers on the arm of my chair and studied this large, cheery American. "Well I must say I'm very gratified to hear that but I can't return the compliment because I have heard nothing about you at all," I announced. There followed a long and stony silence which John eventually broke with a quiet, "Well, I wish you luck with this programme." I was now officially undergoing rehab at the Ley Community.

The Ley was my home for the next six months and it was the place where I started to understand that I did have feelings and that it was possible to manage these wild things without resorting to chemicals. Until that particular afternoon group I had been a cool dude. No, I never got angry or particularly happy either. It was just the way I was....cool. I had a reputation after all for being slick, inscrutable, calculating, but, sometimes, generous. No, I didn't get angry, until that historic afternoon group.

"Why don't you just tell Brendan what you think of him?" suggested Dave. There were twelve addicts in the group and suddenly the unwelcome spotlight had fallen on me. I was surprised because I'd been sitting, quietly expressing my usual aloof indifference to the group theatrics. Brendan was the Ley Community Group Boss and he had completed 12 months of his rehab programme. I avoided him and didn't like the way that he always assumed he knew what I was thinking. Plus, and this item was big in my mind, he'd never touched H. He was a silly dope smoker that's all. "Go on you chicken fucker," yelled Brendan. "Why don't you tell me the truth?" I shuffled on my uncomfortable chair and tried to avoid his attention. It was true; I did have a very unpleasant, stodgy weight of something turning over in my stomach. Were these feelings I wondered? I raised my eyes and looked at him. I could have beaten the shit out of him at the moment our eyes met but, of course, that was not allowed. I had to remain in my chair and 'deal' with my feelings.

Suddenly I exploded. Our eye contact had continued for too long and I went….. "I fucking, fucking, fucking hate you. You fat, bald bastard. I've always hated you since I arrived. You're an arrogant piece of stupid shit and everything you do annoys me. You are a cunt and I hate you. Cunt, cunt, cunt………," I screamed and hollered at our Group Boss across the group. I ranted and ventilated my fury for long minutes until I started to get hoarse. "You cunt, cunt………." I finally wound down and dropped my eyes to the floor. I had been clutching at the arms of my chair until my knuckles were white and prominent. No one will like me after this little lot. I was ashamed at my uncontrolled explosion. No one spoke and after some minutes. I began to think more clearly and I began to feel a strange lightness in my belly and brain. I plucked up my courage and looked up and around me. Instead of the expected hostility and sullen expressions I was met with eleven pairs of smiling and understanding eyes, including Brendan. For the first time ever in my life I had dealt with a feeling without hurting me or anyone else. Dave said, "It feels good doesn't it Joe?"

"Hmm, it does. Very, very good," I said quietly. "Thanks Brendan."

I left the Ley a few weeks after this important discovery. The intense pressure of being rigorously honest with myself and others for 24 hours a day and the hurt of confrontation on a daily basis took its toll with me and I collapsed under the effort. I wanted to use again. When I was leaving I was met by Brendan at the front door. "You know that if you leave this house we'll have to phone the police and inform them that you are in breach of your court order. If you get busted it means that you will have to go back in front of Judge Minette and he's threatened to send you to prison for five years," he warned me.

"I'll take my chances Brendan."

"OK. Good luck Joe," he said.

I went immediately to Emma's pad in Park Town and, surprisingly, she seemed delighted to see me. She said that she'd missed me and I had thought about her constantly. We hugged and kissed and giggled. "I always wanted to go out with a man on the run," she beamed. "I've had enough of Oxford anyway. Let's go to Bath and start a new life. If you stay clean and keep your head down they'll never find us." Little Emma looked so excited at the thought of a new beginning that I was infected by her enthusiasm and readily agreed. "Bonnie and Clyde," I said. "Just like Bonnie and Clyde."

"No, no, you goon, you've got to go straight remember," laughed Emma with that waterfall giggle of hers.

We moved to Bath, got a flat off the London Road, and Emma got a job as a Sister in a nearby nursing home. With time on my hands I began to drink again and one day, on returning from the pub, I found our flat empty of Emma's things. She'd gone. The previous evening I'd slapped her across her face after she'd objected to my drunkenness. My sudden violence was the final straw. A note on the kitchen table said, "I've had enough of your drinking. Don't try and find me because it's over. I still love you, but I have no room in my heart for you and the drink. Thanks Joe. Goodbye." I'd lost the woman I loved because I couldn't control my drinking. I was ashamed, guilty that I'd hit her, and I needed to drink more to cover my loneliness and pain.

I was alone again, with no money, but it was the time of the Walcot Sunshine Festival in Bath and so I had an opportunity to hustle some money. The four day rock and alternative festival was packed with hippies and stoned people. I linked up with a local West Indian dealer called Simpson and began to sell gear around the site for him. He was a tall, gangling guy who wore a knotted handkerchief on top of his pin head. He moved with effortless grace and gesticulated artfully with his long arms and slender fingers when he was carrying out a hustle. After just one day he was very pleased with my sales and began to lay a dozen or more quid deals on me without an up-front payment. That was a big mistake on Simpson's part as I was now rich enough to buy a lot of booze for the next couple of days. When I woke, under the stage, on the third day of the festival I realised that I had absolutely no money and I couldn't return to the West Indian: I already owed him, I needed a drink badly and I was beginning to withdraw. I had 10p left in my pocket. I was frightened and missed Emma.

As I crawled out from under the wooden stage into the warm, morning sun I had a sudden brain wave. I would go to W.H.Smith, just down the road in the town centre, buy a swatch of raffle tickets and then sell them with yours truly as the prize. I'd need to clean myself up first so that I looked appetising for the customers and so I went to the nearby public lavatories and had a good scrub.

At noon, as the day was getting hotter and the field was filling up with stoned people looking for a good time,

I started to make some money. In fact, I started to make an awful lot of money very fast. I'd spy a girl, or a couple, and approach them with my schpiel, "I'm collecting for the orphans of Bangladesh and we are running this exciting raffle. Each ticket is 10p and if you win you get me for 24 hours to do with what you like. I'll paint your house, clean your flat, walk your dog, baby-sit, read poetry to you, tell you how nice you look lots of times, or make love to you for hours on end. I will be your slave for 24 hours." 'Mama Mia!' it was a great pitch. I returned to Smiths umpteen times during the course of the afternoon to buy more books of tickets. It also meant that I had plenty of money to drink and that's what I did. I was amazed at the number of innocent, respectable, young chicks who said, "Let's just fuck now and forget the raffle." I really didn't know what was happening to English morality in those days.

By the end of the evening I found myself talking to a girl wearing a white lace dress and drinking ginger beer. She was blonde, green eyed and spoke as if she had swallowed Roedean whole. She had a strong, curvy body and her body language was often masculine in appearance. Her manner was alarmingly direct and her speech was clipped. "Am I going to win the raffle?" she asked me. We were sitting under a red brick wall some way away from the stage and the music. She was smiling at me in a seductive way.

"Do you want to?" I asked.

"Of course, then I'll employ you to fuck me all night and then tomorrow night I'll take you back to my smallholding in Wales and we'll live happily ever after."

"The prize only lasts 24 hours," I said.

"I suspect that it is going to last longer than that," she smirked.

We made love that night and Dennis, her boy friend, lay beside us throughout the night. I heard Hannah tell him in the middle of the night, "If you really can't take it Dennis, just turn over and face the other way. For God's sake go and pull a chick and fuck her, or have you forgotten how to do it? You're welcome to bring her back here after all."

"I could I suppose," murmured Dennis sadly. I heard him turn over and felt Hannah's fingers searching for my penis again. She mounted me and rode me furiously to her climax. Dennis moaned and exhaled deeply and loudly.

The following evening Dennis, Hannah and I drove to Aberystwyth in Wales. Four miles outside, near the village of Capel Seion, was their four acre smallholding. The ideal place for a man on the run to hole up for a while.

17

THE ILLEGAL DWELLING
IN THE HILLS

Late summer 1978

The sky was a deep blue and the sun was fiercely hot on the day the inspector from the Planning Department arrived. Dressed only in a pair of shorts and working on the stonework at the top of the western gable-end, I heard him before I saw him. "This is an illegal building. Cease work immediately." High on the rickety, wooden scaffold, I turned, trowel in my hand, and looked down to the gate. "Put your trowel down please and come down at once. I need to talk to you," shouted the tall man in the grey suit. Two noisy magpies took off from the big oak near the track and a couple of sheep began to 'baa' at each other. I climbed down the long extension ladder and walked towards the middle-aged, stern looking official. "Good God man, this house is huge. When on earth did you start to build this?" he asked with his mouth open and an incredulous expression on his face. "About two years ago," I replied and brushed a fly from my sweaty face. I started to roll a cigarette and remembered my arrival at Rhoserchan Fach.

The three of us, Hannah, Dennis and I, arrived in the middle of the night at their deserted four acres in Wales. We had travelled in Dennis' battered old mini-van from the Walcot Sunshine Festival in Bath. I was lying in the back on the hard, ribbed, steel floor for hour after hour and I was starting to experience the beginning of the DTs. I had promised Hannah that I wouldn't drink if I came back with her because it was already evident to her that I had a monster problem. We stumbled, in the pitch black darkness, to a small caravan parked beside a ditch and settled down for the night. Hannah and Dennis in the double bed and me on the floor.

During the night I dreamt that the caravan was turning over and over and I woke up screaming and covered in sweat with my heart racing. It was the halucinosis that precedes full blown delirium tremens and it was not a comfortable experience. Of course, despite the spectacular tales of heroin withdrawal, no one has ever died from a lack of opiate, whereas death from alcohol withdrawal was fairly common. It is positively dangerous to withdraw from alcohol without medical supervision and people die during seizures, or fits, caused by alcohol deprivation. I staggered into the field outside the caravan and, in the gloomy half-light of dawn, I took a first shaky look at my new home.

When Hannah had suggested going to her smallholding in Wales I had imagined that I would be spending my days mowing the lawns with a tractor mower and feeding the chickens now and again. I had seen the large, pretty farmhouse in my minds eye a few times and the entire proposition was very attractive to me. I was away from the police that was the main thing. Now I was staring at a derelict cottage, silhouetted against the early morning sky. No roof, walls tumbling down and surrounded by scrub and brambles. I felt a hand on my shoulder and it was Hannah standing next to me. "Am I seeing things? Where are the house and the barns and everything?" I asked in a bemused tone.

"That's what you are here for. You are going to build it all," she announced proudly with a large smile plastered over her face. And I did build it: with no running water or electricity available, I built an energy-efficient, five bed-roomed, three storey house, stables, Dutch barns and an assortment of agricultural buildings. I made everything by hand: window frames, doors, kitchen fittings, staircases - everything. I worked seven days a week for over five years until it was all finished. But I'm getting ahead of myself here. Let me take you back to my first days in Wales.

God, it was hot in the summer of 1976 and the sun shone for weeks on end. At first I believed that I had arrived in Paradise and I hoped and prayed that it would never end. I thrived in the heat. The DTs subsided after four or five days and I gradually began to eat more heartily. Dennis gave me his tent, which I pitched away from the caravan and it felt cosy and safe. Often at the end of the evening meal Hannah would say, "OK I'm sleeping with you tonight Joe," and she'd come to the tent already moist and panting. She had a strange, scented, musky smell that was completely unfamiliar to me and I liked it. What I didn't find so attractive though was her treatment of Dennis. She obviously felt secure in the knowledge that he loved her deeply and therefore she could say more or less what she liked to him. As the warm, summer days progressed I felt more and more sorry for Dennis.

"I'm cooking bean pie tonight Dennis but you won't be having as much as me or Joe because you've done bugger all for most of the day," snarled Hannah. Dennis mumbled something and continued to read, occasionally looking up as we both ate our hearty portions of pie and kissed each other. I was taking a slash into the ditch one day when Dennis came to join me. He was a small, skinny fellow of twenty-eight and he sported a long, wispy beard. By profession he was a metallurgist but he was a homeopath in his spare time and also by inclination. He was intelligent and kind but he preferred studying books on homeopathy than digging foundations for the house. I felt that he was intimidated by Hannah and in awe of her toff accent and background. As we stood peeing together I couldn't help but notice that he had the most enormous cock, it was huge and he was only a little guy. "Joe, you just need to know that Hannah never keeps her friends for long. Sooner or later they find her out, get tired of the abuse and leave. It's always the same story. She can be cruel, she calls it honesty," he confided in me looking even more sheepish than usual.

"I love your knob," I said.

The four acres at Rhoserchan Fach were set on a south facing slope and where the land was not marshy it was not especially fertile either. It was poor quality wet, scrubby land, but it had a bore hole from which we pumped our own spring water and the bottom paddock was filled with glorious Southern Marsh Orchids. The land had never had lots of chemicals used on it and it was open to improvement using organic methods. In that summer of

1976 Rhoserchan was especially beautiful. Facing south it caught the sun all day and was protected by a boundary of cherry and oak trees planted around the three fields. We were just over half a mile, down a stony track. from the village of Capel Seion, which was close to the seaside and university town of Aberystwyth.

Hannah and Dennis had already consulted with one of their alternative lawyer friends in London and he had advised that they should just go ahead and build the place without planning permission. He thought that there was more chance of it being granted retrospectively (if they were caught down the line) than if they applied before they started to build. There was a move to depopulate the countryside at the time and he thought the chances of getting planning permission for that remote spot were slim. So, the plan was to commence building. I'll rephrase that. Hannah's plan was that *I* should commence building. Both Hannah and Dennis were very taken with the notion that the breakdown of law and order in the West was imminent and that soon there would be hungry mobs in the cities, all over the UK, looking for a bit of grub and something to rape. This, they claimed, was a big part of their motivation to have an isolated, self-sufficient, organic smallholding. Such was Hannah's paranoia that she purchased a twelve bore shotgun during that summer.

I'd had a little building work experience in the past but, I figured, I could learn as I went along. One thing at a time, starting with the foundations. Dennis had loads of building construction books which I borrowed and studied avidly. I still got drunk occasionally, still bought codeine linctus and also tapped a local, obliging and hugely gullible GP for amphetamines now and again, but, in the main, I had a lot of clean time in which I could work well. I was gaining weight and getting my strength back with all the healthy living and hard work. Dennis continued to mope and do nothing though. He'd spend the days hiding from Hannah's terrible fury. Red faced, spitting, machine gun anger she would point her carving knife at him and attack, "You do nothing Dennis. For God's sake pull yourself together and get used to the fact that he's staying. You're useless anyway, just dreaming, reading and saying the occasionally smart-arse remark." Gradually, unsurprisingly, Dennis spent more and more of his time at his parent's home in St Albans. Hannah and I were left at Rhoserchan where I worked, with Hannah supervising me.

One night after pumping our tank full of fresh spring water, I sat, half naked, in the long grass, watching the rabbits as they came out of the banks to have their suppers. I felt tears falling down my face. Big, fat, salty drops fell out of my eyes and down on to my chest. Something huge came up from my belly and leapt out of my mouth as a great sob. I knelt down in the scented grass and cried; not from my throat or chest, but from my stomach, from somewhere I didn't know about or recognise. I howled great, heaving sobs, huge moaning sighs. I wept and wept, falling forward off my knees and on to my hands and face. Minutes later I felt Hannah's hand on my shoulder, stroking me. She had heard me and had come to see what the problem was. When I finally lifted my face and looked up at her my eyes were flooded with tears and I couldn't see her clearly. With a final small sob I stopped at last. "I don't know what happened. I don't know what that was," I said quietly.

Perhaps I was mourning the loss of so many things in my life. Perhaps I was sufficiently clean at that moment for my ego to give way to the pent up emotion welling up behind its barriers. Perhaps I was grieving for heroin most of all.

I knew, even in those early days in Wales, that I did not love Hannah. I certainly found her brand of 'honesty' entertaining at first but it was only much later that I recognised her candid confrontations for what they were - cruel controlling behaviour, a device to make others do her bidding. I stayed with her because she wanted me and because I had no choice, I was on the run after all. Anyway, maybe she would change tomorrow and be a person that I could fall in love with.

There were more and more things happening in my life that I couldn't explain. I have the kind of brain that has to understand how things work before I will trust them. But with an ever increasing frequency, funny, strange things were happening. It had started before I met Emma in Oxford when I was attending a Pentecostal church on the Cowley Road. For a time, I went to their Sunday service and I was always drunk out of my mind. Some time before, in some sort of desperation as I was having DTs, I called in at the community centre and asked a couple of the congregation to send someone round to my pad. Two guys arrived, within the hour, and were obviously shocked when I let them into my room.

The room was in total darkness with the black curtains closed. The older, suited man crossed the room and with a smile threw open the curtains. "Let us bring some of the Lord's light into your life my son," he chimed. Now they could see that the room was tidy because that was my nature, to be tidy, but the stink was another thing altogether. There were several cider bottles filled with my urine parked along one wall and if they had cared to open my wardrobe they would have found an old, plastic washing up bowl with a few turds floating in it. Often I was too paranoid to leave my room to go to the lavatory. The guy crossed the room once again and threw open the window. "Let us allow some of the Lord's fresh air into your life my son," he sang again. The younger boy was standing awkwardly near the open door, coughing a bit and looking at the filthy carpet. He looked up once or twice to say amen but mostly he just smiled timidly, nodded and looked ill. They said some prayers with me but they wouldn't have a drink, which was a very good thing because I needed it all. They told me that Jesus loved me and I knew then that these holy men were capable of exaggerating a little bit.

I was in the late, chronic stage of alcoholism and I was now entering a period of extreme and prolonged delirium tremens. Lying on my bed in that Cowley Road room, deprived of alcohol, I was often visited by booze demons. The terror would start with me staring at a small fissure in the ceiling plaster. Suddenly and without warning the crack grew, racing across the canopy, widening as it went. Dozens and then hundreds of black, angular rents splintered off from the main large, charging gap until the entire ceiling was crazed with deep, dangerous and mobile cracks. As lumps of plaster began to fall, I saw small rodent teeth appear, emerging through the walls below and biting savagely at the gypsum. Now there was a dozen or more rat's heads eating their way into my room; two dozen, fifty rats began to pour into my hovel. They raced amongst the fallen plaster and dust and over my body where they began to nip and bite at my feet. I yelled and ran from the room and out into the street. I sat on the front wall and waited until the horrors subsided.

My heart was racing and I was covered in sweat. The collapsing ceiling and the rats were real, they happened. These hallucinations were not like dreams, or the illusions of LSD, or mescaline – they were real. A terrible, frightening experience.

One night, again on the Cowley Road, whilst awaiting a visit from a doctor, who I had called earlier in panic and terror, my door opened to admit a gentleman carrying a doctor's bag. He was wearing a green trilby and a gabardine raincoat. As he closed the door and I heaved myself into a more upright position on the bed, I noticed a long, red tail protruding from the rear vent of his mac. I saw the nice, furry tip almost brushing the floor. He turned and approached me lying on the filthy sheets. Under the trilby was the face of a wicked, slavering fox. I cowered in fear as the animal proceeded to examine me. He lowered his snout to my throat and I could smell his foul breath as he licked at my jugular. With a high pitched and frantic scream I leapt up off the bed and scrambled outside, where I was soothed and consoled by the normal flow of busy traffic.

In my loneliness and absolute desperation I started to attend the services of the Elim Pentecostal Church on the Cowley Road. They were held in a large community hall above a Co-op store. Although I'd been brought up to believe in God and sent to Sunday School with a thick ear every Sunday I had never experienced worship like this before. There were no clergymen, vicars or priests leading the service, just elders. Everybody seemed to be half mad with the 'spirit' and members of the congregation would break out spontaneously in 'tongues' fairly often. The Lord's gift of tongues seemed to have been handed out quite generously on the Cowley Road because a lot of worshipers were at it. It was certainly spooky and heavenly to hear it for the first time. A kind of Italian gibberish with lots of Spanish O's at the ends of words, but I had a drunken half-belief that perhaps this really was God's secret hide-away.

I bumped into Sonia one day in Jericho and I was surprised to see that she had returned early from India. She still looked radiant and beautiful but now she was the golden brown colour of a mulatta and she had lost her junky pallor. She had a house in the neighbourhood and she had made a lot of money during her travels. I suspected that she was working as an international drugs mule to make so much cash. She told me sadly that she hadn't found God and laughed when I enthused about the Elim Church. To my surprise she agreed to come on the next Sunday.

Sure enough, Sonia arrived and sat next to me during the joyful free for all. She was dressed in colourful Indian silks and looked very exotic. But I was appalled to watch her laugh, snigger and tut-tut throughout the service and she left before the end. I tamed my acute disappointment with a slug out of my plastic shopping bag. The following Sunday I was astonished to see her return. She walked in late and stood at the front of the congregation. During that morning her life changed forever. She committed her life to the service of Jesus and became a Christian. She is still a Christian to this day. When she told me later I was flabbergasted and began to see my attendance for the sham that it really was. I stopped going to church and I drank even more.

The first Christmas time at Rhoserchan, Hannah decided to go home and spend the festival with her aging parents in Buckinghamshire. The day she left I headed into Aberystwyth and got drunk. Later, that evening, I was arrested for being drunk and disorderly and during my detention overnight I was beaten up badly by the cops. I can't really blame them because I'm sure that I lashed out first. When I awoke there was a lot of blood about and a young, pleasant, plain clothes officer informed me that I was 'Wanted' for outstanding offences by Oxford CID and they were going to transfer me to Oxford Police Station that morning.

I spent Christmas in Oxford Prison until Hannah bailed me in the New Year. Hannah was disappointed in me but wanted me to stay with her for some reason. In another inexplicable sequence of events Gordon, my solicitor, found a legal loop-hole that meant that I did not have to go before Judge Minette with his 'guaranteed' five year jail term. The 'loop-hole' had something to do with the geographical location of my last bust, plus the minor nature of my offence. He found it amongst a pile of legal books minutes before I was due to appear before the magistrates. The result was that their worships dealt with me in that court, giving me a further term of probation and a strong recommendation that I attend Alcoholics Anonymous. I was free..........again.........to return to building the house.

Back at Rhoserchan the planning officer told me that his name was Scarrott, Mr Scarrott, and he started to wander around the building site, groaning and tut-tutting. Hannah walked down to the half finished house from our caravan wearing a skimpy bikini. Usually she spent most of the day topless, and sometimes bottomless, much to the delight of visiting lorry drivers. But in deference to our official looking newcomer she had covered her breasts. "Who's he?" she asked in a worried voice.

"He's from 'Planning.' He's busted us and ordered us to stop all work," I informed her. "He's looking around now and I think he's impressed with the quality of the work."

"Yah, well naturally, it's first rate," she replied nervously. Mr Scarrott emerged from the back door of the house and I introduced him to Hannah. They shook hands and he said, "Such a pity, such a damn shame. The building work is excellent and from what I can see it's also within Building Regulations?"

"It is," I answered.

"Hmm…thought so. Are you a builder by trade?" he asked me. His manner was softening, helped I'm sure, by the close proximity of Hannah's tanned, curvy body in the summer heat.

"Getting there," I said. "I learn each stage as I go along."

"Well it is impressive but it may have to be torn down I'm afraid," he announced. "Is that timber Greenheart by any chance?" pointing to the main, first floor beams.

"Yah, we bought it in an auction in Kidderminster," said Hannah. "Joe's going to make the staircase out of polished Greenheart later……if he is allowed."

"The place will be worth a fortune. Such a pity, such a pity," he mumbled as he walked back into the house for another look.

After Mr Scarrott had done a thorough inspection he sat down with us. He refused our offer of a cup of tea ('It can be so easily misinterpreted d'you see?') but for some reason he appeared to be fascinated by the 'illegal dwelling' and us. He kept asking question after question and then peering back at the house. "You are almost up to the roof," he observed. "Such a pity, such a pity." He took his jacket off and spread it on the grass beside him. "Please have some fruit cake Mr Scarrott," offered Hannah. "I made it myself."

"No, no thank you very much. Such a pity," sighed Mr Scarrott. Half an hour later he got up from the grass, brushed himself down and said, "I'll see what I can do. You will have to apply for planning permission now and you must not build any further. Do you understand?" He set off up the track and we watched him as he climbed the hill. He looked back a couple of times and, just before he disappeared around the corner, he waved.

18

SOMETHING CAME INTO
MY BEDROOM

Autumn 1982

"It's over then, I'm so glad that it's over," muttered my mother quietly. She said it with such a finality and certainty that I was momentarily taken aback. How did she know my years on drugs were over? She was watching me and clutching her knitting to her chest, wearing her glasses on the end of her nose. It was 1982, the house in Wales, was now built after Hannah and I had successfully won our retrospective planning appeal and I was visiting my mother at her new house in Oxford. My father was dead. He had committed suicide a year earlier.

Six years previously, partly because of my unpredictable behaviour and my insatiable need for money and drugs, my parents had left their beloved city and travelled north, back to their home town of Preston in Lancashire, where they had both grown up. They tried to settle but, for a variety of reasons, it didn't work and they missed Oxford terribly. They eventually returned and after trying a couple of houses they finally moved to a small, terraced house off the Cowley Road which they liked. It was here that Frank started to lose his mind.

The years of repression, suppression, depression and loneliness finally broke my fathers will to live. On an earlier visit of mine to Oxford, when we were sitting together alone, he had asked me in an urgent voice, "How do I kill myself Joe? What drugs will do the trick? Tell me, you know how I can do it." He stared at me with childish, pleading eyes and then turned away, disinterested in my speechless response. I was shocked that he had gone grey, practically overnight, and it conveyed to me his internal anguish. My mother told me later that Frank had frequently woken her at night during these last years. She said he would show her the carving knife from the kitchen and tell her he was going to kill her and then kill himself because everything was so awful. He told her it was better to die now than endure any more of this torturous life. "Weren't you scared mother?" I asked her.

"No, strangely I wasn't. I knew he wouldn't harm me. He just wanted to kill himself but needed me to come along in case he got scared," she said matter of factly.

My mother cut my Pa down a few times before he finally made it. She came home from a shopping trip one day to find him hanging, dead, behind a door. He'd slipped a rope around the door handle, flipped the rope over the other side of the door and fashioned a noose, high up, near the top of the door. Standing on chair, he must have put his head through the loop and then kicked the chair away. Life was over for my dad and I wished, and still wish, that we could have talked more. I wish that the feelings I now have for my father were there, inside me, when he was alive. An accident of time and history prevented this. I knew that there was a quiet, capitulating and acquiescent Frank inside of me but I knew, instinctively, that I had to keep shouting and fighting to keep the silent, passive, hopeless and relentless devil from driving me into the same, black place.

"A funny thing happened a couple of weeks after Frank died," said my mother, screwing up her eyes so that she could count her stitches. "You know that Frank spent some time at Littlemore as an in-patient last year?"

"Yes I heard."

"Well, whilst he was there he got quite chummy with Richard, the Trinidadian nurse, the fellow you used to like so much," she told me, dropping her needles and looking out of the window. "After he died, about a week later, I had to go up to his old ward to see his doctor and collect a few things. Richard caught me leaving the ward and asked me how Frank was. I told him that he had killed himself the week before and I thought Richard was going to have a heart attack, right there on the spot, he looked really frightened."

"Why, what happened," I asked.

"Richard looked thunderstruck. You know he's normally a lovely brown Caribbean colour but he went horribly white after I told him about Frank's death."

"Mother, for Gods sake, get to the point," I badgered, impatient to understand the mystery.

"Richard said that Frank had arrived on the ward two days before. Apparently he'd walked in and caught Richard's eye and seemed to wait for him until he could leave the sitting room and the patient that he was talking to. Richard signalled for Frank to wait, and he did for a minute or two, and then he turned and left the ward."

"But he was dead," I whispered.

"Hmm…..exactly. Why do you think that God fearing Richard went the colour of parchment?" She glanced at me over the top of her specs, nodded a couple of times and sighed deeply.

I'd been out walking around my old town during the day and I had passed the Cowley Road Hospital. It was here, under a tree, in the gardens, that I had taken my last drink in 1978, whilst on a brief visit from Wales. I was born there in the old workhouse, I was busted there for burglary and finally I took my last drink there. I sat under the same tree, in the sun, and watched the passers-by and wondered about my life. My past now only existed in my head; I had realized that during the day. My memories of Oxford and all my adventures here were all that I had. It's odd how I'd believed that the people that I loved in this city would always remain as I remembered them. That everything would be the same and not change, but now I could walk through the city centre, amongst the ancient beauty and dangerous men, and no one called out, "Joe, my darling, come and get a drink," or, "And what have you got for your favourite girl customer today Boss?" We were ghosts. My world, our world, had gone. People change, or die, and leave nothing but memories.

Whilst building the house at Rhoserchan Fach, in Wales, and after my last drink of alcohol I had become increasingly dependent on painkillers prescribed by my doctor. I still hadn't developed a way of handling my relentless and persecuting sensitivity which was such a huge part of me. I ended up using around twenty dihydro-codeine, or DF118s, every day. I was working hard on the house and also doing building work for others during the summer months to raise cash for the house. In fact, I earned all of the money needed to build the place. I handed everything to Hannah at the end of each week and never properly understood why I did that, especially as I was beginning to dislike Hannah intensely. I'd seen Dennis' words come true on a number of occasions through the years. Our friends would grow tired of Hannah's exploitative and rude ways and they would walk away. I was beginning to understand that she was calculating and could be horribly ruthless. It was easier for me to continue swallowing the tablets and working hard.

Finally though, one January morning in 1981, something happened to me which was completely marvellous and, again, wholly inexplicable. I was sitting and contemplating visiting my doctor in town to ask for another supply of painkillers. During the previous month I had tried to stop using and I had endured days of acute discomfort; agony in fact, both emotional and physical. The house was built, looked beautiful and I needed to stop taking the prescribed drugs. I had diarrhoea, vomiting, painful muscular spasms and I hadn't slept for five days. If ever I needed proof of the fact that the disease of addiction was progressive it lay in my pain of the past few days. Many times through the years I had experienced withdrawal and cold turkey from heroin and from alcohol. Both were heavy duty drugs but the withdrawal I suffered coming off these relatively innocuous analgesics was more severe than the times before. I was getting older and the condition was living inside of me and not in the drugs. The drugs that I chose to use were simply medications for my own inherent sensitivity.

The uncertainty of when the pain would stop was always the worst thing for me during cold turkey. If only I could believe that on the coming Monday, say, I would be better, then I had something to work towards and it would have been bearable. The fruits of the poppy did not leave my body without one fuck of a fight. The pain was relentless; day after day of nerves stretched to breaking point. The codeine had effectively filled the dopamine receptor sites in my brain, which controlled the flow of natural endorphins, and now the codeine had gone. It took days, if not weeks, for the brain chemistry to sort itself out and start releasing its own morphine-like painkiller once again.

That cold, grey, winter morning I'd endured five days of screaming pain and emotional terror. I decided that I'd had enough and I was going back to my doctor to score. I put on my jacket and headed for the bedroom door. Before I reached it the thought struck me that I'd given up the last time simply because the drugs were not helping anymore. I walked back to the bed and sat down to think. I stared at the fitted wardrobes that I'd made and at the pink marble top of the table that ran alongside the east wall. I needed to sleep badly and my thoughts were racing through my mind at the speed of light. My legs and arms were thrashing about periodically and, like a bloodhound, I could smell the propane gas that stood outside the house and it made me want to vomit. I covered my head and cowered. I could hear the tap dripping in the downstairs kitchen; I'd have to turn it off soon before I screamed. I could smell the bread that Hannah had baked two days before. I could smell the near shit smell of my own sweat and my brain reeled. I could not possibly take any more.

I got up from the bed and walked, another time, to the door. I just had to score, I couldn't bear this kind of pain. Once there I was stopped again by the realization that the drugs would only be a temporary respite and not a very satisfactory one at that. I needed to get high, so high that I would never come back down into the pain. My hand went up to the door handle and dropped again when I understood finally that my drug taking equipment was forever broken. My body would never allow me to get properly, and wonderfully, stoned anymore. My physical ability to process the stuff was buggered. I'd never, ever, get to that peaceful place again as long as I lived.

I walked back to the bed – back to the door – back to the bed. I sat down and knew that this was one fuck of a problem that I was not going to solve alone. I was obsessed by opiates, compelled to use them but knowing that it would solve nothing. I buried my face in my hands and said, "Please, please help me. I don't know if anyone is there but I need help. I don't know what to do, please help me." Suddenly, I felt cold all over, but it was a very pleasant, bearable chill and I had a strong sense that something, or someone, was in the room with me. I looked up and dropped my hands into my lap. I thought for a moment that I'd gone deaf because there was no sound, there were no awful smells and I was tingling from the top of my head down to my toes. There was something in the bedroom with me. It felt powerful and loving and I was able to know that somehow. My withdrawals had gone. I was still weak and dazed but I knew that it was over.

I slowly staggered downstairs and found Hannah busy in the kitchen. "I think that I've just had a visit from God," I told her.

"Can you watch that the pot doesn't boil over Joe? I have to go and fetch some eggs from the nest boxes," she said as she headed for the back door, putting on her warm combat jacket as she went. I stood there, like a loon, in the kitchen watching the simmering saucepan of beans and tried to understand the events of the last fifteen minutes. Something supernatural, bigger than me, had picked me up and taken away the pain. Unlike my mother I was unable to say that my drug problem was over but, for the first time in my life, I was able to commit myself to staying clean for the rest of that day. When Hannah returned with a bucket full of brown eggs I was still standing in the kitchen but now I was crying.

In the wonderful days that followed I joined a self-help group for alcoholics in Aberystwyth and discovered others who shared the same compulsion to use that I'd had all my life. But it wasn't quite so much the symptoms of intoxication that fascinated me when I spoke to these guys but the inherent characteristics that we all seemed to share. They spoke of feeling apart, of living in a glass bubble, unable to touch or feel close to others or things. They talked of their sharp sensitivity, of their masks of grandiosity and of their self-doubt: of their perfectionism and constant self-criticism. I felt at home and comforted by these people.

Sandy, a recovering alcoholic, had been sitting around in hired rooms for months, keeping the meetings going but hardly anyone came. We got on well Sandy and me. A respectable, middle-aged spinster and a thirty seven year old ex-tart, dealer, con man and recovering junky. Sandy was glad I had arrived when I did and we were company for each other whilst we set about the task of attracting other sick alcoholics to the meetings. Sandy and I giggled a lot. She'd laugh if I caught her eye and sometimes, during the sessions, she'd turn away from me for fear of laughing out loud. Always silly things set us off, but once we were going it was hard to stop.

One newcomer in particular was a trial for us both. His name was Don and he was a young married man with two kids, living in the hills in a remote cottage a few miles out of Aberystwyth. Week after week Don would breeze into the meetings telling us all how well he was doing and how grateful he was to the Twelve Step programme for his new life. The only problem was that he reeked of alcohol. "I've been sober now for five weeks four days and my life is turning round," he'd share with us, breathing out enough dangerous fumes to drive us all to relapse. Sandy and I would eye each other during Don's hypocritical rants and she would raise her eyebrow and then stare at the floor, biting her bottom lip to keep her mirth in check.

We all patiently tolerated a few weeks of Don's denial before I had a word with him after a meeting one day. "Don I can smell booze on your breath. I smell alcohol every time that you come to a meeting. Personally I don't mind if you want to drink, it's your funeral, but I hate the lying week after week."

"No, no you're mistaken Joe. Not a drop has passed my lips for over five weeks," protested a cheery Don, exhaling Polish vodka up my flared nostrils.

"Don wise up, everyone knows you are drinking. We can all smell you before you drive into the car park," I continued, looking into his eyes and touching his arm.

"Ah! Ah, yes I know what it is. Mouth wash, that's what you can smell," spluttered Don.

"Bollocks Don."

"No! Not bollocks Joe, mouthwash," he smiled. Later Don went to a Twelve Step treatment centre in England but even after his stay there he continued to drink and still protest that he was dry. I could never figure out why he bothered to come to meetings at all. Perhaps it was to pacify his wife. The Twelve Step recovery programme talks candidly about people who are constitutionally unable to get hold of the rigorous honesty demanded in order to clean up and I was going to get very familiar with this type of personality later on.

Again, in the early days, and by way of a marvellous contrast, a small miracle occurred in our meeting; a gift for Sandy and me. We held 'open' meetings once every month and it was to such a meeting that Elizabeth came along with her teenage son and daughter. The thin, pretty, chain smoking lady shook and trembled throughout the hour and a half meeting and tried to hide inside her warm, woollen winter coat. Elizabeth was withdrawing from alcohol and she looked like it too. Her son and daughter sat close to her and sometimes gave her small nods of encouragement and little smiles. She listened, fascinated, by the accounts of the other alcoholics and she slowly started to relax. I watched the pain and worry leave her white face. Elizabeth never drank again after that night and later she told me that she had felt as if she had come home at last.

Back in Oxford, during my brief stay, I told my mother of my new life and of the miracles that I'd seen and she was glad. We walked together a lot during that visit. She especially liked to stroll in the University Parks and stand on top of the High Bridge, the lovely arch that John Betjeman wrote about in one of his poems. We watched the ducks, swans and the idiotic punters trying to impress their 'gels' with their punting skills. My mother and father had few friends; they were outsiders, both of them. They watched and observed others but rarely got close. As we walked the city streets, arguing and chatting, I felt grateful to be there with her and I was sure that, deep down, my mother knew intimately of the insane journey that I was taking.

19

Putting on the Roof

Spring 1987

I slept in the tiny tent with a loaded shotgun by my side. I didn't sleep too well because I was alert to every strange sound during the night and in the morning I always woke up stiff and with a gun barrel stuck in my back. I poked my head out of the dew covered door flap and had a quick look at the building site. It was early morning and a glorious spring light lit up the almost completed rehabilitation unit – The Rhoserchan Project. It had survived another night and hadn't been burned to the ground by angry villagers. I broke the twelve bore and climbed out of my tent, stretched, yawned and took a leak under the trees. I reckoned that it was around 7am and I was hungry for breakfast but I had to check the building site first. As I strolled around the site I saw that everything was OK and ready for the three young builders to come in at 9am to finish putting slates on the roof.

In 1984 I had the idea to build a centre for addicts on the four acres at Rhoserchan and in 1986 we won a Welsh Office Planning Appeal to build an addiction rehabilitation unit on our land in Capel Seion. The model of treatment would be based on the Twelve Step programme, known as the Minnesota Model, and I wanted to provide free treatment wherever possible. I knew from independent studies and from my own experience that the best treatment for addiction that existed were the self-help movements of Alcoholics Anonymous and Narcotics Anonymous and also the treatment centres, worldwide, which based their programmes on this philosophy. They showed a consistent average recovery rate of 56%, which was nothing short of miraculous when compared with NHS treatment approaches and the other methods, including the Christian based ones and hierarchical concept houses. These showed very poor recovery rates of 1% to 2% with a huge number of people leaving treatment before completion. One of the reasons that made me want to start the project was because of the fury I felt towards the liberal, permission-giving approaches I saw in the NHS and in the Probation Service. Disrespectful methods that robbed using addicts of any hope of recovery and, worse, creating a permission giving environment in which the addict felt free to use and die. The suffering families of their clients were never, to my knowledge, considered by the street drug agencies.

In 1984, after enlisting the help of Maldwyn Pryse, a local clergyman, Bob Davies, a probation officer and Dr Richard Edwards, an Aberystwyth GP, as Trustees of the new charity, I started to look for Patrons and the money to build the unit. Princess Diana wrote, out of the blue, to say that we could use her name in any way we wished in order to promote Rhoserchan. The word was out that I wanted to provide excellent, low cost treatment for addicts and soon after, Anthony Hopkins, the actor and film star, became one of our Patrons and I began to raise the money necessary to build a rehabilitation centre. Things were looking good until the villagers of nearby Capel Seion began to object to the siting of the rehab. They were frightened and angry that a temporary home for thieves, thugs, child molesters and violent drug addicts was to be set up less than a mile from their village.

After the Trustees and I had submitted our planning application for the new building we decided it would be polite and politic to explain to the whole village exactly what we were about to do. I had the simple, naïve belief that everybody in the world would welcome something that was geared to helping their sons, daughters, mothers and fathers with addiction problems. I was disabused of this notion one night in the village school. The large classroom was packed to the rafters with villagers. I never imagined that our tiny village had so many people living in it. I thought that they must have dug up some ancestors to swell their numbers that night. Our audience was quiet, unsmiling and looking to derail my dreams. Dr Edwards, Richard, opened up our presentation and then I followed him with a description of the rehabilitation process and how disciplined and well run it was going to be. I pointed out that no patient would be allowed to leave the unit unaccompanied and they were welcome to visit any time. They were not impressed or swayed by my talk; they jeered and sometimes booed during the course of the evening.

One local farmer suggested that they should hang me there and then and get it over with. After that outburst, a stream of threats of one kind or another were made. I looked at the hostile faces and thought, 'This is the wrong tactic folks, you're just making me want to fight and win even more now.' Suddenly, amidst the foot stamping and finger pointing one old fellow from the village stood up and spoke, trying to calm his neighbours with a flapping hand gesture, "We have to be careful here everybody," Emrys stuttered, addressing the unruly crowd. "We know there is a huge drug problem in England and it won't be long before it's here in Wales and affecting my kids and yours. One day we may be glad of a facility like this, that's all I'm saying." Emrys sat down, red in the face and trembling slightly. His wife patted him on the back for his courage and smiled at him gently.

There was relative quiet for a bit as the warning was digested and then the anger erupted again. "We won't allow it, not in our village. Over my dead body," shouted a burly villager known for his extravagant drinking habit. I looked at my three Trustees and felt grateful to have them. They were all local people but they stood firm with me against these panicky and frightened villagers. "The best thing to do is close the meeting now," whispered Richard. "Let things simmer down for a few days." With that he thanked everybody and said goodnight. I sat there, feeling both stupid and humiliated. I had really believed that they would welcome the unit with open arms, glad to know help would be available for people in Wales with addiction problems. But no, addicts and alcoholics were not a part of their community, they came from elsewhere and they would be dangerous.

After I'd done the morning inspection of the unit I walked back to my new house with the shotgun in my hands. Hannah was sitting in the dining room with our two boys. Simon, the four year old, rushed at me as I came in through the back door, a happy smiling little boy dressed in his rumpled pyjamas; he giggled as he hugged my legs and grinned up at me. Alfie was just a few months old and he was sitting on his mothers lap with a breast in his mouth. There was a delicious smell of toast in the air and it made me even more hungry. "Uneventful night?" asked Hannah without looking up from her son's face.

"A fox came in the night to sniff the tent but that's all," I answered, slicing the home-made bread for toast. Both Simon and Alfie were born at home and I was present at both the births. I had attended special classes beforehand to learn pain reducing techniques so that I could help Hannah during the actual birth, in case she lost it and needed encouragement or guidance with her breathing technique. They were lovely boys and I adored them both.

I knew though, that I wasn't cut out to be a father and I'd have been happier not to have had kids at all. I was either over responsible or highly irresponsible and I couldn't seem to hit a compromise, therefore parenting for me was one long anxiety. When the subject of having kids was originally discussed between us I explained to Hannah about my reluctance to be a father. She assured me that she would be the main figure in their lives and I was not to worry. After they were born, of course, I loved them deeply and ended up, as usual, doing most of the hard work.

I sat down with everybody to eat my toast before I showered and shaved, ready for the day ahead. "Len called you late last night. He sounded worried about something," announced Hannah. Len was a young recovering heroin addict who had cleaned up in the drug self-help group that I had started in Aberystwyth a few years before. It was the first of its kind in Wales to survive for any length of time and, at that moment, it was flourishing with recovering people. Len and his wife had been on the brink of suicide when they first came and now they were clean and had a new baby daughter. Len was a stalwart member of our group. "He's chairing a big open meeting on Saturday and I suppose he wants to talk about it," I said.

Another member of the same group called Dean was currently away at Broadway Lodge Treatment Centre in Weston-super-Mare training to be one of our future counsellors for Rhoserchan. The training was rigorous and included a spell as a patient which was particularly challenging. I had serious doubts about Dean. He seemed reluctant to own his feelings and happier to act out a kind of complacent, phoney serenity. I didn't trust his sly charm or his motivation for being a counsellor. I felt that he had an inflated ego and lacked intelligence, which was worrying for me as the Programme Co-ordinator of the unit. Still, he was clean, and he wanted to help others no matter what his motives were. I didn't have a huge amount of people to choose from anyway. Recovering addicts, the 3% who made good counsellors that is, were a rare breed indeed, especially so in wild and woolly Wales at that time. Apart from one other young woman who seemed slightly detached from reality, I felt fortunate to have found the others who would make up the Rhoserchan staff, including Elizabeth who I first met in that marvellous open meeting. I came to love them all very much over the years.

"How is the treatment plan coming along," asked Hannah, detaching Alfie from her tit and sipping her tea. I was excited by the program I was writing. It was based on the Twelve Step programme but had the very best elements of the concept houses built in to it. It was devised to introduce addicts to their feelings for perhaps the first time in their lives and then to show them how to manage these previously frightening emotions. I wanted my guys to accept and embrace their anger, sadness, guilt and joy and understand that none of their emotions were bad and in need of change. All that had to occur was recognition of the feeling and then an acceptance of it. I wanted my fellows to ride their lives and not fight against their own emotions. I knew that this new programme could work, because it had worked so well for me.

Hannah handed little Alfie over to me and I kissed his rosy cheek. His lips were wet with Hannah's milk and he stared at me with his large brown eyes. Simon came and stood by me and pointed his finger at Alfie's nose, trying to make the child go cross-eyed. He succeeded very well once or twice and giggled softly. I loved these two boys, but their mother scared me. I knew that as a recovering addict and as someone about to run a treatment centre, my behaviour had to beyond reproach; I had to be whiter than white. But I suspected that Hannah could wreck it all with her special brand of madness. Our 'thing' was not good. Just as I was slipping into despair and panic the phone rang. Hannah answered it and said it was Bob, the Trustee who handled our accounts, and he wanted a word.

When I started to raise money to build, after achieving charity status, I asked my Board never to allow us to go into the 'red.' It was agreed that we would not go into debt and it proved to be a great principle that served us well. "Hi Bob, how are you?" I said into the receiver.

"Joe, I've just looked at the books and we are out of cash. Sorry to drop this on you at such short notice but I've been so frantically busy with other things and haven't checked our balance for a while. You'll have to tell the builders to quit. We have enough to pay them until about now but that's all," said a sad Bob.

"What about the £10,000 from the Elizabethan Trust," I asked desperately.

"That is due to arrive in three months time and is allocated for staff training and equipment," Bob answered in a concerned tone. "Go and tell the lads to get off the roof."

Gloomily I strolled up to the top field where the Rhoserchan Project was being built. Jason, Frisbee and Spliff were already hard at it nailing new asbestos slates to the roof. It was satisfying work and it looked great. The three young fellows were hippies from Birmingham who had chosen to live in the Welsh hills to try an alternative lifestyle and I liked them a lot. During the early days of building I had fired the local Welsh contractor because he was scared of repercussions should it get out that he was working for me. His heart was not in the job and he was scared to be seen on site, consequently he rarely turned up to supervise the men. He obviously thought that he may lose future contracts in the area if the Capel Seion villagers started to broadcast the news about the Judas builder.

After I sacked him Jason, Frisbee and Spliff stayed with me and took on extra responsibilities as well. The week before I had watched Frisbee as he caught sight of Lucy's daughter, from his vantage point on the roof. She came into the site to give me a message from her mother. Lucy lived in the village and she was going to be my future manager. Her daughter, Tilly, had walked down the lane, in her school uniform, with her note. At fourteen years old she was one of the most beautiful creatures that I had ever seen. Frisbee stopped his hammering on the roof and stared, mesmerised by this young beautiful girl beneath him. He was transfixed and drooling as Tilly turned into the lane and walked back towards her house in the village. He watched her go and then after a little while he glanced down at me and said, "What a shame. Oh God, what a shame," and resumed his banging on the roof. It made me smile because it summed up my feelings about Tilly also. I'd look at her beauty and think, "What a shame, what a shame."

"Amigos, I've just had a phone call from one of my Trustees. We've got no money left so you have to stop work," I told them glumly. The three of them dropped their hammers and sat on the roofing battens to roll cigarettes. They started muttering to each other but I couldn't hear what they were saying. After a few minutes they resumed their roofing tasks, picking up the new slates and nailing them to the wooden battens. "Didn't you hear what I just said guys? I can only pay you until now, no more. Come down please lads," I pleaded.

"No," said Frisbee turning his back on me.

"What do you mean, no," I asked, puzzled by his response.

"We talked and we are going to stick with you, pay or no pay," he said.

"I don't know what to say. I don't know what to say," I said.

"Well then, don't say anything and fuck off," said Spliff, talking through a gob full of copper nails.

"Thanks boys," I said, walking back to the house and trying to swallow the lump in my throat on the way.

When I reached the house I searched my fund raising files to try and find a solution to my immediate problem. So far I had raised over £140,000 for the unit and we wouldn't need too much more to launch the thing. I had spent hundreds of hours writing to charities listed in the Directory of Grant Making Trusts and received positive replies from around 5% of the organizations that I approached. Subsequently, I learned that 3% was a good return but the anxious 'waiting days' were unpleasant to live through. At that moment though I couldn't see where to get an immediate donation from. After lunch there was a knock at the door and I opened it to an elderly lady dressed in a colourful, woollen cardigan. "Are you Joe South?" she said smiling pleasantly.

"I am," I replied. "Would you like to come in?"

"You don't know me, but I know you. I'm Josh's mother. Katherine Macmillan."

"Lady Macmillan?" I said, amazed at her sudden appearance.

"Lady Lisburne has told me that you are building an addiction rehab here and I want to help you," she whispered, staring at me with wide eyes. "For Josh's sake, you know."

For the whole of that afternoon we talked about Josh and of the problems in her family. At that point I was badly in need of a wealthy sugar mummy and here she was, bang on time! Unbelievable! We walked up to the site and she admired the building and talked to the hippies on the roof. I told her that they were working for no wages at the moment and explained what had happened that morning. "How much do you need? Look, here's £5,000 now," she announced, reaching for her cheque book and pen. "Well, what are you waiting for Joe, go and tell those good and loyal men they are back on the payroll." Thus began my friendship with Lady Macmillan and Lady Lisburne. They not only became Patrons of the unit, they also supported me with their friendship during the coming years.

After Lady Macmillan left that afternoon I returned to the site with Alfie in a papoose on my back and with Simon running around my legs and bashing things with his big stick. The afternoon felt good and full of hope and, for a time anyway, I was relieved of the burden of responsibility of urgently hustling money. Jason, Frisbee and Spliff were still working on the roof as I passed beneath them and entered the building. I thought of their gesture this morning and felt grateful for their friendship. I walked around the interior and saw that we were only months away from completion.

Hannah and I had found the pre-fabricated sections of the building at an old army camp in North Wales and bought the whole lot for a song. With the help of a friendly, young, local architect we set about designing a building tailor-made to be a rehabilitation unit for addicts. In a sense I was lucky to be able to do this because most treatment centres began their lives in old houses, or mansions, that really were not suitable for the job envisaged without extensive changes to the structure of the buildings. These changes often robbed them of their original charm, elegance and grace. We were starting from scratch with our 'shed in the hills.' The architect and I consulted with the department of social services during the drawing up of our plans so that come registration with them, as a care home, there would be no problems.

As I walked around the night block I was thinking about Dean and Zara, the two members of my future staff, who bothered me. When I was training as a counsellor at Broadway Lodge Treatment Centre, Ted Marlowe, the Treatment Director, had told me, very wisely, that my major concerns would not be with the patients but with the staff. He knew Dean from his time at Broadway and he advised me to fire him before we started and I said I'd think about it, as I watched how he progressed. I saw a few counsellors whilst I was at Broadway who never seemed too healthy to me. Like some members of AA and NA they seemed to have transferred their dependencies from booze, or junk, to their recovery, or counselling careers, or food.

It was almost as if they were in role play because they were frightened of finding out who they were underneath their protective veneers. My daughter Johanna had once told me that her mother never spoke to her anymore since she found Jesus. "If I have a problem she just quotes the Bible at me. It drives me mad and I don't feel special to her anymore." Like my ex-wife these evangelistic AA members, or counsellors in treatment centres, covered every eventuality and predicament with a series of slogans and quotations from the Big Book of AA. Some addict friends found it a help but some, including me, found it demeaning and disrespectful. Unfortunately, these clone type counsellors lacked intelligence and sensitivity and I really did not want to work with people like that. I wanted the people who worked at Rhoserchan to be absolutely comfortable with themselves and others. It was common knowledge that some personality disorders (psychopaths, sociopaths etc) got past the screening process for patients, on admission to treatment centres, but it was not commonly accepted that there were counsellors with personality disorders operating all over the world. Ted said that he didn't think that they did a great deal of harm to the other patients but he was quiet when I asked him what harm he thought they did to other counsellors.

After supper that night I bathed my boys and dressed in their pyjamas they went to their bedroom for their nightly bedtime story. Of course little Alfie was too young to understand a word but night after night he was content to snuggle in my arms and listen, sometimes dabbing a moist, pink digit at the Greendale characters on the pages. This half hour was special to me and I never tired of reading the same favourite story over and over again. The three of us were together, safe and inhaling the soap smells from their bath. When I turned a page I could hear three people breathing and feel three hearts beating. I thought that life was precious, but fragile.

20

HILARY

Autumn 1989

I was back to living alone in one bedroom of a large, shared house in Aberystwyth town centre and I was happier than I'd been in years. When I left Hannah I felt as if I had just walked out of a particularly harsh prison sentence. I was free and I was in love with a girl called Hilary. Although I luxuriated in my new life I still worried about my sons constantly. After the Rhoserchan Project had opened Hannah's behaviour became more and more bizarre and not only was I finding it impossible to live with her, the Rhoserchan staff were also beginning to experience difficulties with her behaviour.

For several months, just after the unit had opened, I had looked after Simon and Alfie whilst their mother underwent treatment for her emotional problems. At one point during her treatment it was agreed that I would care for the boys in the future, but later, Hannah decided against this move and said that she would not agree to that arrangement. Although Hannah no longer worked as a gardener for Rhoserchan, the unit was built on our land

and she lived a stones throw away so I was compromised as to what I could do or say at that point. The welfare of my boys and the safety of the unit's future were my priorities so when it came to legally dividing the property, Hannah received the lions share. I literally caved in to all her demands because I could not cause a fuss for fear of jeopardising the centre and its future. I thought that if Hannah was content with her side of the deal, big house, some land etc, then it would reflect on the boys and therefore I agreed that she should have the house and an acre of land, whilst I took the land where the centre was built. I was glad to be away from Hannah and it was inevitable that we would split up one day but I wondered how Simon and Alfie would react to her guidance alone. For the time being though I was allowed to see my sons at the weekends. I felt angry that the law always presumed in favour of the mother even if the evidence showed that the man was more responsible.

I was looking forward to Hilary coming to my tiny little hide-a-way today. It was a Friday evening and I had finished work for the week, although I was still on call via a bleep that I had to carry 24 hours a day. Hilary was working in Leeds in a Social Services hostel for the mentally ill but I had met her four years before on a hot, sunny, summer day in Aberystwyth. Dean and I had just returned from talking to an alcoholic who had asked us for help. We'd spent an hour with this young man as he cried and chucked pebbles into the sea.

After our talk by the crashing waves we'd decided to go to Dean's workshop at the harbour where he was making hideous kitchen furniture from reclaimed timber. As we approached his place I saw a girl leaning against a garage door. She was wearing shorts and she was smiling as we approached. "Who's this?" I asked Dean.

"It's Hilary. She's a student, but she is living with me at the moment," replied Dean. He looked reluctant to give me anymore information than that.

"She's nice, she's got blue eyes," I whispered because we were now close to where she was standing. Hilary was smiling, in an uncertain way, at Dean as he greeted her casually with a, "Hi," and a wave. "Been waiting long?" he asked her. "I'll have to give you a key of your own." She glanced quickly at me, smiled a hello and followed Dean in to his workshop-cum-home. I loved her clear, blue eyes, her girly legs and her ready laugh. I liked Hilary from the very start.

After a few months Dean dumped Hilary for someone else, a woman he met in the recovery rooms. Hilary, for a while was heartbroken, and came to live with Hannah and me at Rhoserchan Fach whilst she got over her love affair. I felt for her as she cried and moaned over the wicked Dean. She found it hard to accept that he'd been seeing the other woman while he was living with her. It was his dishonesty that hurt her the most. However, after a couple of weeks of her wailing and me saying, "It's over Hilary," she began to come back to life. I found that she was easy to be with and I felt comfortable with her. During the light summer evenings we would play badminton together and she would laugh at my antics. I once beat her using a rubber Wellington boot as a racquet and she howled with merriment, unable to play for laughing. We were getting close and I once went too far at breakfast one morning by telling her that I loved her blue eyes. She looked up from her muesli and stared at me. I stared back for a few seconds and then we both continued with our breakfasts.

Hilary had just obtained her degree at Aberystwyth University and she wanted to work with Rhoserchan when it opened. I was glad to have her because I thought that she was kind, intelligent and reliable. But after the Dean bust up she came and found me on the building site one day and told me that she was leaving Aberystwyth to work in Leeds. "I can't work along side Dean, it would be impossible. I have to go. I'm so sorry Joe," she told me with tears in her eyes. I didn't want to lose her and I was shocked by her announcement.

It was evening and the light was fading fast. It was starting to get chilly as we walked to the house. Inside, we drank our tea and the boys made their usual fuss of Hil. They both loved her and Simon even had a special name for her. It was Monya. We were mystified by the name and couldn't figure out where he got it from, but to Simon, Hilary was definitely Monya. I knew that Rhoserchan was losing a good member of staff but I saw the wisdom of her departure. As she said, it would not have been healthy for her to work alongside Dean. But, buried deep inside of me, was a terrible sadness at the thought of losing my friend. "OK it's the best thing I agree," I said to her across the cluttered table. "I'm going to miss you." She climbed into her Volkswagen Beetle and drove away.

Over a year later and sometime after Hannah and I had spit up, I phoned Hilary at work in Leeds. I was staying with Elizabeth at the time, before I got my new place in town, and she agreed to come and stay with us for a weekend.

I was glad to see her. I was with my pal again and I'd missed her. That first evening I hugged her for just too long and stared at her too much. Before we all went to bed I'd managed to kiss her in the kitchen, secretly and away from Elizabeth's gaze. She returned the sweet kiss and held me close. I didn't have to work on the following Saturday and we walked a lot and later we held hands. Everything was funny and we giggled and laughed at everything and everybody. The waves crashed on to the beach, the seagulls squawked and the wind blew our hair. I looked at her laughing face and olive skin and I was happy. Sunday evening came much too quickly and she had to return to Leeds to work the next morning, but, by now, there was a bigger love between us.

Weeks later, when we finally made love, it was worth waiting for. We started kissing, caressing, petting, licking and loving at 5.30pm one evening and, at last, sank into an exhausted sleep at midnight. We fitted, us two, we matched, we worked.

The unit was going extraordinarily well and people were getting well. Already we showed a 70% recovery rate which, to me, was miraculous. I had also developed a treatment programme for anorexia and bulimia which was particularly exciting and proving to be highly effective with sufferers.

Stephen Rose, a documentary film maker for BBC2 had heard a programme about Rhoserchan on BBC World Service whilst driving in his car one day and had sent his researcher, Jane Stephenson, to talk to me about making a film. When Jane arrived I instantly warmed to this young, intelligent woman but I was wary about what she and Stephen had in mind. They thought that the Rhoserchan recovery programme was ground breaking and exciting and they wanted to film the process in some depth. Sitting in my office with Jane I listened as she outlined the plan. "We would bring a team in for a month and follow the progress of that particular group of addicts through their treatment. We would want to film everything," she told me earnestly.

I had recognised that if a BBC2 film about Rhoserchan was to be shown, possibly worldwide, it would have tremendous publicity value for us and possibly attract future funding. I desperately wanted to provide quality treatment, for the less well off, and I needed publicity just like this to achieve my aims. I also recognised that any involvement with film makers was inherently risky. I was suspicious of Jane and Stephen's proposal. "Well, filming one-to-one interviews is out straight away Jane. There is the big issue of client confidentiality and so the rest of the film could only go ahead with the patient's agreement, the staff's agreement, the Trustee's agreement and my agreement," I declared, shaking my head.

"Naturally," she agreed, shifting forward in her seat.

"Of course I'd want full editorial control," I said.

"No. You'll never get it in a million years," she said forcefully. "Freedom of the press and all that..."

"Freedom to show what you like to the world pre-supposes that you will be responsible in your presentation of Rhoserchan and that is the bit I don't trust. Stephen could film everything and then cut and edit to make a movie that says what he wants to say but it doesn't reflect accurately the work of Rhoserchan." I argued. It was a warm afternoon and the sun shining through my office window lit up Jane's face when she smiled and said, "True, but what can I do to make you trust us?"

"Hmm....OK. Presuming that permission was forthcoming from all parties I would want you to come into treatment, as a patient, looking only at your own defects and assets, for two to three weeks. Then, subject to your progress and how the group like you, I'd see about starting to trust you," I said, flicking my pen, irritatingly, head over heel. I knew that Jane had been in group a few times and had talked with the current guys in treatment and I knew that she knew it was very, very tough. This plan was a problem solver for me because I assumed that she'd never dare to do it. "OK, I'll do it. I'll be scared but I trust you and your team and I know I'll benefit from it. God knows I could do with straightening out a bit," she chirruped.

'Fuck,' I thought. 'You and your foolproof plans.' I'd badly miscalculated and was humbled by Jane's bravery.

Not only did this intrepid BBC researcher survive her spell in treatment she gained a lot from it in terms of learning how to manage her feelings and life situations. She became very enthusiastic about the Rhoserchan approach and could now speak from personal experience. I obtained everyone's permission to go ahead and Stephen Rose and his camera crew arrived to make the film. During the filming I became aware that documentary film making was essentially a lie. I observed that when a camera was present, no matter how accustomed to it you were, you acted differently. People were self-conscious and masked the discomfort in varying ways in front of a camera. We were posing. I realised that there was no such thing as filming 'real life' or 'cinema verite' because the presence of a camera changed the people in front of it. It was the small ingredient that changed real life to theatre. I was disturbed by my revelation but it was now too late to stop the filming. However, after the film was shown, we received a great many compliments and it put our unit firmly on the treatment map as more and more people came to us for treatment.

As I waited for Hil to arrive for the weekend I thought about my last visit to Oxford and I remembered how something that happened there could have killed my happiness and the Rhoserchan Project stone dead and made me very, very rich. I was walking up Cornmarket just after I'd bought a jacket in Austin Reed and I heard a familiar voice hail me from across the busy street. "Joe, Joe, hold up my brother. I've been looking for you all fucking year," yelled my old criminal compadre Freddie Smith. He danced between the traffic and grabbed me, kissing me on both cheeks. This was a Smith family custom, adapted I suspect, from their distant soul-cousins in the Cosa Nosta.

"You old cunt. Where 'ave you been my darling? I've been looking all over," said a breathless Freddie. "Someone said you were in a Russian jail." It was great to see this villain again and we went to the Grapes to celebrate our chance encounter. "What the fuck are you drinking? Don't tell me it's Perrier?" asked Freddie, aghast at my choice of drinks.

"No drugs, no booze, no cigarettes. Nothing for a while now Freddie. I had to stop mate, or die. As it happens I've found it suits me fine. I like being clean," I told him. Freddie stared at me, lifting his pint to his lips, "Fuck me Joe. I'm going to ring the Pope about this. Get it certified as a fucking miracle mate," said the stupefied Freddie.

"Why were you looking for me?" I asked him.

"Ah! Well Joe, what I reveal to you later, at my pad, will make you reach for a drink. I guarantee it. It's shocking news coming up for you. It'll blow your bollocks off. Come with me my man."

Freddie was still living in Jericho but he now had a larger place and he looked like he was a bit more prosperous. "Have you got a woman Freddie?" I asked on the way to Walton Street.

"Eight."

"Eight?

"Eight and I fuck 'em all when the fancy strikes me," he declared proudly.

"You're a pimp! You wait until I tell your mother you immoral bastard."

"She already knows, smart arse. She's the receptionist at my 'igh class establishment." We stood outside his garage as he fumbled for his keys. "I've been waiting to talk to you for a year about this lot in 'ere. I couldn't trust anybody else." He slid the door up and after we had ducked down and entered, he pulled it down again, leaving us inside with a large, white transit van.

"Let me explain what 'appened," said Freddie, carefully removing a stack of timber which was leaning against the back door of the van. "Last year I wanted to score some weed from the Wilson Brothers in North London. You know 'em, don't you? Anyway, I drove up to their patch and took Fritzy with me. It was evening when we arrived at Johnny's place. He's got no class that boy, he lives on a council estate," recounted Freddie, leaning against the back door of the battered vehicle and staring at the garage ceiling as if he found the thick cobwebs there very interesting. "I park down the street a bit and see Jimmy the Turk get out of this van, which he's just parked outside Johnny Wilson's place, and walk to the back and pull the door to make sure it's locked."

I'm interested now in Freddie's tale and can guess what is coming next. In his best Oxford Town cool he continued, "We're not going in Fritzy," I says, "Radical change of plan boy. We're going to nick that van and take it back to Oxford. So, we waited for Jimmy the Turk to go into Johnny's and then I moved. I didn't fuck about; thinking speed is of the essence 'ere, in case they come out to the van again to 'ave a butchers. I put a wheel brace through the window, 'opped in and I was off. Back to Oxford with Fritzy following in my car. Sweet eh?" Freddie was smiling now like Paul Newman and enjoying telling his tale to an appreciative audience….me.

"During the drive back the doubts set in Joe. I don't mind telling you. The van might be empty of anything valuable after all and then I've risked everything for sweet FA."

"What made you think the truck was loaded?"

"Just the way he looked around and tested the door after he parked. He looked like me when I've got something valuable on board. Dead fucking shifty."

"Did you say anything to Fritzy?" I asked to eliminate any future weak links.

"No, as far as he knows I just nicked the van for its own sake. Strip it, re-paint job and re-sell it kind of thing. He's not fucking Einstein our Fritzy. Thank you

God." Freddie, now grinning like a loon, released the padlock and swung the rusty doors of the transit open. They creaked horribly and rust flakes dropped off them as they moved. Inside were ten tea chests and nine or ten large cardboard boxes, each covered with a new, fresh potato sack. Freddie whipped off one of the sweet smelling Hessian covers and revealed, inside the tea chest, lots of polythene wrapped one kilogram packets of a white substance – cocaine. With a theatrical flourish Freddie removed the other covers, "Voila Brother Joe. The Great Coke, Dope and Doll Robbery of the Century." As far as I could see the chests contained cocaine, eight of the cardboard boxes housed marijuana and the remaining two were full of blow-up dolls (three-hole type with real hair.) Enjoying the incredulous expression on my face Freddie found a ready blown up doll behind the boxes. "I 'ave tested the product myself Sir and she was 'ighly satisfactory. In particular I enjoyed sodomising this very attractive, if a bit floppy around the arms and legs etc, girl and I 'ave now divorced my old lady." He looked so pleased with himself and I was stunned at the audacity of the heist. I also felt honoured that Freddie had waited a year, and then told me alone, of the robbery. I was touched by the trust that he had in me.

"How much is here Freddie?" I asked, picking up a bag of white crystals and admiring the white/blue light the coke gave off.

"Darling, I am proud to announce that I 'ave in my possession, half a ton of cocaine, half a ton of marijuana and one hundred beautiful rubber women."

"Fuck! Let me sit down Freddie."

"Will you 'elp me move it Joe. You know where to place it and I trust you boy," said Freddie looking into my eyes as he sat down with me on the bed of the van. We would be very, very rich if we flogged this lot there was no doubt, but this time something had changed for me. Before, I would have seen only the pound notes and all they could buy: girls, tropical sun, a house and a pool somewhere – bliss. Now I saw, in my minds eye, the children of coke and heroin addicts, abandoned as their parents used their days pursuing the drug. Now I saw despair, hopelessness, violence and an absence of soul in the white crystals. Thus far, how many people had I already killed, indirectly, by my dealing and, more importantly perhaps, how many children had I robbed of their secure, happy childhoods and bright futures?

"'Elp me Joe," whispered Freddie, touching my arm. I looked at my friend and knew that I had to walk away and never come back. "Things have changed for me Freddie. I've changed. I don't want to hurt anybody, anyone. I want to help, not destroy."

"It's the dealers that do the killing boy, not us. We just supply the dealers," he argued, his eyes frantic with worry as he read my reaction to his request.

"I've got to go mate," I said, getting up from the van and walking to the garage door.

"What can I do?" pleaded Freddie.

"Burn it, or chuck it in the sea," I suggested, knowing it was a ridiculous proposition for Freddie.

"Yeah," said Freddie very quietly. The trust he had for me had now gone from his eyes. Our friendship was over. I was now an impediment, a liability, a fucking non-entity. He opened the garage doors and I walked

266

away from a fortune and a life of luxury. It felt good and I breathed in the Oxford air and felt the sunshine on my face. Later, I thought about my friend Freddie and I was sad. Years later I'm still grieving for Freddie.

Today, back in Aberystwyth, I was happy and my little room was decked out with flowers waiting for Hil to arrive. I knew that she would jabber non-stop for an hour or two after she came and then we'd walk on the Promenade, close to the sea, and we'd be together. It was good to be clean and good to be doing the right thing for a change.

21

BIG SHARE

Late winter 1993

Today we were celebrating five years of successful operation as a treatment centre for addictive illnesses and the whole of Rhoserchan was waiting for its friend and Patron, Anthony Hopkins, to arrive.

It was fair to say that the Rhoserchan Project was now pretty well established and respected as an addiction rehabilitation unit. We had Welsh Office support and financial backing from many charities that liked what we did. Lucy, our manager, had through the years, worked tirelessly to make the money needed for this ambitious venture. When she first came on board, during the early, fraught days of operation, I would often catch her walking the corridors and bedrooms of the rehab with a panic stricken look on her face. Her unfamiliarity with addicts meant, I suppose, that she was expecting to be jumped on at any minute and be raped, or robbed. Plus, she had the unenviable task of raising the wages for nine staff by the end of the month.

She was aided and abetted in this by Marcie, her personal assistant. I knew Marcie was a sensitive and fearful person and I admired her courage when she faced every fear and undertook every daunting task that she was presented with. I loved them both and felt lucky to have them. The nine staff were all united in the belief that we could provide the very best of treatment for a minimum cost. We met and talked through every difficulty and gradually became a close knit team.

My two main worries on the counselling team had eventually resolved themselves. Zara became pregnant and left to look after her new baby and Dean left us after two years to work at another treatment centre. I was happy to say goodbye to both of them.

Rhoserchan offered a twelve week residential programme for addicts using an adaptation of the Minnesota Model. I believed, and still believe, that the unit was only successful because we used the Twelve Steps of Alcoholics Anonymous as a base for our programme. The Twelve Steps are a work of genius in my opinion and are entirely appropriate for obsessive/compulsive addicts. Therefore, we were able to treat alcoholics, anorexics, bulimics, drug addicts, sex addicts, gamblers and compulsive helpers using the clinically interpreted AA programme with abstinence as the foundation for recovery.

But the thing that was going to make Rhoserchan special was the 'feelings management' training which we developed and used so successfully over the years. I realised then that this particular programme could only be used if all the counselling team were completely integrated as personalities. Loving, objective and tough.

Later, I was to watch, with great sadness, as a future Programme Co-ordinator at Rhoserchan, dismantled this revolutionary approach. In my opinion he discarded it because he was frightened of what he thought he may discover about himself had he continued. Denial of self and problems were pretty impossible under my approach, but will flourish under less confrontative regimes.

We had booked the local theatre for the celebration later that evening and we expected to fill the 350 seat auditorium. Rhoserchan alumni, family, friends, Trustees, Patrons and representatives from Social Services were going to attend. It was an exciting occasion and I felt proud. Elizabeth spent the day ducking around the rehab and organising everybody to cover her nervousness and pride. We were all waiting for Anthony to arrive, when we would eat a sumptuous buffet, prepared by Jenny, our long suffering cook, and then pile out to the Theatr y Werin for the Big Share. That afternoon I had rehearsed the show with the main players and the lighting technician in the theatre.

Out of respect for Wales and its language I wanted to open with Wynford Ellis-Owen, a Welsh TV actor and scriptwriter, recounting his story of alcoholism and recovery at Rhoserchan in his native tongue, followed by the beautiful Lizzie telling her story of recovery from alcoholism and bulimia. Then, Anthony Hopkins would take centre stage and share of his journey into 'hell and back.' After the interval Michael, one of our more flamboyant counsellors, would host a grand free-for-all of sharing from the audience. I'd choreographed everything but now we all needed some luck and divine help to make the evening sing. I felt nervous and edgy during the day.

271

"I can't believe that I'm sitting next to Hannibal Lector," said the young female drug addict. "Can I touch you?" Tony was busy munching on salmon sandwiches but he smiled and gave her the go ahead. He seemed happy and even happier to be talking to people who shared his problem. I watched him from across the room and saw this great actor as fragile and vulnerable. He'd supported me since 1984 with my dreams of launching the centre but sometimes, when we met, he seemed trembly, uncertain and afraid. Later, he confided in me that he thought that he was sometimes an empty vessel just waiting to be filled up with the characters that he played and it was this sensitivity that was his gift as an actor. The young woman was giggling as Tony leaned towards her and threatened to 'eat her liver with Chianti and fava beans.'

I wondered if Jake would be here tonight. Big Jake had gone through the Rhoserchan programme during our second year and he was still clean and sober, now living in London. He was huge was Jake; an ex-mercenary and alcoholic. I remembered an afternoon in my office three years before. "I need to tell you something Joe," said Jake, shifting his bulk in the squeaky, wicker chair. "It's difficult.......hard like." With that he got up quickly and rushed to the lavatory in the corridor and I heard him vomiting inside. He returned, some minutes later, and eased his big body back into his chair. "I need to tell you something Joe. Something's preying on my mind like," he said in the deep, melodic, Swansea accent that I loved so much. He was sweating and he kept swatting, with his right hand, at an imaginary fly. Well, at least, I couldn't see it.

Big Jake had been a regular soldier for many years and after he left the army he couldn't seem to settle and he began to drink heavily and get into trouble with the law. Seeking something that would pay him for his soldiering skills as well as tolerating his drinking he shipped out to Asia and became a mercenary soldier. "I arrived at a village in the jungle where I had to meet my future commander in a bar there," Jake began to relate. "I'd been drinking for a while when he finally arrived. Chatting up the local talent I was see. Happy as a pig in shit I was when he walked in and changed everything. A small German bastard with a very arrogant manner. That upset me straight away, but I knew I'd have to overlook it because I needed the job so badly," Jake stopped his narrative to stretch out in his chair, look down at the carpet and sigh. He looked full of terrible guilt.

"Do you want to puke again Jake?" I asked him.

"No. Give me a minute and I'll be alright." After a little while he carried on with his tale. "The Kraut introduced himself like and bought me a drink. He spent an awful lot of time studying me and he finally asked me to stand up. I did and he seemed impressed with my size. He asked me if I'd killed anybody and I told him that I had, many times in battle. No, he said, have you killed anyone in cold blood? I shook my head like I was signifying that I hadn't." Jake raised himself up once more and made for the loo and I heard him vomiting again.

He returned, sat down and started once more. "The guy put a revolver on the bar and left it there for a bit. Finally he says, pick it up and follow me. We went outside the bar, nothing more than a thatched mud hut really, and the German points to two small boys sitting on a beer crate behind the shack. He indicated the bigger lad in a striped T shirt and told me to shoot him in the head. I shot the boy Joe. No hesitation at all, I killed the young fella to get the job. I killed him in front of his brother, in cold blood," Jake stared at my shoes, horrified and licked his dry lips. He started to weep, his great body jerking up and down, back and forth in his chair. I stayed quiet and willed him to continue. "I passed the test Joe and worked for the Kraut for years. I'd kill anybody and the terrible thing is I grew to like it. No, 'like' isn't strong enough, I loved it. I looked forward to machine gunning the opposition, innocent villagers, anybody. This is why I'm scared Joe, because I know that I enjoyed it. Maybe I'm beyond redemption?"

Jake, in my view, was not a psychopath. He was empathic, sympathetic, loyal, honest and he carried a guilty conscience. He was not Hannibal Lector. He was a living example of how chronic addiction could drive a person to do terrible, unthinkable things. He sat, weeping in my office, for some time and then he looked up at me, "I'm beyond fucking hope I suppose Joe. How could I do such things.........and enjoy it?" I was shocked by his revelation but encouraged by his admission/confession I suppose. For Jake, the healing process had begun, but for his victims it was too late.

I could tell that Tony was enjoying himself talking to the addicts in the Rhoserchan sitting room. The whole bunch of them were laughing when I sidled up to him. "Tony will you do me a favour before we go to the theatre?" I asked him.

"What's that?" he replied in his film star voice.

"One of our ex-residents is in the local hospital and she is dying of cancer. The poor old girl has been clean and dry since she left us over a year ago but now she's on her last lap. She's always dreamed of meeting you Tony, she's your number one fan. Will you come and see her with me before the Big Share?" I pleaded.

"Lead on Boss," he said and got up from his seat amongst his cheering, delighted fans. They loved the fact that he was going to see Margaret and going with such spontaneity and willingness. He was one of them and so was Margaret.

As we entered the hospital I briefed Tony that she was not expecting him and it would be a huge surprise. As we walked through the corridors of Bronglais Hospital nurses, doctors, patients and porters stopped and stared at the famous film star. I swear that when we got in the lift with one nurse she was on the verge of fainting. Tony looked very content with his present role and smiled at the young woman. She returned his smile shyly.

Margaret was lying on her bed and reading when we entered her four bed ward. She looked up, saw me and broke into a huge grin. "Joe, how lovely to see you and I thought that you'd be so busy tonight of all nights," she raised herself up into a sitting position and she looked to be in pain with the effort. Tony pinched some extra pillows from another bed and stuffed them behind her. "I've got so much to tell you," she said brightly, totally unaware of her idol's presence.

"Margaret, I've got someone here who......."

"Joe, just let me show you my latest poem," she cackled, opening her bedside locker drawer and rooting around inside the untidy jumble of papers.

"Someone is here to.........."

"Now, what do you think of that first line my friend?" she asked thrusting the poem at me. By that time a smiling Tony had moved from behind me and stood at my side.

"Hello Margaret," he said, bending forward to embrace her.

"Oh! Ohhhh! My God! Are you a ghost? Am I seeing things?" she screamed, loud enough to attract several nurses and patients to the ward. After her outburst she lay on her bed panting and staring at her hero. "I'm in Paradise," she whispered, holding his hand. Days later Margaret died and I was so sad to lose her, but at least she'd seen Anthony Hopkins before she checked out.

It was a privilege to be there that evening, in the hospital, with Margaret whilst she talked so excitedly to Tony. I had seen that close bond between two recovering addicts many times in the past and it never failed to move me, especially in group therapy, where there was always a kind of magic present. People would be willing to tell their deepest secrets simply because they'd heard similar things from others in their group and it had given them permission to disclose and begin to heal. I remember many incidents in group where I was moved by the tremendous courage shown by addicts in treatment. The young woman who had sex with her pet dog, the man who was addicted to eating human excrement, the man who stole from his daughters piggy bank to buy drink, the housewife who beat her children, repeating what her mother had done to her as a child, the woman who could touch nothing without washing her hands until all the skin had gone. I'd heard many, many incidents of the shameful side effects of chronic addiction. Talking about this guilt and shame is the first step in climbing out of the chains of dependency and the platform for that was group therapy.

"I need to share something with the group," said Peter, a thirty something guy from the North of England. He was a big fellow and had been a petty criminal, alcoholic and drug addict for most of his adult life. He looked frightened and he was fidgeting and red faced. I knew that Peter had done something in his past that haunted him. He began, "I was drinking in a public toilet and I was masturbating at the same time. I looked down and there was a guy in the next cubicle who was lying on the ground and pushing his penis under the partition. There was a big gap of around twelve inches between the wall and the floor. I'd always been straight and never been with another man before but when I looked down at the guy masturbating his dick it made me really randy." Peter looked up from staring at the floor and glanced at his peer group to check their reaction thus far. Obviously their expressions gave him permission to continue and he blushed scarlet before he began again.

"I pulled my pants down and lay down on the floor. It's strange because I noticed the piss and dirt on the tiles but it didn't stop me. I wanted him to fuck me up the arse really badly and I reached behind me to grab his cock to guide him. I felt him draw back and I wondered what he was doing. My arse was half under the partition and my head was resting against the base of the toilet bowl. Then I heard him, it was an old man's voice, I heard him say to me, 'Your arse is dirty, you'll have to wash it first.' I got up from the floor and sat on the loo. I'd never been so ashamed in my life. I was drunk out of my mind but I was blushing like crazy. It was as if I'd been rejected for being too filthy. I'd made a decision to partake in a degrading sexual act and I'd been turned down. Why? Because I was unclean." The other members of his group were quiet and watching Peter with concern in their eyes. We'd all been there, or in very similar situations and the empathy felt was strong. There was no need for me, as a facilitator, to do anything but be there for Peter. The healing was happening in the quiet of the group room.

A similar peace, tranquillity and acceptance followed another honest disclosure from a young Welsh woman. Beth was anorexic, bulimic, a drug addict, alcoholic and she was developing coping strategies in the form of compulsive shop lifting. She had entered treatment in panic and desperation. Her best friends: food, drugs, booze were not working for her any more. They no longer offered this pretty, bright girl respite from her frantic and sensitive mind. She felt betrayed and was now alone with her punishing and insane thinking. Her drugs and obsessive/compulsive behaviour no longer functioned to remove her pain.

"I woke early one morning and my husband was still asleep by my side. I remember thinking that he looked sweet and peaceful and I felt so guilty that I had neglected him in every way," Beth recounted to her group. She was terribly thin, had a slight lisp and she could not maintain eye contact with anyone in her group whilst she told her story. "It was dawn and I remembered the events of yesterday and felt so guilty. I'd spent most of the day in the bathroom vomiting into a bucket. Forcing food down my throat and then throwing up. I was naked to avoid splashing my clothes with puke and bits of food. I was in there for several hours before I gave up, mainly because I was so tired. Remembering that and the terrible things I'd done during the past year I decided that I had to stop. I stared at David's sleeping face and promised him, quietly, that I'd stop. I'd had enough. I'd get help from Rhoserchan and start a new life."

Her group knew what was coming next. I could see them studying her with keen interest. When someone is being honest in group therapy, the other members will respond to it by respectfully keeping quiet and being still. However, denial, or dishonesty, is greeted with confrontation, a checking of the addict's account until the truth is exposed. Often the group, especially the young female drug addicts, reminded me of a bunch of terriers, worrying at a large juicy bone. Denial or dishonesty is difficult to hear and sit with in group, whereas frank and candid accounts bring an automatic silence of respect.

"After David left for work I went to the kitchen and took down the birthday cake I'd baked for my mother a while before. I ate it all, throwing up the whole time into the kitchen sink. I drank the milk and yogurt in the fridge and saw that if I was to carry on I'd need stuff from the freezer as the cupboards and fridge were almost empty. I took frozen bread and pizzas out and started to break them into small frozen pieces, but I was so desperate to eat that I began to consume the hard, frozen dough. By mid-morning I was getting exhausted and I started to drink the whisky that I'd bought for my fathers Christmas present and swallow more laxatives.

Normally, I'm meticulous about cleaning and clearing everything away to hide my tracks but now I was drunk, desperate and didn't care. David woke me up at six that evening, naked on the kitchen floor. My body was covered in vomit and the floor was knee high in discarded food and wrappers. I'd lost control of my bladder and bowels when David discovered me. I'll never, ever forget how frightened he looked and how concerned he was for me. I had no control anymore. I was powerless over my illness," she finished with tears flowing down her cheeks but we all knew that she was finally on the road to recovery.

The auditorium was packed and the air of expectation, celebration and excitement was palpable. I'd spent half an hour hugging and greeting ex-residents, families and counsellors from other treatment centres. There was a lot of gratitude around in the Theatr y Werin on that evening. Hilary had nabbed the local Social Services funder and was pounding the poor guy with reasons why he should refer more of his clients to us. "Look the evidence of an effective and inexpensive recovery programme is all around you. Just look at these clean, smiling faces," she pointed out the walking miracles to the brow beaten social worker. It was hard for me to understand that we, the Rhoserchan team, had completed five years of successful operation and during that time we had been honoured to help these addicts and their families.

Because I was separated from my children and only saw them at weekends I became particularly aware of the children of Rhoserchan's patients. Everyday I worried about Simon and Alfie's welfare but I knew that I had to be content with my role as a 'dad in the background.' To follow my instincts and fight over custody issues would not be good for my children or me. Hannah had decided to educate them at home and I was opposed to this decision but I could do nothing about it. I doubted

Hannah's ability to teach them and I wanted my kids to come into contact with all sorts of other children in order to develop their personalities and social skills. I felt cheated and compromised but I was powerless to do more. I just hoped that one day Simon and Alfie would make me a part of their lives. Annie was living in Oxford and, as far as I could find out, was having her own problems with drugs. I made several tentative approaches but she showed no inclination to meet up. She knew that I ran a rehab and that may have put her off contacting me while she was using.

The first half of the evening, before the interval, had gone well. The audience seemed interested by Wynford, entranced by Lizzie and impressed by Tony. They laughed at his recollection of recovery in the AA rooms of California and they were moved by his humility. But the real show came in the second half when Michael, our counsellor, encouraged anyone from the audience to share about their problems and recoveries. As the alcoholics, junkies, sex addicts, gamblers, food addicts and their family members shared their very moving testimonies, I scanned the audience from the side aisle of the theatre. People, unaccustomed to the honesty of the 'rooms' seemed transfixed by what they were hearing. Perhaps some were thunderstruck and shocked by the accounts of our ex-residents and their families but I could see that it was an experience unlike any they had heard before.

Maybe it was OK and safe for us humans to drop our silly masks and admit to our mistakes and defects of character. Perhaps it was fine to say 'thank you, I appreciate you and I love you.' It was OK to be vulnerable with others. We didn't lose anything, we gained, won friendships and respect along the way. In the half-light of the auditorium, people that I did not recognise were smiling and crying at the same time. I felt hopeful leaning against the theatre wall in the darkness. I'd helped to create something good.

Michael ended the evening by thanking everybody: Lucy, Elizabeth, Jenny, our Trustees and Patrons and then he thanked me. As the clapping audience began to stand up I wanted to run away. I was in a blind, frozen panic and I wanted to escape. I really did not want this, a standing ovation, I wanted to go home with my pleasant memories of the evening, but the whole damn place was up on its feet now and yelling for me. There was nothing else for it but to go graciously to the stage and accept this wonderful gratitude. I stood, momentarily blinded by the lights, and, as the applause faded, I heard myself leading everybody in the Serenity Prayer, " God grant me the serenity to accept the things I cannot change, courage to change the things I can and the wisdom to know the difference."

22

THE BELLS, THE BELLS..........

Early autumn 1997

I never missed an opportunity to take my clothes off. I was lying in my garden, overlooking Cardigan Bay, half naked and cooking in the hot sun. My mind, however, was in a turmoil of despair and near panic. Earlier that fine summer day Richard, my doctor and Rhoserchan Trustee, had told me that I had Hepatitis C. He told me in the street, outside a shoe shop. I'd bumped into him and his children and he had informed me of the results of my recent blood test. He said, "It's a great shame but you appear to have Hepatitis C." I'd heard him say something different, there on the hot, sunny pavement. I heard him say, "It's a shame; it's a pity that you are going to die."

I had left Rhoserchan a couple of months previously after working as its founder and Programme Co-ordinator for almost ten years. I had felt more and more tired, exhausted almost, especially during the last two years. I assumed that my fatigue was because of the nature of my job and the massive amounts of energy that I had expended there. I wanted a change of direction, a new experience. Hilary and I now lived happily together in our lovely town flat and life was good. We were travelling lots during our vacations and we had grown to love New York, returning there three years in a row, but the news I had heard that lunchtime threatened to change everything.

After leaving Rhoserchan I visited Richard to ask him for a medical examination. I thought that I'd eliminate the physical causes of my fatigue before I entertained the idea of emotional exhaustion associated with the job etc. "I need an examination Richard," I said. We were sitting in his cheery surgery and it was always a pleasure to see him.

"Why do you think you need an examination Joe? You look terrific, much younger than your years and you are fit for your age." I suppose it was true that I looked toned and fit. I had done exercises religiously since I was a kid and, obviously, although I hated the discipline of doing them every day, they had helped me tremendously. Even during my thin, junky years I walked miles every day.

"I feel so tired though Richard and I just wanted to eliminate the possibility of any physical ailments hovering about," I pleaded.

"Take it from me, you're as fit as a flea, you don't need a medical," he said.

After I left the surgery I was dissatisfied with Richard's response and I decided to go back and plead my case again. Days later, when I sat with him again, he finally agreed that I should have a private physical at Bronglais Hospital and he booked me in to see a consultant there. The doctor I saw knew of my work at Rhoserchan and after I'd taken off my shirt he remarked, "I'm telling you now there's nothing wrong with you Joe. I can see that you are healthy just by looking at you. Pointless wasting your money really," he concluded.

"Please just go ahead Doc. Just humour me for my own peace of mind." He proceeded to give me a very full physical examination, blood tests, x-rays, everything. The next time I saw the good doctor he was so apologetic I felt sorry for him. "I'm sorry to have doubted you Joe. The Hepatitis C that you have would account for your chronic fatigue of course. I am terribly sorry." During my bizarre past I had wanted to end it all so many times but now that I was staring death in the face, I wanted to live.

Lying there on the grass in the sun I was waiting for Hil to wake up. She was on a night shift at the local psychiatric unit and I didn't want to tell her about the horrible result until she'd had a good sleep. Two hours previously she had got up and wandered into the garden and I was desperate to tell her but knew I couldn't until she had had her rest. "It's not good to sleep in the sun, go back to bed," I urged her. Finally, after a lot of nagging she went back. At lunchtime that day I'd visited the local NHS HIV nurse, Julia, to ask if Hilary could see her later as I was petrified that I'd infected her, although the possibility of transmission of Hep C, via the sexual route was fairly rare according to her. As I lay there in the sun I was trying to calculate the number of people that I'd have to notify. Hannah, Alfie, Simon and lots more besides. It was a nightmare. I thought back and tried to figure out when I could have become infected and reckoned that it must have been around 1962, when I contracted Hepatitis B. It was now known that if intravenous drug users contracted Hep B then the chances were strong they got whacked with the more alarming, insidious and life threatening Hepatitis C at the same time.

The tiny virus was only discovered in 1989 and, at the moment, there is no certain cure. A course of Interferon and Ribavirin can work for some, but not all. You can have it for years and not know it until a random, or routine blood test picks it up. Having the virus means that you have a chance of developing cirrhosis or cancer of the liver and dying from that disease. Unlike Hepatitis B it did not run its horrid course and then leave the body, Hep C stayed and multiplied. I was scared for me and terrified for Hilary.

At last five o'clock came around and Hil got up to prepare for her night shift. She was lying in the bath when I raised the subject. "Hil, I need to tell you something. I saw Richard today and he gave me the result of my blood test. I've got Hep C," I said hesitantly, watching her face. She stared at me and didn't seem to comprehend what I'd just said. "I've probably had it since 1962. I've already made an appointment for you with Julia, the HIV nurse. She says that you are not to worry because the chances of you having it are miniscule," I said, trying to reassure her. I was frightened that she'd leave me. "If you want to leave me I'd understand."

She didn't speak for a long time but continued to stare at my face.

"You've seen Julia already?" she asked.

"Yeh, you can go on Monday at 2pm," I replied.

"I'll be alright, don't worry and I don't want to leave you. How could you suggest such a thing," she said, smiling a sad little smile. "This is why you have been so tired?"

"Yup, I reckon that is the reason," I said.

As she got out of her bath she hugged me and told me, "We'll be OK, don't worry." Later we sat in the garden and the sun was still hot as the evening shadows lengthened. We could hear the seagulls squawking and we stared at the sea and the cloudless, blue sky. It struck me that the world was carrying on, as usual, even though I had Hep C. I thought of Simon, Alfie and Annie and I missed them.

Hilary and I were developing a new programme for the treatment of the emotionally ill and she hoped to open her new unit, Tukes, in 1998, the following year. We had been planning this new approach since 1993 and we were both excited by its possibilities. Hilary had worked hard to establish the charity and we believed that it would be the first of its kind in the world. It offered a 16 week programme for people suffering from food dependencies, anxiety states, depression, phobias and obsessive/compulsive conditions. It was a revolutionary programme whose main thesis was that manifestations of these illnesses were simply medicines chosen by the sufferer to deal with an underlying hyper-sensitivity. The coping strategies became addictions and, therefore, recovery could only occur when abstinence from these behaviours was achieved.

We had already seen many people get well in Emotions Anonymous and, of course, in Overeaters Anonymous, so it wasn't too difficult to believe that a clinical model would work very well. Hil was to pack up her job as a psychiatric nurse and launch Tukes, as its Programme Co-ordinator, the following year. About this time I also co-operated with a former ex-patient and trained counsellor,

George, to establish a drug and alcohol street agency in Aberystwyth. I'd had the idea for years and now the time was right to develop it. 'Contact Ceredigion' went on to forge a great reputation as a resource for people suffering from drug and alcohol problems and it also won an award for its highly imaginative and helpful website.

I was beginning to believe that addictions and neurotic illnesses were mostly part of the same continuum; that these conditions were caused, or triggered by a brain malfunction, perhaps resulting in a lack of dopamine or endorphins to the sufferer. The resulting hyper-sensitivity was the reason that people reached out for drugs, or phobias, or anxiety states, or depression, or food as a way of coping. Psychopathy, however, was a different kettle of fish altogether and whilst it was relatively simple to differentiate between drunken/drugged anti-social behaviour and psychopathic behaviour it was more difficult to separate the so called 'co-dependency' condition from psychopathy. I came to believe that there are more psychopaths in our world than the odd Hannibal Lector who is, of course, an extreme example.

Often co-dependent people, showed these 'personality disorder' signs and symptoms: self-centredness, a lack of guilty feelings, never learning from bad experiences, an inability to form long-term relationships, an ability to rationalize the most outrageous behaviour and outright lying. It was difficult to work with someone displaying these behaviours because their ego told them that they were always in charge and winning the game against all comers. They showed a flexible values system and moved the goal posts of recovery targets constantly, ensuring that they remained 'in charge.' I saw that psychopathy, albeit mild psychopathy, was much more common than I'd previously supposed. I'm not familiar with any known cure.

Working within an established treatment framework Rhoserchan was run largely by its residents in treatment. Events were announced by the 'bell boy' ringing the brass bell loudly in day block and night block shouting, "Group therapy" or "Lecture" or whatever. There was lots of shouting at the unit and it encouraged our recovering people to assert themselves and to believe that they had a right to be heard. Whenever a member of staff wanted to talk to the Group Boss we just stuck our head out of our office and hollered, "Group Boss!" and usually he or she would come running. Shouting was also encouraged in group therapy and 'facing fear' assignments to ventilate blocked anger and come to understand that the feeling of anger was not wrong or sinful. Anger was normal and healthy, violence was not.

Rhoserchan had its own tuck shop where you could buy cigarettes, tobacco, sweets, toiletries etc. and this was run by one of the addicts. Invariably he, or she, was known as Mr Arkwright, after the 'Open All Hours' TV show. There was tremendous camaraderie in the unit and the sound of laughter was ever present in Capel Seion. Visitors were always impressed by how clean and tidy the whole place was and often their preconceptions about 'addict types' were severely dashed.

I liked giving lectures to the patients and also enjoyed facilitating group therapy. I believed strongly that in order for information to 'stick', in lectures, the listener has to have some kind of emotional response to what they are hearing. So, I found that personal anecdotes were useful to illustrate my lectures. They provided an empathic, telephone line of communication direct to the listener's memory. It was gratifying to hear people, years later, saying they still remembered my talks.

The sensitivity that had dogged me all my life began to play a major part at Rhoserchan, especially in group. I relaxed totally in this setting, and could assess situations and the patient's responses very rapidly. This hyper-sensitivity served me and my addicts well during my time there and led Stephen Rose, the BBC2 director, to believe that I had extraordinary mind-reading capabilities. "Don't be ridiculous Stephen, I'm just aware that's all," I told him.

"Well, whatever it is you've got, it's scary," he replied. I have learned, over the years, when to use the gift and when to ignore it.

I ran a continual battle against the emerging, liberal drug and alcohol programmes during my time at Rhoserchan as Programme Co-ordinator. I hated what they did and confronted their perverse activities whenever I could. The drug street agencies, set up by the NHS, were generally staffed by untrained young men and women, often secret drug takers themselves, who believed that their friendship and permission giving attitude could save their clients. These vicarious thrill seekers were endlessly manipulated by addicts and some facilities in Dyfed and Wales were forced to close because they were out of control and had become unmanageable. The alcohol agencies insisted that controlled drinking was a viable option for alcoholics but when they were asked to present proof, in the form of recovery figures, they never came up with the goods.

I once told a civil servant from the Home office that I felt like an eminent brain surgeon who had been forced to watch the local butcher do his job in the operating theatre. "It's that bad is it?" Alan asked.

"Worse, these guys are failed nurses, failed grocers, failed junkies and living in an imaginary TV film in which they star as the hero," I replied. "Why do you allow this shit to happen Alan?"

"The answer, my dear Joe, is because we don't understand addiction and therefore, like everybody else, we can be manipulated and we tend to grab at anything that is on offer. Don't forget we are under pressure to provide services for our escalating drug and alcohol problems. It's costing the country billions and we don't always know what to do about it."

I resented my taxes paying for these awful, dreadful services and I worked hard to expose them. I don't think that it did much good apart from branding me as a maverick and a nut case in some quarters, but at least I slept at nights. A lot of my Twelve Step colleagues elected to work with these guys, hating every minute of it, but they rarely confronted them with what they secretly complained to me about. They said that they were forced to co-operate with these services in order to safeguard future government funding but I thought that they were cowardly and short sighted. In my opinion only two men stood head and shoulders above all others in maintaining the integrity of the Minnesota Model and they were Dr Robert Lefevre, at Promis, and Peter McCann at Clouds House and, later, Castle Craig. Sadly, most treatment centres also now had a unhealthy population of active food addicts, gamblers, and compulsive helpers, working as counsellors for them. My dream of the perfect addiction treatment was diminishing slowly. One of my counsellors was fond of joking, "This would be a great job without the patients," and I felt the same about the emerging treatment centres, "This would be a great treatment programme if we didn't have to have counsellors."

Western culture was also moving towards the 'cult of the individual' and away from 'conservation of the community' and this did not help us reinstate a new values system with our people in recovery. Some drug and alcohol agencies were saying to their clients, loud and clear, 'if it feels good, do it,' and some were even offering advice on the best ways to take illegal drugs. This approach did not work in the 60s and it 'aint working now.

The following morning, after I had received the news that I had Hep C, Hilary woke me, coming in from her night shift and told me that Princess Diana had been killed. "Christ, what a day, what a day!" I murmured. The Princess had supported me and Rhoserchan from its inception and I was sad to lose her. Like most other people I felt for the two Princes, robbed of their mother at such a young age.

During my final months at Rhoserchan we set about trying to find a new Programme Co-ordinator. I knew that it was going to be difficult for various reasons. Rhoserchan was geographically isolated, the programme demanded a self assured, knowledgeable, charismatic and fearless leader and, finally, he was going to be leading an already established family; all experts in their particular jobs. He would have to have been an exceptional human being and counsellor to be accepted and respected by the team.

By this time I was exhausted and could only think about leaving and going on my travels. Later I was going to bitterly regret my lack of application and attention during this phase and I believe that I put the whole future of the unit in jeopardy. I suppose it's easy for me to say that now, with my new found energy, but then, I was frazzled beyond belief. Eventually, we chose a nice guy to be Programme Co-ordinator but he failed within his first few months and was forced to leave by the existing staff. It was my fault and now I feel so sorry that I didn't work harder to secure a safe future for Rhoserchan.

Later I heard that Dean had returned to Rhoserchan as the Programme Co-ordinator and I learned that he had immediately set about dismantling the treatment programme there. He ceased to publish recovery figures in the Annual Report and he abandoned the highly effective 'anger management' programme. Presumably this was a move to satisfy politically correct funders and I wondered if Dean had ever properly understood the Twelve Step Programme with its emphasis on principles and trust. He seemed more concerned with making money and moving the unit to a grand country house than preserving a small, high quality, treatment unit.

I was glad to learn eventually though that Hilary was free of the Hepatitis C virus and so was everybody else that I had contacted. I decided that the discovery that I had Hepatitis C was not going to dissuade me from my plans to travel and I started to plan my future adventures.

23

LA VIDA DULCE

Spring 2000

The noon-day South American sun beat down on the two of us as we sat together on the pedestrian bridge in the centre of Cali, Colombia. My friend, on that tropical day, was Soledad, a blind, black woman who begged on the skinny, concrete bridge for hours at a time. I'd known her for three weeks now and she could recognise my footfalls as soon as I hit the top of the steps, at least twenty feet away from where she squatted with her begging bowl. She'd yell, "Hola Senor Joey!" when I was yards away from her and the other pedestrians would look and wonder what all the fuss was about.

Soledad had told me that her husband had pushed a red hot rifle barrel into both her eyes eight years ago. "He thought that I was sleeping with his best friend but it was a lie. My husband imagined all sorts," she said in a sad voice. She was tall and beautiful in spite of the horrific attack. She supported two children and her aging parents with her daily begging. "I'll give you a few pesos each day but you'll have to work for it," I told her.

"What shall I do?" she giggled.

"You have to teach me two Spanish swear words every day," I replied.

"Vale, trato hecho," she said, laughing and shaking my hand.

Cali was one of the most dangerous cities in the world but I came to love it very much during my stay: hot, sensual, and rhythmic. I learned, with fascination, that the high murder rate was not down to FARC or drug cartels but to domestic violence. Women shooting men, men killing women. Latin passions, unbridled jealousy and wild imaginings meant that these guys lost it easily. When I was flying into Cali, from Miami, I was seated behind three women from the city that we were headed for. They were all dressed in black and they were lovely. I'd read somewhere that Cali was home to the most alluring women in South America and they were known as Las Calenas.

Two of 'las chicas' were very drunk and pestering an obliging, male flight attendant for more drinks whilst the third was content to chat with me over the back of her seat. Suddenly the woman on the aisle noticed our conversation and swivelled around to face me whilst kneeling on her seat and clutching a miniature scotch. "Where are you going?" she enquired in a slurred, accented voice.

"Yo voy a Cali Senora."

"Don't go there! Turn around immediately and go back," she screeched. "It's too dangerous. It's the world's most violent city."

"Oh," I exhaled, terrified by her histrionics.

"Go back!" she shouted, pointing to the back of the aircraft.

"Hmmm......difficult without a parachute," I replied. The sober beauty intervened and told her friend to be quiet, "Can't you see you're frightening him. Stop it." The rest of the passengers were now getting more interested in our discussion and some were moving up the plane to see and hear us better. "Do you know why I'm going to Cali?" the black dressed screecher asked.

"No."

"To attend the funeral of my sister who was shot dead by her bastard Colombian husband. That's why! Don't you understand that Cali is dangerous? Everybody kill everybody. I moved to Miami to escape this hell-hole and you want to go there? You are mad, loco. It is the worst place on earth." This was my terrifying introduction to Cali. I was grateful that this was not my first trip into Latin America and that I already had some idea of life in the Spanish speaking world. I had first learned about its passion, craziness, music and idiosyncrasies in La Habana, Cuba.

Hilary had got Tukes off the ground in 1998 and she was determined to give it five years before we could discuss our next move together. For the first time in twenty years I had no responsibilities and I wanted to take this opportunity to indulge my love of foreign cities, so I headed first for Havana in Cuba and fell head over heels in love with Latin life.

It was October 1997 when I first arrived at the Hotel Nacional on El Malecon in Havana. I had stepped off the Cubana plane at the airport and entered a different world. The heat and humidity were overpowering and it was late in the evening. This tiny, defiant nation existed on its own, in enemy waters, and I felt their surreal isolation within minutes of arriving. It was as if I'd flown into a dream world unlike anything I had experienced before. I noticed the exceptional beauty of the Cubans, both men and women, during that first night. Women with golden skin and violet eyes, yellow eyes, black eyes, emerald green eyes. They moved like dancing snakes and flashed their white smiles generously. The handsome hombres were tall, muscular and charming.

A week later whilst talking to a Cuban doctor on the Malecon I asked him, "Tell me why there is this abundance of beauty here. It's extraordinary to see and it must be unique in the world. Tell me the reason for it?"

"You're right. There is a physical reason that Cuba is famous for its exquisite people," he replied, puffing out his chest and smiling proudly at me. "During the 1700s the black slave ships from Africa would sale into Havana as their first port of call. The French sugar plantation owners came down to the docks to inspect the human cargo whilst the poor black men and women stood, in chains, on the side of the harbour. The rich plantation owners would then select only the fittest, strongest and most attractive as their slaves. The remaining unfortunates went on to Jamaica and to other Caribbean islands. "So, Havana got the best of the crop," I said, amazed at his explanation.

"Yes, a kind of selective breeding programme and that is why you see all this incredible beauty around you," he finished. It made me realise how lost our popular Western culture was these days. We worshipped fame and celebrity but here in lowly Cuba there was a country of men and women, who would easily knock the spots off our top models and film stars and some of them were sweeping the streets or cleaning sewers.

The Hotel Nacional was the pride and joy of Cuba. Their top hotel, it was built by the American gangster, Meyer Lanksy, at a time when the gringo hoods ruled the roost along with the dictator, Bautista. I loved this flamboyant hotel but stepping out of the luxury into the decaying, dusty streets of the city was a savage contrast and one I found difficult to handle. Ordinary Cubans were not allowed into the hotel and brown suited secret service men were always on hand to stop it happening. There was luxury and plenty of food for the foreign tourist but not a great deal for the native Cuban. I'd always assumed that all Cubans were pro-Fidel and I had admired his stand for a more egalitarian society etc., but I was to learn over the coming months that most Habaneras were sick and tired of their ranting leader and just wanted him to die, painfully if possible, por favor!

Often, on a Sunday afternoon, you could see the 'bearded one' giving a speech on the local TV. His tirades lasted for between two and three hours most times. The camera would pan his audience from time to time and you could see the people desperately trying to stay awake. In the September before I arrived he was said to have given a speech for thirteen hours, beating the world record set by his friend and rival, Khrushchev, by two hours. This gave you some idea of how mad the Cuban leader really was. To believe that anybody can listen to someone, no matter how fascinating they are, for more than an hour, indicates an ego the size of Everest. The truth, I was to learn, was that everybody was afraid of him.

One day, when I was exploring Habana Vieja (Old Havana) a street hustler approached me and asked if I wanted to buy some PGG. He was small, dark skinned, with abundant, curly hair and he danced from one leg to another, smiling the whole time, in the tradition of street 'jineteros' throughout the world. I liked his intelligent, mischievous face immediately. "Que es PGG?" I asked, in my baby Spanish.

"You take it before you make love to a beautiful Cuban chica and it makes you hard........like stone," he explained, tapping the cobbles beneath his feet with his toe.

"Hmmm.......I don't think I need it then. I'm hard all the time," I replied.

"Seriously? Do you want some Cuban cigars then, the very best?"

"No, don't smoke thanks. But I do want someone to show me around this city. I'll give you $10 to be my guide for the day," I offered, knowing that $10 was a fortune for a Cubano. The pay rate then was $4 a month for everybody: doctors, mechanics and street cleaners. He accepted gleefully and shook me by the hand. "I'll teach you Spanish too," he said. "My name is Anibal."

"And my name is Joe."

"Ahh! Joey, un placer!"

We spent most of that sun filled morning inspecting the important historical buildings of the capital and I loved the flaking, crumbling, splendour of the city. It oozed romance and great, untold stories and the Cubans were friendly and smiley. Having lunch in a bar near Parque Central I asked him where he lived and I said I'd like to meet his family. "I'll take you there this afternoon.

It's not my real family you understand, my parents are both dead, but I live with a married couple and a girl from Santiago, in a small flat. We help each other. Life is hard for us."

That afternoon Anibal and I wandered into the grey, dusty district behind the Hotel Inglaterra. As we walked through the slum streets shiny black faces gave Anibal the thumbs up. Perhaps they were going to kill me and eat me later. "Where are we Anibal?" I asked.

"El Barrio Colon," he replied. I distinctly remembered that Rough Guide had advised its readers not to go into this tough area, but I thought, 'what the hell.' The sound of Salsa came from the old buildings and dead rats and mangy dogs populated the narrow streets. We finally reached Anibal's flat in a large multi-occupancy building and I met Lino and Adalia, the married couple, and Marisol, the large, comely girl from Santiago de Cuba. I loved this little family and we spent the afternoon chatting and laughing. I wanted to know about Cuba but, they of course, wanted to know about England. They fed me and accepted me during those hot, lazy hours and I didn't feel so alone with my Hepatitis C.

Much later, when I was staying in Santiago de Cuba, Marisol arrived at my guesthouse and told me that she was coming for me the next day and I had to be dressed in white. She duly arrived the next morning in a taxi and she too was clad, from head to foot, in white. When Marisol emerged from the battered cab she stumbled and then fell on to the pavement. Despite her height, her radiance and her African heritage she was the clumsiest person I ever met and she was always banging into things and falling over. If anyone ever tells you that all blacks can dance, don't believe 'em. Marisol had as much sense of rhythm as Queen Victoria. She was completely un-coordinated but her white, wide smile made up for everything.

Marisal took me to El Cobre, a church a few miles from Santiago where miracles were supposed to occur. She wanted to pray for my recovery from Hep C. When we knelt before the altar and I realised what she was doing I felt so grateful for her love and friendship. I thought then, before that gaudy altar, I could live here, with these people, for ever.

One humid, sultry evening back in Havana, we all went to an authentic Cuban nightclub called the Nacional. (Nothing to do with the five star hotel) This was the genuine article, not a tourist hang out. Located in a basement it consisted of tables arranged around a rickety stage. The small orchestra and stage to the right and the darkened bar to the left. We had settled, with our drinks, when the heavy, but threadbare curtains squeaked open to reveal the eight piece band seated behind their music stands. The left hand curtain got stuck half way open and so the drummer had to get up and yank it free of the obstruction. Although there was a singer on stage dressed, on one half of his body, as a man in evening dress and on the other half, like a woman in a ball gown, I became fascinated by the young trombonist in the front row of the orchestra. He was obviously new and hadn't a clue where the rest of the band were playing on his heap of music sheets. After flicking through his pile for a while he began to attempt to catch the attention of other band members to ask for help.

Finally the trumpeter, next to him, stopped playing his piece and leaned towards the lost trombonist. After listening for a while he shook his head and carried on playing. The handsome young musician tried several other guys during the song but they all pretended not to know what he wanted. The band played on and the apprentice gazed out into his audience with a lost expression on his face. Eventually the drummer caught me watching and gave me a massive wink and pointed at the young man. Obviously it was the trombonist's first night in the Nacional and this was his initiation ceremony as a rookie. They had removed the relevant sheets for that evening's performance Occasionally I caught a member of the band peeping at their victim and trying not to giggle as he searched and fumbled for the missing sheets.

The tall, graceful, black dancing girls, with their heavily darned, fishnet stockings, had just left the stage as the curtain closed on the band, signalling the end of the first half of the evening's entertainment. Anibal, Marisol, Lino and Adalia were laughing at my attempts at Cuban street talk when I noticed smoke coming from the stage. Suddenly, the entire orchestra jumped out from behind the curtain, clutching their instruments and yelling, "Fuego! Fuego!" The smoke thickened and the entire population of the basement club moved towards the door. I was amazed at how calm everybody was, even smiling and polite to each other, as we formed an orderly queue to exit the joint. The manager was at the bottom of the stairs handing back a full refund in return for our tickets and apologising for the fire. Men from the barrio outside were already rushing into the club with buckets of water and I assumed that the small blaze was soon put out. That incident, and the behaviour of the Habaneras made me want to share this magical place with Hilary and

I began to hatch a plot to move to either Central or South America with her, after she finished at Tukes.

I returned to Havana several times in the next couple of years. After my first visit I woke early one morning in Aberystwyth and told Hilary, "I've got to go back. It's no good I have to go." Hil believed that I'd taken leave of my senses but tolerated my madness, perhaps because she was too busy with her treatment centre to bother about a barmy, fifty two year old suddenly deciding that he was a Latino after all. After my first fabulous month in the five star Hotel Nacional I decided to stay, in future, with the Valdez family on Calle 21. I lodged with these lovely people many times and felt a great affection for all of them: Graciano, the ex-rock guitarist, turned hotelier, his serene and dignified wife Consuela and their lovely, bubbly, teenage daughter, Marita.

One morning, after a breakfast of fried eggs and strong black coffee at Casa Valdez I was chatting with our neighbour, Luz, about the Cuban system. "No one ever dreamed, when the revolution came, that Fidel Castro would turn into the monster that he has," she confided. "Everybody is waiting for him to die. Can you imagine Joey, how can he believe that he can turn the world's greatest capitalists into communists? The man is loco, I tell you my friend."

"Why don't you all rise up and get rid of the bastard then?" I asked.

"Because everyone is afraid. Everywhere you look there are uniformed policeman serving our leader. Mostly they come from Santiago and dislike the Havana folks, especially the intellectuals, and they are very willing to police and inform on them. You agree there are a lot of cops here?" she asked me, poking me with a long, brown finger.

"Yes it's true. I never felt safer," I replied, rubbing my arm where she had jabbed me.

"And so you should because if anyone is caught robbing you they will go to jail for a hundred years," she laughed, making her point. "Now listen to me. We are so afraid because for every uniformed cop that you see there are six secret policemen and an informer on every block in Cuba."

"Fuck, scary."

"Another thing to tell you; Consuela, who you love so much, is one of Fidel's nieces," she told me.

"Oh no! I've had long discussions with her about Fidel and his regime," I replied, instantly imagining the inside of a Cuban jail.

"Don't worry," she said, tapping the side of her nose. "First and foremost Consuela is a mother and second she is an Habanera. So don't worry."

"Perhaps I should stop talking so openly to people," I suggested. "Like Senor Large Gob."

"No, please, for the love of God. We rely on tourists and travellers criticising the system. We need discussion and information brought in and taken out to help us. We are prisoners, don't you see. We are trapped." Luz leaned over and gave me a hug. "One day we go to the Habana Café and dance some Salsa to Los Van Van eh?"

If I was to need proof of Luz's theory about Cubans being prisoners I was to get it a few nights later. I was carrying Marisol's bags from the railway station after meeting her off the train. She had returned from visiting her family in Santiago and she had come back to work the streets again – a dollar a fuck. My arms were dropping off when we turned into the Barrio Colon from Parque Central. As we rounded the corner I saw that the wide crossroads outside Lino and Adalia's flat was flooded with army trucks. It was a regular street clean-up and the fuzz and the soldiers were arresting anyone without papers, or anyone they didn't like. I already knew that people from Santiago had to have government permission to travel to, or live in Havana; therefore Marisol was a possible target for them.

"Don't look at them. Keep your eyes down," I ordered her as we stumbled past the huge, dark green trucks. She tripped a couple of times, which was normal for Marisol, but she kept her eyes down until we reached the corner. At the last possible moment she just couldn't resist it and she glanced back over her shoulder. "Don't, for fuck's sake Marisol." Too late, they were hissing for her to stop. I was furious with her and I glared at her as the young officer approached us. Three problems coming up: she was black, very black, shiny black, she was from Santiago and she was a hooker – she was well and truly buggered.

The policeman pushed me against the wall and escorted Marisal to the lorry. I watched them in the glow of the street lamps whilst he checked her ID and contacted someone on his ancient radio. A few minutes passed and then he took her to the back of the truck and made her climb up into it. She was under arrest. I walked over to the vehicle and told the cop that I would take her back to Santiago in the morning but he refused to talk to me. I couldn't do business with this stern, young man. I waved up at Marisol and tried to reassure her that I'd try and fix it. As I was walking to the Barrio Colon flat, Chepe, the Barrio chief hood, stopped me, "Senor Joey. I fix it, give me $20 quick." Chepe was small, had only one eye, a vicious scar cleaving his right cheek in two but he was built like a tank. I liked Chepe a lot. I had no hesitation in handing over the $20. "Go back to Lino and Adalia's place. I'll get Marisol." True to his word a fat, relieved, idiot of a Marisol arrived after half an hour. She was embarrassed and sorry to have volunteered herself for so much trouble. I kidded her for weeks after, "You'll have to up your price now with your clients because Chepe paid $20 for you."

I so loved my times in Havana I felt as if I'd come home and would have dearly liked to live there permanently. In a short space of time I made many friends and I had fallen in love with La Salsa. The vibrant colours, the steamy heat, the sensual people, the love and friendship of this tiny, beleaguered island stay with me still.

Back in Cali, on the bridge with Soledad, I remembered my Cuban adventures. "Come on you lazy beggar, let's go and have lunch somewhere," I said to a delighted Soledad. She rose up and felt for her long stick with the little Y shaped thumb grip at the top. Apart from the odd tap here and there she walked with confidence and everybody in the park greeted her as we passed. We walked to a café I liked called La Palma and we sat near the entrance where I could see the passers-by. I watched Soledad with fascination when her rice and chicken dish arrived. She quickly located the position of each item of food on her plate with a touch of her long, thin fingers and then proceeded to eat hungrily. I swear that she did not drop a single morsel from either her fork or her mouth during the whole meal. I watched her and tried to imagine what her life was like. She couldn't see a thing but she had a family to support and she could still smile. I was a little bit in awe of Soledad.

As we sat there in the light filled restaurant stuffing our faces, Jim entered and came over to sit with us. Jim was staying in La Mariposa, the same guesthouse as me, in the centre of Cali. He was a builder from Birmingham who had walked up to Colombia from Tierra del Fuego in Southern Argentina. On the way he'd met an Argentinean doctor, also on a walk-about, and they had fallen in love and travelled together through Chile, Paraguay and Bolivia. Apparently things started to go wrong in La Paz and they finally split up. He had told me the story with tears in his eyes. I thought he loved her a lot.

As far as I could make out there were only four or five English guys in Cali, it was too dangerous, so it tells you something of the character of those who were there – utterly crackers, the lot of us. The popular, daily newspaper was filled with macabre pictures of mutilated corpses in the city morgue next to pages of happy wedding snaps. After I introduced Jim to Soledad I pointed across the crowded restaurant at an elderly guy eating by himself. "Look Jim, it's Frankie Howard," I exclaimed. Jim turned his great frame to have a look and, in his thick Brummy accent, replied, "Good God man, you're right. It's dear old Frankie."

"What's he doing in Colombia? I thought that he was dead," I said.

"Obviously it was a cunning Frankie ruse. Look, it's definitely him and hiding here in Cali," replied Jim.

"Remarkable."

"I'm off to get his autograph," said Jim and he went over to the old fellow's table with a paper napkin. I watched him borrow a biro from a passing waitress before he asked the Frankie Howard 'look alike' for his autograph. The old gent looked puzzled for a while but finally signed the napkin. Jim proudly brought the serviette back to our table and displayed the flamboyant signature, "Look, he's living under the name of Enrique Costas. Would you Adam and Eve it? I'll probably sell this information to the Sun when I get back." He folded the paper napkin carefully and pushed it in to his pocket. "Would you like an ice-cream Soledad? I'm going to have one," he asked her.

Earlier in the week, at La Mariposa, I'd visited Jim in his small room. The door was slightly open but I knocked just in case……. "Come in," He yelled. "No need to knock."

"I thought I'd better in case you were having sex, or wanking or something," I answered tentatively.

"Well, I was actually."

"What? Having sex?" I asked him.

"Yup. With a nice chicken." He stretched his muscular frame over the old, grey blanket.

"A hen? Where is she now?"

"Probably hiding under the bed. You can have a look if you like." I bent down and searched under his single, rickety bed. There was nothing there, apart from dust and old condom packets.

"Oh yes, I see her," I said. "Oh she's lovely isn't she?"

"She is," said Jim. "I love her."

"What's her name?"

"Celine," he replied. That night as we were leaving the house to go to a salsa joint Jim turned to me and whispered, "Listen, you won't let on about my affair with Celine will you? People might think I'm a bit strange."

"No, of course not. Safe with me mate."

After we'd eaten lunch in La Palma we walked back to Soledad's pitch on the bridge. She was happy and taught me at least three more swear words on the way back.

24

THE ISLAND OF BONES

Early summer 2002

Officer John Baldwyn was around six feet five inches tall and about three feet across the shoulders. 'Old John,' as he was affectionately called in Key West, was a big, big man and he was not at all happy with me at that moment in time. "She has a right to enter Pelican House. Stand aside and let her in," the huge copper ordered in his drawling, Florida accent.

"No, I'm sorry; she's not coming into the house. I refuse to let her back in," I replied, staring the blue uniformed monster in the eyes.

"Let her in," he commanded me again.

"Nope." He turned on his heel and walked over to his patrol car. His partner, a rookie cop, was watching the unfolding scene with his mouth open and his hand on his gun.

The year was 2002, nine months after the 9/11 attacks, and I was a volunteer at a mental health facility in Key West, Florida. I had answered an advertisement in the Guardian asking for volunteer workers at an organization called the US Alliance and I'd arrived to work there eleven months before. After I had returned from my South American travels I spent a year, in Wales, injecting myself with Ribavirin and Interferon in an attempt to eradicate the Hepatitis C virus. The side effects of the treatment were unpleasant to say the least and at the end of nine months I still had the virus and my doctor and I decided to halt the drugs. I recovered fairly quickly and looked for something to do while Hilary attempted to get Tukes off the ground and complete her five year stint there. This year in Wales gave me the opportunity to work on persuading Hil that a move to Latin America was a great idea. I used a subtle drip technique with her, introducing a new wonderful fact about South American life into our conversations every day or two. It was unthinkable for me to live without Hilary and so I had to infect her with the Latin virus, which lived so happily in me, in order to carry out my plan.

I watched across the darkened Key West street and saw the cop reach inside his car for his mobile. Carmen, the patient I had refused to re-admit to the house was sitting amongst her scattered belongings on the porch. She was a Cuban immigrant, schizophrenic, paranoid and sometimes aggressive. For some weeks now I had watched her as she bullied and threatened the other patients at Pelican House. I was willing to tolerate bad behaviour for quite a while but when it began to upset the stability, peace and safety of the other residents I had to make a decision. Carmen had come to me in the glass fronted nurses station earlier and hissed, "Gringo bastardo, I go now. I leave Pelican House." She shook her flaming red hair and flashed her dark blue eyes at me, flexing her fingers in a strangling motion. "Where are you going Carmen," I asked her quietly.

"To my 'usband," she replied and started to transport her things from the women's dormitory to the porch outside. When she'd finished, I found her sitting on her bags and smoking a cigarette. "I call 'im, 'ee's coming now." She screamed.

"If you leave now, it's without my consent and I won't allow you to come back in. OK?" I handed her the 'leaving against staff advice' form and she signed it. "Bastardo," she muttered, lighting another cigarette.

I was soon to discover that Carmen had not phoned her ex-husband, but the Key West Police Department, and that is when 'Old John' had arrived at Pelican House. I heard him bellowing into his phone and I assumed that he was talking to Terri, my manager. "The problem is not the Cuban; the problem is the Englishman in my opinion. Doesn't he know we have laws in America?" From across the street I heard Terri's croaky, deep voice yelling at him down the telephone wire, "I trust that man with my life. If he says she 'aint going into Pelican House there's a damn good reason. Where's your respect for a professional Officer Baldwyn?" Nothing like support from your boss I thought as I crossed the road to whisper in the rookie's ear, "When your companero gets off the phone tell him that if he forces me to accept Carmen. I'll document it and if any violent or dangerous incident happens tonight he'll be the one to blame." He nodded and looked nervous and uncertain. As I walked back to my porch I turned and added, "She needs to go to the State Hospital you know, why don't you take her there? They will have the facilities to handle a patient in remission…..we don't." I watched as Terri continued to rant at the cop.

He was holding the phone down by his waist but we could all hear her loud and clear. "Do us all a favour John and take her to the State Hospital." Old John said a quiet "OK, bye," into his phone and I watched as the faithful, but confused rookie, relayed my message. After a couple of minutes they helped a yelling, screaming Carmen into their car. Before he drove off 'Old John' turned briefly and delivered a hard stare at me, standing Clint Eastwood style, on the darkened porch. Dolly and Faye were waiting for me inside the house and Dolly asked with wide eyes, "Has she gone Joe?"

"Yup, State Hospital."

"Praise the Lord," sang Dolly. The whole house was relaxed and happy the next day, with their tormentor off the scene. This was one more occasion when I lamented the passing of the old fashioned lunatic asylums. Carmen would always have had sanctuary and some kind of attention in these institutions and it was the worldwide political move towards 'care in the community' which made life so difficult for schizophrenics like her.

Four days later Officer John Baldwyn arrived at Pelican House and asked if he could see me. We sat together in the nursing station as he quietly and humbly apologised to me. Instantly I understood that it took such courage for him to do this and I also understood why he was so popular in Key West. "I apologise for not hearing you out as a professional Joe. The Florida law does clearly state that you have the right, just like a hotel, to discharge anyone that you regard as a danger or a nuisance. I was wrong and I'm sorry." This great big man's humility and honesty touched me deeply and it made me ponder the vanishing, old fashioned, virtues of honour and chivalry.

There were ten patients at Pelican House, five men and five women. Mostly these guys were suffering from psychotic illnesses: schizophrenia, bi-polar disorders and clinical depression. I felt for them because they were truly victims of their illnesses and there was nothing that they could do about it except take their medicines to stave off the horrid, incessant symptoms of the disease; the frequent, unrelenting voices and thoughts that sometimes were so persecuting of their host. These conditions were unlike the obsessive/compulsive dependencies that I had helped to treat in the past. Once addiction is recognised and diagnosed then there is a clear, laid down, path towards recovery, but the psychotic patient can only sit, often in awful mental anguish, tolerating as best they can, the unpleasant side effects from the medication and wait for someone to discover a cure.

Pelican House was on Highway One and if I walked across that busy road I could stand and stare at the Mexican Gulf. But if I walked for 10 minutes or so in the opposite direction I could watch the pelicans fishing in the Atlantic Ocean. Much more of the global warming lark and Key West would be the new Atlantis. In some places the island was barely a foot above sea level.

The house itself was quite a rarity in construction terms in the Keys because it was built of rendered concrete blocks and not of the more common timber, clapboard design. It had a large wooden veranda and the patients spent many happy hours mooching, away from the hot sun. The ground floor was given over entirely to the patients and was light and airy with an efficient air conditioning unit cooling their troubles. The volunteer staff lived on the floor above with windows protected by special hurricane shutters.

The US Alliance of Florida had Pelican House, Pelican Apartments (in another part of town) and a large house in Marathon, a few miles up the Keys. Key West is the most southerly point of the USA and is connected to the mainland by a chain of small islands and spectacular long road bridges. Juan Ponce de Leon, one of Christopher Columbus' mates was the first European to set foot in Florida and when he discovered the Island of Key West it was covered in old Indian bones, probably a tribal burial ground, and he named it Cayo Hueso, the Island of Bones. Later this was to be corrupted into the English 'Key West', by the Americans.

I always had grave doubts about Clara, the boss of the US alliance. About her suitability as a charity head and the way she conducted her business. Later I was able to influence the Board to remove her from the charity. My predecessor, an English fellow called Alex, was leaving only six months into his twelve month contract because he was at his wits end with the woman's abusive manner and lack of management skills. I quickly came to see that he was right and that she presented as a manipulative, arrogant and cold individual.

In particular she abused the Japanese volunteers, asking them to use their own uninsured vehicles for Alliance business, expecting them to work very long hours and then making them wait months for their airfare refunds etc. She knew that it was easy to use these girls because they were so desperate to work in the US and escape from the Japanese constraints of their homeland. I learned later that they had actually paid an agency $1,000 each in order to secure their volunteer posts at the Alliance.

I'd been at Pelican House for four days when Terri, the manager, called me into her office and asked in a pleading tone, "Joe, please will you consider being the Assistant Site Manager here to help me out?"

"Hold on Terri, I came here as a volunteer only. I'll work hard for you but I'm not prepared to take on that amount of responsibility," I replied. I was pissed off at the suggestion that I do a large part of her job for peanuts.

"The Board reckon that you have such good credentials that they would really like you to help the Alliance," she purred.

"OK I'll tell you tomorrow," I said. The next day I saw Terri in her office and said I'd do the job. I had a think overnight and saw it as an opportunity to improve life for the patients, implement a new daily structure in which the guys took more responsibility and as a chance to oust the crazy boss of the Alliance. With Terri's, "Great, great!" ringing in my ears I turned to leave her office when I spotted a printed staffing structure pinned to her wall and it was dated four days previously. My name was at the top as Assistant Site Manager!

I set to work putting some structure and stability into the lives of the Pelican House residents. I set up weekly house meetings where all the patients and the staff came together for an hour to discuss anything to do with their lives there. I encouraged the patients to be honest about their grievances and feelings towards each other and the staff, believing that buried resentments were the chief source of discontent and friction in any community. I also banned sleeping during the day except for a two hour siesta in the afternoon. This had its effect within days and the irritability, aggression and sleepiness that I'd seen in the guys when I had first arrived started to disappear. They were awake during the day and sleeping at night and not the other way around.

I was aided and abetted in my work at the rehab by other volunteers. Paul, a young guy from England and Miyuki, Reiko and Keiko from Japan. I came to value the Japanese girls and I loved working with them. They were punctual, meticulous, polite, kind to patients, physically strong and all had wicked senses of humour. Once, during one of Hil's visits to Key West, we were sitting, late at night, in the staff quarters, comparing national anthems with Miyuki and Reiko. "Go on, you sing yours first, I'd really like to hear it," I suggested. They began to sing so sweetly and harmoniously it took my breath away. Hil and I exchanged, with a glance, an unspoken 'how do we follow that' and then we began to sing God Save the Queen - a flat, raucous rendition of the anthem. We finished with me trailing sadly behind Hilary. "Ahh...so! Which one of you sing right tune?" asked small, mischievous Miyuki who had a habit of dumping me in the poo whenever the opportunity arose.

Terri often brought her tiny, miniature, brown Yorkshire Terrier into work on a Friday. He was covered in little red and blue ribbon bows and she would lovingly park the tiny animal on our desk where he would scamper amongst the important papers and growl at the anti-psychotic tablets. I used to dread the boss bringing her dawg to work because of the damage it did to the Anglo-Japanese system of running Pelican House. We'd spend hours after the tiny terror's visits searching for prescriptions, pills and dollar bills. One Friday, Terri arrived, with dog in arms, and I was obliged to greet the small pooch in my normal mock-affectionate way, scratching under the mini-mayhem maker's chin and generally cooing nicely. After Terri had left for her own office Miyuki pointed at me with an accusing finger and said, "Why you love dog? When Terri not here you say fucking dog!"

I simply had to have my revenge on Miyuki and the opportunity arose on the evening of December the 7th 2001. All the staff and patients were gathered together for the evening meal when I entered and I asked everyone in a loud voice, "Today is an anniversary folks. Does anyone know what happened on this day sixty years ago?" The patients, Miyuki, Keiko and Reiko stared at me looking blank and clueless. After a decent, quiet interval to build the tension I announced, "It's Pearl Harbour Day everybody. The day when the Japanese attacked and sunk the great American Pacific Fleet. Isn't that interesting?" I sat down to my meal and later glanced over at the Miyuki. She was watching me, half bowing, half rocking in the Japanese way and then she lifted her finger and pointed at me as if to say, 'It's war now my friend.'

Miyuki and I were sitting in the office months later when Mark, one of our paranoid schizophrenic patients, came in. Mark was tall, around 35 years old and very suspicious of everybody. He chain smoked and was forever running out of his allowance because of his addiction to tobacco. "Can I call my brother Joe? He's in a half-way house up in Homestead." Mark looked at me with his big, blue sad eyes. He had so much anguish and pain in his sun burned face it was difficult not to look at him and reveal the pity that I felt inside. My heart went out to these haunted people. "Of course you can." He dialled the number and after a couple of quick transfers he got through to his brother.

Way into the conversation in which Mark was advising his brother against marrying anybody under the age of sixteen years old I heard his brother ask, "Who is there with you Mark?" There followed a long awkward silence whilst Mark searched the office walls and table looking for inspiration for a reply. Finally he said, "He's a four star British general here at Pelican House. He's doing R&R after fighting the Japs in the jungle. Goddamn General Joe has got so many medals they weigh him down. He asked me to clean them yesterday but I said that I was far too busy to spend a week shining his damn medals." I turned and Miyuki was quietly giggling in the corner. She turned in her seat and saluted me.

Quite by chance one day I peered out of my bedroom window above the patient's quarters at Pelican House and saw Errol getting out of a brand new four by four Range Rover in our car park. He left the shiny, expensive vehicle and strode proudly into the house. I dived downstairs and caught him just as he was going into his dormitory. Errol was a well built, medium height, black American. He'd had a fine education and was a natural musician and singer. When he had first arrived at Pelican House he'd been living on the streets for months, eating discarded food from trash bins around Key West. He'd had no medication for his mental illness for a long time and he was slow and trance-like in his manner. He had nothing but a filthy, white vest and a pair of torn pants. He had no shoes and so his feet were covered in cuts and sores. If you asked him a question Errol would consider it for some minutes before answering and often we'd forget what we'd asked him in the first place. He was gay and he had a soft, gentle, girly voice. He responded well to the love and care he found at Pelican House and soon began to stabilise. He bought outrageous clothes from thrift shops and quickly accumulated a vast wardrobe for himself. He dressed in a different outfit every day and became the neighbourhood dandy.

"Errol, there's a big car outside," I said. He turned towards me casually flicking his sky blue cashmere cardigan over his shoulder and twirling a set of car keys. "Oh, Hi Joe. You like my car?" he asked with a wide smile.

"It's not your car Errol," I said.

"Of course it's mine Joe. They left the keys in it for me, down near the harbour."

"Obviously they were being careless Errol. You have stolen the vehicle and you could be arrested for theft," I argued, hoping to persuade him of his dishonesty.

"No, you've got it wrong. They left the car for me. Look I have the keys, my keys," he explained, emphasising the indisputable fact by twiddling the set in his fingers.

"Errol, I want you to take the car back to the harbour and if you get stopped you will have to apologise and hope for the best." I wanted Errol to face the consequences of his escapade and I hoped that he'd learn from the event.

Errol clambered, reluctantly but elegantly, into the four by four and drove off. Half an hour later I received a call from the police who'd arrested him as he pulled into the harbour. Luckily he only had to spend two nights in the county jail before he was released with a caution. The experience of the couple of nights in the slammer frightened the sensitive Errol and whilst I remained at Pelican House he kept his nose clean and had no more run-ins with the law.

Between shifts and on my days off I would sit on the beach and watch the pelicans diving for fish. I was entranced by these big, ugly, brown, sea birds. How could something so ungainly turn into such a beautiful and co-ordinated hunter in the air and under water? It was a mystery to me and I watched these big birds turning and diving together, perfectly in time, for many hours. One day I was sitting watching when I saw a girl, in a bikini, scrambling out of the surf which was gently breaking on to the beach. The seagulls screamed overhead as she walked towards me, sitting alone on the sand under a palm tree. As she approached, glistening with sea water, I could see that she was of an Indian appearance, maybe Singhalese, with her round, pretty, brown face. "What are you doing here?" she asked standing in front of me with her hands on her hips.

"Cooking in the sun and watching the pelicans," I replied, momentarily puzzled by the directness of this stranger.

"I'm lost," she said. "I don't know how to get home. Do you know my home?"

"Do you live in Key West?" I asked.

"We live all over the world and I'm here with my mother, but I've forgotten the name of the hotel and where it is."

"Did you swim straight from your hotel?" I asked, worried because she looked so frightened.

"I don't know," she replied. "I'll swim back again." She turned and walked towards the sea. I heard her as she walked down the beach, "Everyday I get lost. We are rich but I don't know where I am." In a sudden feeding frenzy five pelicans began a synchronised diving attack to her left and she stopped, waist deep in the water to watch. Later she turned and waved at me as she began to swim in the direction that she had come.

At about this time I learned from my sister that my mother had died, while staying with her in Devon. She had suffered an infection in her heart which had come on fairly swiftly. For weeks after her death I used to find myself half way to a phone, intending to talk to her, before I realised eventually, that she had gone. A trick of denial I suppose. I missed Annie, our walks and our fights, and I still do.

I was feeling hopeful and happy after my visit from Big John earlier in the day and I was enjoying a game of Monopoly with Eleanor and Patsy, when we were interrupted by Mark. "Joe, come quick. Doris took some knives from the kitchen and hid 'em under her dress," he whispered, wide eyed with panic.

"When did she do that Mark?"

"About five minutes ago," he said. I rushed for the female dorm and saw that it was empty of patients. I found Doris in the adjoining communal shower area, naked, sitting on a white plastic chair and covered in thick, red blood. Her dress lay to one side, neatly folded on the white tiles and her blood was splattered across the walls and floor of the shower. She'd slashed both her wrists and her right thigh. As I raised both of Doris' arms in the air I saw Eleanor and Patsy peeping around the corner to try and see what was happening. "Don't come in girls. Please wait outside," I said and the heads disappeared. I had a problem now. How could I reach the phone to call an ambulance but ensure that Doris kept her arms above her heart? "Doris, hands up and keep 'em up. Do not drop them," I commanded her.

As I left the shower, trying not to slip on her blood I looked back to check where her hands were. She was watching me with a curious, trusting expression on her face and her hands were held up, high above her head. Her eyes said, 'Help me.' When I returned, after calling 911, I discovered that she had remained sitting with her hands held aloft. She was still bleeding, but much less. As I took her wrists to support her, she looked up at me with her pale, sad face and said, "It's getting worse," in her slow Floridian accent. I knew what she meant as I returned her gaze and we waited quietly in the blood drenched shower room for the US Cavalry to arrive.

Unlike my stays in Latin America I was glad to leave the USA. Although I had always loved so much about the American way, these days the superficiality and greed were beginning to sicken me and I wanted out. It bothered me that such a wealthy nation had no health service, that some states still executed people and when it came to television the lowest common denominator ruled, plus wall-to-wall advertisements – unwatchable! I was sad to leave my patient friends and I was going to miss my Japanese pals but we said we'd keep in touch.

With Hilary's agreement the way was now clear to plan our escape to somewhere in Central or South America.

25

THE LOST PARADISE

Early winter 2006

"What on earth brought you to Paraguay?" asked the shrill, American evangelist. She was pinched and had the cold, judgemental eyes of fundamentalists from every faith everywhere. "Nobody comes here to live apart from fugitives and Mennonites." Her name was Wanda and she was a guest in our pension, here in Asuncion. We'd lived here for three years.

After returning from Key West to Aberystwyth I got a job with an organization called Hafal, which was the new name for the Welsh branch of the old National Schizophrenia Fellowship. I worked in Aberystwyth town centre, in a place similar in operation to Pelican House in Key West. I enjoyed my time at Hafal and got on well with the delightful staff and patients. My spell there gave me plenty of time to thoroughly research our forthcoming move to Latin America, a year later, after Hilary had finished at Tukes.

We had decided to try and earn our living by running a guesthouse and now the only question that remained was where? I wrote to all the London embassies representing Central and South American countries and read all I could on every place. To give us some guidelines for a final selection I decided to discount countries without a democratic system of government, to avoid countries where malaria was widespread and those that suffered natural disasters like hurricanes and earthquakes. Whilst I was in Key West I gained first hand knowledge of the devastations that hurricanes cause when, during a violent storm, I was told to take 38 mentally ill patients to the local jail. It was one of the very few stone built constructions on the island and consequently offered us some degree of protection. It was a constant anxiety and preoccupation for the home owners of Key West that one day their houses would be blown to bits in a hurricane. People who inhabited the Caribbean Islands and the countries surrounding the Mexican Gulf lived in fear from June until December every year and, frankly, it was not a good way to live. Paraguay looked to be a likely winner early on in my studies and the decision was made for us when we received a letter from the Paraguayan Embassy in London who ended his friendly, informative letter with the words, 'Welcome home.'

Wanda and her husband had lived as missionaries in Paraguay for many years, setting up their brand of religion in various places throughout the country. Now they were making a return visit and staying with us for a couple of weeks while they saw old friends. Quite by chance another American couple was staying with us, in the adjacent room to Wanda and Bill. They were friendly young Mormons from Florida and the husband had been a Mormon missionary in Paraguay a few years previously and he had fallen in love with the place. He wanted to introduce his new wife to his old Guarani friends. The oddest thing was that although both these couples shared a faith based on the teachings of Christ they did not see eye to eye at all. "A lovely young couple but normally we wouldn't have anything to do with them. Such a pity," commented Wanda one morning.

Like evangelists everywhere it seems they only get along with their own gang. Religions are systems of theology invented by man that actually appear to divide us rather than bring us together. As I grow older I fail to see where God fits into these self proclaiming and exclusive churches. They all, almost without exception, proclaim to be the only, true way to salvation. Time for a spiritual rethink? or maybe it's too late? Even the local English speaking church here in Asuncion likes to distinguish between 'Christians' and 'non-believers' in their congregation; they call them 'members' and 'attenders.' The assumption is firmly made that your God, your faith, whatever it is, is simply not good enough.

My talk with Wanda was interrupted by a visit from Ramon, my plumber friend. "We've got a leak somewhere Ramon. I don't know where but the water meter is whizzing round really fast," I explained to the smiling plumber and his three sons.

"Bueno, muy bien, Senor Joey." With that the four of them dived down on to the red tiled floor and, on their hands and knees, crawled around, occasionally lowering their ears to the deck to listen for the leak. The evangelist and I watched, mesmerized, as the four guys searched the house listening for the tell tale hiss from underground. After a short while Ramon located the leak and proceeded

327

to dig up the floor and repair the corroded old pipe. The job took about two hours and cost £10. This was the Paraguayan way.

Hilary and I arrived in Asuncion in October 2003. It was a grey, wet Sunday afternoon when we checked into our hotel, the ManduAra, on Calle Mexico. After we had unpacked and set out through the deserted streets to discover the nearest supermarket I recalled the slogan that I'd read about Paraguay. 'You cry when you arrive and you cry when you leave.' I hoped to God this proved to be true because our first glimpse of this grey, shabby town was thoroughly disheartening. As we strolled past the Plaza de los Heroes in the drizzle I said to Hil, "It's taken me a year to decide on Paraguay and it's the wrong decision. I've made the most monumental cock up."

"We can always move on to Chile," said a bedraggled, jet lagged Hilary.

The next morning the sun was shining, people were smiling and friendly and Asuncion didn't seem so bad. The Maca Indians were sitting on the square flogging their colourful jewellery and handicrafts. Everyone, it seemed, was sucking on their silver straws, drinking cold terrere in the heat. Like Cuba and Colombia I was instantly struck by the beauty of the people: the soft, brown, doe eyes of the men and the women – gentle and accepting. I found it humbling to be surrounded by this deluge of human beauty. In particular, the female posterior was a sight to behold. Of course the women were proud of their shapely bums and deliberately celebrated their assets by wearing tight pants.

Our senses were assaulted that first Asuncion morning: bright blue sky, vibrant colours, blossom everywhere, the occasional whiff of urine in the street, the street vendors, the pretty and obedient children, the mad hurtling traffic and the stares. Everywhere we walked people looked at us. I remembered what Jim, the Birmingham builder, had once told me in Cali. I'd asked him what he was going to miss most about South America when he returned home. "Being stared at," he replied. "It's lovely. I feel special. No bugger looks at me in Birmingham, but here I'm a star." It was true, he was right; it was nice to be ogled.

Paraguay is a country the size of Germany but it has a tiny, tiny population, around six million these days. It is situated slap bang in the middle of South America and has no coast. This lost paradise is bordered by Bolivia, Brazil and Argentina but has access to the sea via the River Paraguay, which becomes the River Parana lower down and finally the River Plate in Argentina. Paraguay suffered greatly under a succession of dictators until the overthrow of General Stroessner in 1989 when he was ousted by General Andres Rodriguez who introduced democracy to the country. Nicanor Duarte Frutos, the current president, despite a promising start, seems to be as bent as the gangsters who went before. Most of our poor Paraguayan friends remember, with some nostalgia, the time of Stroessner and say that they would like to return to that time when they felt safer, more protected and more content with their lives.

The good people of Paraguay are even more laid back than their other South American neighbours. They have a philosophy that makes them take one day at a time and they don't seem to worry too much about tomorrow. The dictator, Dr Gaspar Francia (1766 – 1840), known as the 'Supreme One,' passed a law that Paraguayans could not marry from within their own race. The Spanish had to marry the indigenous Guarani Indians and vice versa. The Indians held that if one had a full belly then that was enough. This attitude still prevails today and is probably the reason why this little paradise is not going anywhere very fast. The Guarani language has also survived and many people here use it as their first language. It is based on the sounds of the forest, bird song and animal sounds and is beautiful to hear. The Indians also have almost as many words as Latin to describe plants and their medical uses, something that is currently of great interest to our huge Western drug companies.

We found our beautiful house in the district of Villa Morra, just a couple of miles from the centre. It is a large, hacienda style, traditional Paraguayan construction and boasts a very beautiful, antique, red tiled floor. Villa Morra is a wealthy area with cobbled streets and large, posh houses. We have a swimming pool and a garden which is Hil's pride and joy. Jasmine and Oleander scent the house and all manner of exotic, colourful birds visit us each day to feed from our bird tables. Hilary is the President of the Damas Britanicas, a voluntary organization that helps the poor and disadvantaged of Paraguay and we have also been instrumental in helping an Asuncion children's home get off the ground. We are happy here and feel very fortunate to have found the place. Looking back over my life I can see that I've had one lucky escape after another and so, like the Guarani, I'm grateful for each day that comes along.

I have many regrets about the way I've handled my life, in particular I would like to be much closer to my children and my nephews. One day, maybe we will be together. I am sad that so many of my friends have died because of their love for drugs. I am sad that I didn't know, in those far off days, that something as superb as heroin comes with such a terrible price tag but I am glad that I have taken so many risks on my journey. I have been frightened all my life but today I reap the rewards of confronting those fears that have hounded me. Sometimes it feels as if my life has not been real........perhaps it has been a long, long dream. Today I'm not sure who I am or why I am here and I'm asking the very same questions I asked myself as a small boy. My life has been a wild, sometimes out of control ride, but the large questions remain unanswered in my mind. Paradoxically though, I'm grateful that on this hot, hot day in Paraguay I'm wondering what I can do next. I dream a dozen dreams every day and then, disconcertingly, one takes on a life force of its own and appears in its three dimensional form in front of me. Of course, by then, it's too late, the dream is real.

    Joe South   Asuncion Paraguay South America

ABOUT THE AUTHOR

Joe South was born in Oxford in 1944. During his teenage years he became addicted to drugs and promiscuous sex. Later he spent 13 years as a registered heroin addict. Breaking free of his narcotic habit in 1981 he went on to establish Rhoserchan, an addictions rehabilitation centre in Aberystwyth.

He and Rhoserchan were the subject of '*Nowhere Else to Go*,' a documentary film in BBC2's '*Your Life in Their Hands*' series. He has made numerous radio broadcasts, TV appearances and has written in various professional publications on the subject of recovery from addiction. He is the author of '*Poppy Dream - the story of an English addict*' and lives in Asuncion, Paraguay, South America. Together with his partner Hilary they run a guesthouse in the city and support several projects addressing poverty.

Printed in the United Kingdom
by Lightning Source UK Ltd.
133093UK00001B/3/P